OF CABBAGES AND KINGS

"The time has come," the Walrus said,
  "To talk of many things:
Of shoes — and ships — and sealing-
    wax —
    Of cabbages — and kings —
And why the sea is boiling hot —
  And whether pigs have wings."

Lewis Carroll
Through the Looking-Glass,
  ch. 4 [*The Walrus and*
  the Carpenter, st. 11]

Of Cabbages and Kings™ 2

THE YEAR'S BEST MAGAZINE WRITINGS FOR KIDS

Selected by Kimberly Olson Fakih

R. R. BOWKER
New Providence, New Jersey

Published by R. R. Bowker,
a division of Reed Publishing (USA) Inc.
Copyright © 1992 by Reed Publishing (USA) Inc.
Introduction (pp. xiii–xv) copyright © 1992 by Kimberly Olson Fakih
All rights reserved
Printed and bound in the United States of America

International Standard Book Number 0-8352-3165-8
International Standard Serial Number 0000-1376

Grateful acknowledgment is made to the magazines and other copyright owners for
permission to reprint their materials. All possible care has been taken to trace ownership and
secure permission for each selection. If, in some instances, this has proved impossible, or
if any have been inadvertently overlooked, we will be pleased to make the necessary
arrangements at the first opportunity.

All copyright notices can be found beginning on page 293.

ISBN 0-8352-3165-8

9 780835 231657

CONTENTS

4
KIDS IN CHARGE

PART II. REACHING OUT!

PART III. HOME PLANET EARTH

5
EVERYWHERE ELSE BUT HERE: EXPLORERS AT LARGE

6
WHEN OUTDOORS AND INDOORS
ARE ONE

7
REGARDING DINOSAURS

PART IV. THE COMPANY
OF OTHERS

8
FRIENDS

ACKNOWLEDGMENTS

Exploring the children's magazine field has been, needless to say, both rewarding and enlightening. Whatever it is not, it *is* an important aspect of both mass culture and a child's cognitive make-up. And if there is one lingering thought after the long travail it is this: that the fundamental difference between truth and advocacy lives on. Praise be.

I would like to utter the words "thank you" to each of the many people and institutions listed in the table of contents, index, and copyright notices. The inclusion of those writers and artists depended first on some so-far nameless folks working behind the scenes of this winding paper maze of false starts and return-to-senders, who helped in so many ways. I extend my gratitude (alphabetically) to Mary Algozin and Thomas Hunt (whose material should have appeared but did not, due to last minute, unforseen space considerations) at *Odyssey,* Gerald Bishop at *Ranger Rick*/National Wildlife Federation, Karen Donald, Ron Beuzenburg, and Craig Neff at *Sports Illustrated for Kids*/Time-Warner Inc., Sarah Hale at *Cobblestone,* Mary Ann Hocking at *Cricket,* Elizabeth Kneeland at the Cousteau Society, Jacqui Lieberman at Shooting Back, Ron McCutchan at *Cricket,* Elizabeth Rinck at the Children's Better Health Institute, Larry Rosler at *Highlights,* John Rutter at the National Geographic Society, and the very cordial "Al" from *Scienceland.* Also Will Steger for allowing me use of his slides and his words, David Chen, Laura Cornell, Edward Duarte, Julie Englund, Elaine Evans, Susan C. L. Fogden (for those faxes!), Suse Greenstone, Donna Johnson, Zoraya Mendez-De Cosmis, Susan Neill, Shirley Peterson (working in behalf of *Weekly Reader*), Maggie Ruiz, and Susan Thompson. Many thanks to the people at Bowker: Angela Szablewski and Judy Balsamo. For steadfastness and good company, Marion Sader, and, of course, Dorothy Markinko.

INTRODUCTION

"You'll never eat lunch in this town again!" This is *not* what the people of Parrott, Virginia, said to a local boy when he talked the folks at Rand McNally into putting their town on the map (p. 57). Instead, they threw him a parade. And when a group of school children decided to buy up a piece of the rainforest in order to save it, they weren't run out of town on a rail (p. 57). Kids in the nineties are in charge as never before, utilizing the meager elbow room they have in ways beyond adults' expectations.

Perhaps what kids would like to hear around *their* kitchen tables is what adults have been preaching—to the beat of a tin drum or two—for generations: "I don't agree with a word you say, but I defend to the death your right to say it!" Since no one's telling kids that, they're trying to take things into their own hands. Even though they may feel powerless over such things as weather changes, wars, or divorces, they *can* save a three-leaf clover from extinction (p. 60), start a small business (p. 54), or even just put on a pair of skates and head to the rink (p. 278).

Evident throughout magazines for children and assembled in this volume are some of the ways in which children, who seemed unaware just how helpless they were to change the world, went out and changed it anyway.

The gap between grown-ups and children is already vast. Sometimes even the gulf between people who put together children's magazines, books, TV, and film and the children who use them appears yawningly wide. Perhaps more than any other medium of (what is called) popular culture, magazines help close that gap, even a little, if only because they make it look like everyone—children and adults—is on the same side. In these publications there are clear and distinct instructions for crossing into and surviving the world run by, made for, and yes, jumbled by adults.

Also offered, rather than prescribed, in some of these same magazines are mirrors—looking glasses or reflections of the territories that are kids' own. Concerns or issues that may look a bit silly to ever-busier adults are treated with importance. If the parts of a real day include sibling squabbles, school friends (and foes), playground fights, afterschool surfing, and safe journeys between home and the world, then so do these magazines include them. If shelves in a boy's or girl's bedroom include spaces for a twig picked up on an autumn walk, a stone that performed admirably as an astronaut in an invented game of space travel, or a favorite pair of high-tech, pumped-up sneakers, then so do these publications include like objects, in newly penned stories, favorite old poems, enchanting illustrations, and bright-eyed photographs.

Kids aren't themselves the center of the universe in these magazines, but their *view* of the world is, and counts as the main attraction: how you are when you are alone (who am I? what am I not?), how you are when you are with others (people, animals, Martians), what it's like to be (and really belong) indoors, what it's like to be outdoors (traveling, exploring, or expanding your horizons). And it doesn't matter whether outdoors is just what's beyond the bedroom window or the rest of the universe. You might say, "It's all about me and the world I share with others like me, or different from me."

How magazines convey both their entertainment and their information may be, however, as various as the number of colors and frame styles of eyeglasses. Each one has a way of seeing and discussing a topic (that's what adults call point of view), and there's a whole supermarket of these. Many people consider *variety* and free speech as essential democratic ideals for children as well as adults. Some parents and others may hope that children will subscribe—not only to a certain publication, but to the ideas within it. Luckily, they are a benevolent bunch, and know that one magazine cannot be all things to all children.

So there are plenty of publications to choose from. Who can afford to read them all? (Well, some, like yours truly, can. Let's leave that out of it. And those children out there with a wad of money or unlimited allowances, pipe down.) Even if someone could afford to, who would want to? (Well, again, this reader, for one, does. More on that later.) It would be like facing two or three dozen televisions, all at once, each one tuned to a different channel. Nor would children want to face one channel, all the time, without any choices over what they watch.

In the kingdom of television, there's a remote control button.

In the realm of children's magazines, perhaps, this anthology is the next best thing. Because this volume brings together the best, most representative articles published in the last year (September 1990–August 1991), children have a place to start . . . a place to be entertained, and engaged, to discover what children's magazines have to offer. (I really did like reading all those magazines. I really didn't like all of the articles. And I knew you wouldn't either. But it was important for me to see what I *don't* like as much as what I do.)

And then the only thing left for any adult to do is to back away, quietly, and leave behind the remote control. Children can use it, then go off to get the publications they want, by subscription or in the library. This annual volume takes for granted that kids are not powerless, but they just don't know the ropes as yet.

It's a big, wide, world out there, and someone has to give kids a hand in coping. But if this volume was intended as a source to empower children, it ended up as a chronicle of some of their awe-inspiring events. While the stereotypical TV child is holding his or her hand out for an allowance raise, real kids are making their own businesses into successes. While the rest of the world believes that the next generation is going to grow up and throw away their earthly inheritance, the next generation is taking out the garbage and recycling it. And while adults, perhaps, decry the fate of the earth and wring their hands over global warming, some children face tasks large and small—like those mentioned in the first part of this introduction, and like others, in the pages ahead.

What's happened since the first volume of this annual series was published? Kids *happened* to grow up a whit. You'll find these children in the next 300 pages, but only because the publishers and editors of magazines for children found them first, and printed stories and articles about them. You may be inspired to go out and do a little world-rearranging of your own; the half-pint behavior of a few well-intentioned souls is enough to give anybody hope.

Kimberly Olson Fakih
January 1992

Part I

HOME ALONE

There is a place each of us stands when we are by ourselves—or as one boy, when asked how he knows who he is, said, "Me. My name. Who my father is." He then pointed to himself, his legs, his arms, adding, "Here. Not there. Not you. Me." That's probably all there is to know.

1. A Place of One's Own

Emily Dickinson, the poet who said, "I'm nobody! Who are you?/ Are you nobody, too?" is known to have spent a good deal of her time inside one room. From there, she turned her thoughts and actions and feelings into lasting treasures. Perhaps you are a poet, too. No matter, what you think and do and feel are what makes you who you are—whole and distinct from anyone else.

Girl in a Room

illustration by Laura Cornell

from U*S* Kids

The following piece is a bit like the song that goes a little something like this: "Make the world go awaaaaaaay." If you've ever felt like belting out a few bars of that tune, read on, for words on privacy that are bound to hit home.

A Space of Your Own

from Current Health

In very early times, families lived in one open room. They ate together. They got dressed and undressed together. When two members argued, everyone could hear. When one told a joke, everyone had a chance to laugh. They slept together. They did not have privacy as we know it.

Can you imagine living like that? Luckily, most of us don't have to. Times have changed. And people's need for privacy has changed, too. Having time alone is something Americans of the 20th century feel they cannot do without.

Privacy: Hard to Find

Although your home may not be as cramped as it would have been long ago, privacy often seems just as hard to find. In fact, some days, you may feel as if people are forever looking over your shoulder, that you have no privacy. There's nosy Peggy in math who listens in when you talk with your best friend. Then Emily grabs your lunch box to see if you have anything worth trading. The kids on the school bus yell in your ear the whole ride.

When you get home, the neighbor's stereo is blaring your least favorite music. Your parents ask you about your day. Your little brother, who thinks you're so great, tries to follow you everywhere. Even your dog keeps putting his head on your book, hoping to get a pat. During days like this, you may dream of escaping to a desert island. With no airplane ticket in hand, you try to find a corner of the house empty of brothers and sisters, parents and pets, chores and responsibilities.

Why's It Important?

Why is this privacy, this time alone, so important? For one thing, it gives you a way to relax and unwind. When you are with people, you must think about how you act. You must be aware of what you say and the effect it has on others.

When you are alone, you don't have to be polite. You don't have to work to get

5

along with anybody. You can just be yourself. Getting away from other people for a time gives you the energy to return to the world and enjoy it.

Privacy also gives you a chance to explore who you are. After all, ever since childhood, you've been learning how you ought to be. Your parents tell you who they think you are and who you should be. Your friends expect you to do things their way. Teachers believe you should have certain goals. Commercials on television try to tell you what to eat, what to buy, and what to like. Your world is buzzing with everyone else's ideas about what they expect you to do. It can be very easy to lose sight of what *you* expect of yourself.

When you have time alone, you are able to explore your own ideas about what you think about things and what is important to you. With privacy, you can sort out whether you really want to try out for the team or are just doing it to compete with your older brother. You can decide whether you should support your friend in an argument she's having, even though you think she's wrong. It's hard to know what you think and feel if you don't have the time to explore your thoughts and feelings.

Sometimes your private daydreams can help this exploration. Even though daydreaming isn't something you should do in school, it is a very helpful tool in understanding what you believe and feel. That's how Jesse often uses his time by himself.

Learning About Yourself

Last week, for example, Jesse ran to his room after school and closed the door. Almost before he stretched out on the bed, he started going over in his mind what had happened that morning. He had just watched silently while his classmate Mike picked on a younger kid. But in his day-

dreams, Jesse changed his part in the drama: He stepped in front of Mike and stopped him from being mean.

By having time to daydream, Jesse learned several things about himself. He began to understand that he didn't like the idea of a big kid picking on a small one. He also realized he did not like his own role as someone who did not stand up for what he thought was right. Daydreaming helped Jesse find another part to play just in case he was ever in the same situation again.

Some Chance to Daydream

You may wish you had a few more chances to daydream yourself. Here are several ways you can find a little time or space to call your own:

1. Find some activities you can do alone. It may be something physical such as jogging or riding your bike. It could be a hobby like baseball card collecting. Any of these things will give you new skills and a chance to spend time alone.

2. Keep a journal. Buy a book that locks or find a good hiding place so you are sure your writings will be yours alone. Then fill your diary with your private thoughts and dreams.

3. Build the walls of a private space with music. Slip on your Walkman earphones and get into the music.

4. Is your house filled with people, pets, and noise? Go outdoors to find a private place. You may not have to go any further than the front porch or your backyard. Walk to a neighborhood park. Perhaps the local library can give you some peace and quiet.

5. Suggest your family buy an extra long telephone cord so each of you can have private conversations.

6. If you work hard to respect other family members' privacy, yours will be respected, too. Knock on doors before enter-

ing a room. Don't open or read someone else's mail without permission. Don't eavesdrop when your sister is talking to her best friend in the kitchen.

7. Share a room with your brother or sister? Try to schedule your days so each of you can occasionally have the room to yourself. Perhaps you both can carve out a corner that is yours alone.

8. Find some private space within. Even if the world is humming around you, climb inside yourself and daydream. Move into your imagination; you'll find privacy there!

You're never more alone than when you're sleeping—if you can keep all the dweebs, nerds, and twerps from invading Mr. Sandman's space. Here's how.

Why Do People Count Sheep to Fall Asleep?

from National Geographic World

illustration by Laura Cornell from U*S* Kids

If you toss and turn at bedtime, a little boredom might help. Boredom can dull the nerve cells in the brain that signal you to stay awake. Some people try to imagine an event happening over and over again, such as one sheep leaping after another. By concentrating on a single thing, they forget about other things. The people may actually bore themselves to sleep! The technique can work no matter what you count.

8

Invasion of the Couch Potatoes

illustrations by Joey Ahlbum
from Sports Illustrated for Kids

Kids are getting fatter. Today's 10-year-olds weigh about three pounds more than 10-year-olds did back in 1973, according to a study. Kids today also have higher levels of fat.

Dr. Gerald Berenson, the director of the Bogalusa (Louisiana) Heart Study, says that kids are fatter today probably because they watch too much TV and get too little exercise. Dr. Berenson also thinks kids are eating too many fatty foods.

This is all bad news, because kids who don't exercise regularly and don't eat balanced diets risk having health problems later in life. These problems can include high blood pressure and heart disease.

Unfortunately, some schools have been cutting back on their physical education programs to save money. This means kids have to take responsibility for getting lots of exercise.

"Learn to take care of your body," warns Dr. Berenson. "Nobody else is going to be as interested in it as you."

2. A Sense of Self, Kind Of

We probably don't realize that there is more to our senses than we could possibly see, hear, touch, taste, or smell. Follow Ms. Ackerman's journey, and find out what your nose—and the rest of you—really knows.

Explore the Science of the Senses

by Diane Ackerman, excerpted from A Natural History of the Senses

from Current Science

Land of Instant Memories

Nothing is more memorable than a smell. One scent can be unexpected, momentary, and fleeting, yet conjure up a childhood summer beside a lake. Another scent can spark memories of a family dinner of pot roast, noodle pudding, and sweet potatoes. Hit a tripwire of smell, and memories explode all at once.

Smell is the most direct of all our senses. When I hold a violet to my nose and inhale, odor molecules float into the nasal cavity. There, the molecules are absorbed by odor-sensing cells called *olfactory receptors*, found at the upper end of each nostril. We need to smell only eight molecules of a substance to trigger an impulse in an olfactory receptor. But 40 receptors must be aroused before we *smell* something.

One theory of smell maps the connections between the geometric shapes of mol-ecules and the odor sensations they produce. When a molecule of the right shape happens along, it fits into an olfactory receptor. Musky odors, for instance, have disk-shaped molecules that fit into an elliptical, bowl-like site on receptor cells. The fitting of an odor molecule and a receptor triggers a nerve impulse to the brain's smell center, which identifies the smell.

Wrinkling Aids Smelling

Because our noses jut out from our faces, odors have quite a distance to travel before we're aware of what the nose has probed. That's why we wrinkle up our noses and sniff—to move the molecules of smell closer to the olfactory receptors hidden awkwardly in the backmost recesses of the nose.

The tissues that contain smell receptors—called *olfactory bulbs*—are yellow, richly moist, and full of fatty substances. The deeper the shade of yellow of the olfactory bulbs, the more acute is the sense of smell. A human's olfactory bulbs are light yellow. A fox's are reddish-brown; a cat's, an intense mustard brown.

The animals with the keenest sense of smell tend to walk on all fours, their heads hanging close to the ground, where the damp, heavy, fragrant molecules of odor lie. Pigs can smell truffles under 6 inches (15 centimeters) of soil. Even on stormy nights, bloodhounds can track the few odor molecules that seep through a person's shoes and land on the ground when the person walks.

Pity us, the long, tall, upright ones, whose sense of smell has weakened over time. When we are told that a human has five million olfactory cells, it seems like a lot. But a sheepdog, which has 220 million, can smell 44 times better than we can. Still, we do have a remarkably detailed sense of smell.

What Causes Odors?

Before something can be smelled, it has to be airborne. Only substances volatile enough to spray microscopic particles in the air can be smelled. If you heat cabbage, it becomes more volatile, meaning that some of its particles *evaporate,* or turn into vapor. Many things we encounter each day—including stone, glass, steel, and ivory—don't evaporate when they stand at room temperature, so we don't smell them.

We see only when there is light enough, taste only when we put things into our mouths. But we smell always and with every breath. Each breath passes air over our olfactory bulbs. Each day, we breathe about 23,040 times and move about 438 cubic feet (13 cubic meters) of air. It takes

about five seconds to breathe—two seconds to inhale and three seconds to exhale—and in that time, molecules of odor flood our systems.

As Helen Keller once wrote, "Even as I think of smells, my nose is full of scents that start awake sweet memories of summers gone and ripening fields far away."

Small but Powerful Buds

Seen by a scanning electron microscope, our taste buds look as huge as volcanoes on Mars. In reality, taste buds are exceedingly small.

Adults have about 10,000 taste buds, grouped by theme at various sites in the mouth. We taste sweet things at the tip of the tongue, bitter things at the back, sour things at the sides, and salty things spread over the surface but mainly up front. Inside each taste bud, about 50 taste cells busily relay information to neurons, which alert the brain.

Just as we can smell something only when it begins to evaporate, we can taste something only when it begins to dissolve. And we cannot do that without *saliva,* a fluid in the mouth that breaks down starch.

Smell contributes grandly to taste. We often smell something before we taste it, and that's enough to make us salivate. Smell hits us faster. It takes 25,000 times more molecules of cherry pie to taste it than to smell it. A head cold, by inhibiting smell, smothers tastes.

The other senses may be enjoyed when one is alone, but taste is largely social. We usually eat with our families. Weddings end with a feast. Our friends offer us food and drink—a gesture that in ancient times meant, *I will endanger my own life by parting with some of what I must consume to survive.* Those desperate times may be ancient history, but the part of us forged in such trials accepts the token drink and piece of cheese and is grateful.

Skin: The Keeper of Touch

Our skin is what stands between us and the world. If you think about it, no other part of us makes contact with something not us but the skin. Weighing 6 to 10 pounds (2.7 to 4.5 kilograms), the skin is the largest organ of the body. It is waterproof, washable, and elastic. But most of all, it harbors the sense of touch.

Touch is the oldest sense, and the most urgent. If a saber-toothed tiger is touching a paw to your shoulder, you need to know right away. In fetuses, touch is the first sense to develop. Soon after we're born, although we can't see or speak, we instinctively begin touching.

Feeling doesn't take place in the topmost layer of skin, but in the second layer. The top layer of skin is dead, sloughs off easily, and contributes to that ring around the bathtub. Safecrackers are sometimes shown sandpapering their fingertips, making the top layer of skin thinner so the touch receptors in the second layer will be closer to the surface.

The Many Faces of Touch

It takes a troupe of touch receptors to make the symphonic delicacy we call a caress. The egg-shaped *Meissner's corpuscles* cover hairless parts of the body—the soles of the feet, the palms, the tongue, and the fingertips (which have 9,000 Meissner's corpuscles per square inch).

Meissner's corpuscles respond fast to the lightest stimulation. These receptors record low-frequency vibrations—the feeling of a finger stroking a beautifully woven sari, for example, or the soft, angled skin inside another person's elbow.

Pacinian corpuscles respond quickly to changes in pressure. They tend to lie near joints, in some internal organs, in the genitals, and in the breasts. Thick, onion-shaped sensors, Pacinian corpuscles tell the brain what is pressing on the skin or what the skin is pressing on and how the joints are moving. It doesn't take much pressure to make Pacinian corpuscles respond fast and rush messages to the brain.

Our menagerie of touch receptors also includes

- saucer-shaped *Merkel's disks*, which respond to continuous, constant pressure;

- *Ruffini endings*, which register constant pressure;

- various free nerve endings, which respond more slowly to touch and pressure;

- temperature sensors;

- heat sensors;

- and the most familiar, but oddest, touch receptor of all—hair.

Hair Club: Mammals Only

Hair is special to mammals, although reptiles do form scales, which are similar to hairs. The average body has about five million hairs. Because hairy skin is thinner, it is more sensitive to touch than smooth skin. If something presses a hair or if the skin around a hair is pressed, the hair vibrates. This vibration sparks a nerve to fire a touch message to the brain.

Still, the nerves can't be firing all the time or we would be driven crazy by the feel of, say, a light sweater against the skin. When we put on a sweater, we're acutely aware of its texture, weight, and feel against our skin. But after awhile, we completely ignore it.

A constant, consistent pressure registers at first, activating the touch receptors. Then the receptors stop working. This touch-receptor fatigue doesn't happen in the deep Pacinian corpuscles or the Ruffini's organs in our joints, because if they nodded off we would fall down, midstride.

But the other receptors, so alert at first, after awhile say the electrical equivalent of "Oh, that again" and begin to doze, so that we can get on with life.

Sound = Moving Molecules

Outer space is silent, but on Earth, almost everything can make sound. Mothers sing their babies to sleep. A campfire wouldn't be as exciting if it were silent. Hikers revel in the sounds of birds, river rapids, skirling wind, and dry seedpods rattling on the trees. What we call *sound* is really an onrushing, cresting, and withdrawing wave of air molecules that begins with the movement of any object and ripples out in all directions.

Sound waves hitting the eardrum vibrate the first tiny bone—the hammer or *malleus*. The malleus's head fits in the cuplike socket on the second bone—the anvil or *incus*—and vibrates it. The incus then vibrates the third bone—the stirrup or *stapes*—which presses like a piston against the soft, fluid-filled inner ear.

In this area is a snail-shaped tube called the *cochlea*, containing hairs whose purpose is to signal the auditory nerve cells. When the fluid vibrates, hairs in the cochlea move, exciting the nerve cells. These cells telegraph their information to the brain, and we hear.

What we hear occupies quite a large range of intensities, from the sound of a ladybug landing on a caladium leaf to a launch at Cape Canaveral. But we rarely hear the internal workings of our body—the churning of our stomach, the whooshing of our blood, the flexing of our joints.

Our ability to move some sounds to the almost unnoticeable rear and to drag others right up front is truly astonishing. We can do this because we actually hear things twice. The outer ear is a complicated reflector, which takes sound and hurls some of it straight into the hole. But a tiny fraction of the sound is reflected off the top, bottom, or side rims of the outer ear and directed into the hole a few seconds later.

As a result, there are delays in hearing a sound, depending on the angle the sound is coming from. The brain reads the delays and knows where to locate the sound. Because of this delay, you can slice through the noise of a party to hear a conversation between your boyfriend or girlfriend and a flirtatious stranger.

Our Photographic Eyes

We think of our eyes as wise seers, but all the eyes do is gather light. The eye works a lot like a camera. To focus a camera, you move the lens closer to, or farther away from, an object. The eye's rubbery, bean-shaped *lens* achieves the same result by changing its shape. The lens thins to focus on a distant object, which looks small; and thickens to focus on a near one, which looks large.

A camera can control the amount of light it allows in. The *iris*, a circular eye muscle, changes the size of a small hole, the *pupil*. Light enters the eyeball through the pupil.

At the back of the camera, film records the images. Lining the rear wall of the eyeball is a thin sheet of tissue called the *retina*, which includes two sets of photosensitive cells, *rods* and *cones*. We need two sets of cells because we live in the two worlds of darkness and light.

A hundred and twenty-five million thin, straight rods construe the dimness and report in black and white. Seven million plump cones examine the bright, color-packed day. Mixed together, the rods and cones allow the eye to respond quickly to a changing scene.

When the retina observes something, neurons pass the word along to the brain through a series of electrochemical handshakes. In about $\frac{1}{10}$ second, the message reaches the *visual cortex*, the part of the brain that makes sense of the images we see.

Seeing doesn't happen in the eyes, then, but in the brain. We often remember scenes from days or even years earlier, viewing them in our mind's eye. We can even picture completely imaginary events, if we so wish.

One of the most profound paradoxes of being human is that the thick spread of sensation we relish isn't perceived directly by the brain. The brain is silent, dark. It tastes nothing, hears nothing. All it receives are electrical impulses.

The body is a *transducer*, a device that converts energy of one sort to energy of another sort. And that is its genius. Our senses, which feel so personal, reach far beyond us.

Life began in mystery and it will end in mystery. But what a savage and beautiful country lies in between.

The Kiss: A Loving Touch

When I [Ms. Ackerman] was 14, my boyfriend used to walk five miles across town each evening just to kiss me. There are many theories about how kissing began. Some authorities believe it evolved from the act of smelling someone's face in order to gauge mood and well-being.

Zoologist Desmond Morris is one of a number of authorities who claim this fascinating origin for kissing: "In early human societies, before commercial baby food was invented, mothers fed their children by chewing food and then passing it into the infant's mouth by lip-to-lip contact.

"This almost birdlike system of parental care seems strange and alien to us today, but our species probably practiced it for a million years or more. Kissing today almost certainly stems from these origins."

The Big Picture—that's what the folks at Scienceland (a very underrated magazine) want you to see. Here are two pieces for your perusal.

The Blink
&
The Side View of the Eye

from Scienceland

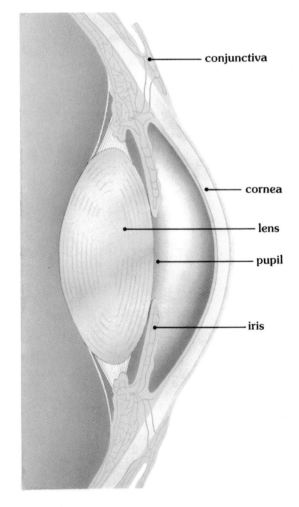

conjunctiva

cornea

lens

pupil

iris

Did you know that our eyes blink every two to ten seconds?* That would be thousands of blinks in one day. Each blink protects the eye by (1) washing away old tears, (2) coating the eye with fresh tears to keep the eye clean, moist, and slippery or lubricated *loo'brikātəd*, and (3) keeping the eye free of germs with a germ-killing liquid lysozyme *lī'səzīm*.

At each blink, tears flow into the tear sac. At the same time the tears in the sac are squeezed out. They empty into the opening behind the nose, drain back into the throat, and are swallowed.

The eye can also be made to blink by itself or by reflex. Whenever anything comes too close to the eye or is felt by the eyelash, the eyelids suddenly blink.

*Every ten seconds means six times a minute and 360 times an hour. If we are awake from 7 o'clock in the morning to 8 o'clock at night that means 4,680 blinks (360 blinks an hour times 13 hours).

Franklin Watts/London

Body Language

by Joan Daniels Gozzi

from Humpty Dumpty

Hips wiggle
Tummies sag

Shoulders shrug
Tongues wag

Toes tap
Feet patter

Scalps tingle
Teeth chatter

Hair curls
Nails break

Chests heave
Backs ache

Arms fold
Legs jump

Ankles sprain
Hearts pump

Elbows bend
Fingers snap

Noses twitch
Hands clap

Skin wrinkles
Knuckles crack

Knees knock
Lips smack

Thumbs twiddle
Eyes blink

Heads nod
Brains think!

Kids and grown-ups already know all about "Chin up!" and "Keep your nose clean." And now for a few words on posture . . .

Standing Tall

by Donna E. Hicks, illustrations by Mark A. Hicks
from Jack and Jill

Did you know that you are a vertebrate? You can thank your backbone for that. All animals with backbones are called *vertebrates.* Your backbone, or spine, is the central support for your whole body. It allows you to bend down and pick up a penny or reach up on your tiptoes or twist to either side. That's why it's important to take care of your fine spine. You don't want to end up flat on your back.

Your Back Bones

Your backbone is not really one long bone. It is made up of separate, small bones called *vertebrae.* You have twenty-six vertebrae. These bones look a bit like spools of thread. Between the vertebrae are disks of rubbery cartilage that act as shock absorbers. Without this cartilage, any kind of running or jumping would really be a pain—in the neck, head, and back.

Worms are invertebrates. In other words, worms have no backbones.

Plugging into Your Brain

Your spine has an important job. It protects your spinal cord, which is your body's telephone line. Your spinal cord carries messages from your brain to your body and back. These messages travel very quickly from your spinal cord to the outer areas of your body along thirty-one pairs of nerve trunks.

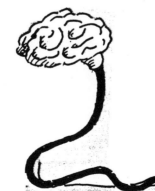

DISK

VERTEBRAE

Keeping It Straight

Posture is the way you hold your body when you stand, sit, or walk. When you have good posture, your bones and muscles are working together the way they should. When you sit up straight in school and at home, you will look better and feel more comfortable. You will notice that you won't get tired as easily, either.

Have you ever worn shoes that were either too big or too small for you? Not only do your feet get sore, but your back may also begin to hurt. A space of about half an inch should be between the tip of your big toe and the tip of your shoe.

Other things also affect your posture. Be sure you get enough sleep, exercise, and the right kinds of food. Otherwise, you're bound to wind up looking and feeling droopy.

Spine Time Game

To play this game, you need two buttons, a penny, and a friend. Flip the coin to start. Heads means you move one space. Tails means you move two. See who reaches finish first.

Spiny Spine

The stegosaurus had double rows of tough, triangular plates all along its spine. The spines were two feet tall and helped to protect the dinosaur. Stegosaurus also had a large nerve center on its spine to help control its back legs and tail. It needed the extra help because its brain was only the size of a walnut.

Back Talk

Even though a spine is quite flexible, it still can't do everything.

Sometimes a disc will squeeze out beyond the vertebrae. This is called a slipped disc, and it hurts! To avoid a back injury, do not strain your back muscles. Lift heavy objects using your leg and arm muscles, not just your back muscles.

3. Where Home Is

Dorothy said it for many of us: "There's no place like (youknowwhat)." And from the looks of these few pages, no matter who the dwellers are, people or animals, it's home sweet home for all. And they know it.

Home Tweet Home

from Ranger Rick

Sometimes animals just don't do what we think they should do. Take a look at what happened in Tina Garcia's backyard:

"I made a birdhouse for wrens with my Girl Scout troop last winter," Tina explains. "My friend and I found a lot of old wood and dragged it to our meeting place. Then we all carefully followed directions for sawing, sanding, gluing, and nailing the birdhouses together. Whew—what a job!"

When Tina finally put the birdhouse up in her yard, she could hardly wait for a wren family to move in.

"I went to a lot of trouble, but some house wrens really fooled me!" Tina says with a laugh. "They found a wet garden glove hanging on our clothesline. Before long the wrens had made their nest inside the glove! Well, that meant my mom had to do without her glove until all of the babies hatched and flew away.

"But my carefully built birdhouse got used after all," Tina continues. "A pair of robins came along, and look what they did."

New Homes from Old Tires

by Elizabeth A. Foley

from Dolphin Log

Just what can you do with old tires? Build a house, according to Michael Reynolds, an inventive architect in Taos, New Mexico. Americans throw away 240 million tires every year, which means there are plenty to reuse. To build a tire house, the tires are pounded full of dirt and stacked like bricks. Then they're covered with mud to make a smooth surface. The walls, about two to three feet thick, remain at a constant temperature, warming the house in winter and cooling it in summer. Tire houses don't need additional cooling or heating systems. It's cheaper than building wood houses and uses up tires that would otherwise be in a dump.

A Dog's Life

illustration by Patrick Girouard

from Kid City

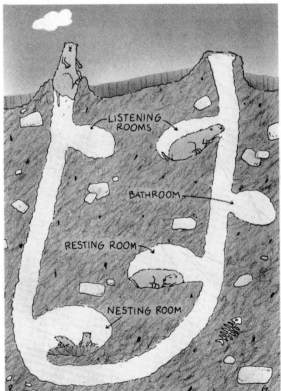

This mound in Africa can shelter many creatures besides a single aardwolf. It's an abandoned termite mound. Millions of the insects once lived inside. Meet the amazing builders and explore their secret world.

The Secret World of Termites

from National Geographic World

You've probably heard of termites only as destructive pests that chomp through wood, damaging and sometimes destroying houses. Yet termites are among the most valuable recyclers in nature. They break down dead wood, often fallen trees, so that it goes back into the soil. There it helps nourish new plant life. The little munchers help keep the world from suffocating under masses of decaying wood and litter.

Termites turn up nearly everywhere, but their favorite places have warm, moist climates and plenty of woody plant material. Large numbers of termites live in the rain forests of Africa, Australia, and South America. There the insects build mounds of soil mixed with saliva. The mounds dry and harden.

Inside a mound termites scurry through a maze of tunnels and rooms. Like ants, termites are masters of organization. Every individual has a job to do.

The queen lays eggs—at least five or six thousand a day. That is her only job.

Workers build and repair the mound. They take care of the queen, her mate, eggs, and young. They gather and store food for the whole colony, or group.

Soldiers have large heads with built-in weapons: armor, needle-sharp mouthparts, and spraying devices. They use these weapons to defend the colony against its main enemy—ants.

Workers and soldiers are blind. They rely on keen senses of smell, taste, and touch.

So well does the system work that a termite colony may survive for nearly half a century. After it dies out, the well-engineered mound remains, often providing shelter for other animals.

You may have thought about all-purpose sponges, but probably only when you had a bucket and mop in your hands. A sponge sitting on the ocean floor—minding its own beeswax or catching up on its reading—may end up as food for one critter or home for another.

The Sponge: An Absorbing Story

by Bill Harrigan
from Dolphin Log

Sponges are very simple animals—they have no eyes or bones or hands or feet. They don't even move around. They lead uncomplicated undersea lives, filtering water in for food and oxygen and pumping it out to get rid of carbon dioxide and wastes.

Because they are invertebrates, or animals without backbones, sponges don't have skeletons, but they do have a special way of keeping their shape. Sponges have spicules, which are slender bits of calcium or silicon, imbedded throughout their bodies. The stiff spicules allow the sponge's soft body tissues to form and hold their shape.

Sea sponges are different than the sponges found in supermarket aisles next to the soap and cleaning supplies. Sea sponges used to be taken from the sea and dried, then used like the supermarket

sponges of today. But supermarket sponges are made of synthetic, or man-made, materials. They aren't the remains of living animals.

To breathe and eat, sponges take in water through thousands of tiny holes, or pores, on their outer surface. The cells in the sponge take food and oxygen from the water as it is passed along a network of canals. Special "collar cells" pump the water through the canals to all the other cells of the sponge. The water is eventually pumped back out through a large hole called an osculum.

Except for this circulation of water, the cells of a sponge don't function together very much. In spite of their simple structure, sponges can regenerate themselves from very small pieces. That means that a small chunk of sponge can grow into a whole sponge again.

Sponges normally reproduce by releasing sperm into the water. The eggs in another sponge are fertilized internally if this sperm-laden water is absorbed. Some of the resulting larvae develop in the parent sponge, but others are expelled, and drift with the currents before settling onto the bottom.

Adult sponges don't move around. They are permanently attached to the spot where they first settled. Encrusting sponges look like blobs. They take a variety of shapes by molding themselves to rocks, pilings, ledges, and other solid objects. Some encrusting sponges are called boring sponges because they bore, or cut, into coral heads or shells, taking whatever shape they manage to dig out.

Other sponges are attached only at their bases and grow upward in a tubular shape. Loggerhead sponges resemble fat rubber tires. Basket sponges are also called barrel sponges because they look like wooden barrels.

Many animals make their homes in sponges. Tiny fishes, such as gobies and wrasses, sometimes swim into the osculum of a sponge to rest or hide. Brittle stars, a delicate variety of sea star, like to live in tube sponges. Reef fishes, lobsters, coral, and even other sponges may be found in the large osculum of a barrel sponge.

Some animals dine on sponges. The queen angelfish can frequently be seen munching mouthfuls of orange sponge. One bright-red encrusting sponge is a favorite food of sea slugs. How fast can you say "Sea slugs sometimes snack on sponges sporting spiny spicules?"

They look like blobs, vases, barrels, and tubes, but they're alive. What are they? Sponges!

The hardest part of having a home is leaving it. It may not happen to you for years, but when you go, whether you like it or not, you always take a part of it with you. Believe it, or not!

Bridget's Ghost

by Lynn Bulock
from Cricket

Bridget Flaherty sat by the big stone fireplace and stared into the embers. The letter she was holding would change her life again, and Bridget wasn't ready for more change.

Just coming here to the near wilderness in America had been change enough. When the potato crop had failed back in Ireland and her parents sent her to America, Bridget had started a whole new life. Living in this small frontier town and working for the Brecks had been an education. Every month she sent most of her earnings home, and her family saved it for their own passage to America.

Now here was the letter. It felt almost as heavy in her hand as it had in her apron pocket all afternoon, where it had lain like a stone.

Albert had been so proud of bringing it to her. "Look, Bridget, a letter for you," he said, waving it around over his head. And Mrs. Breck had been surprised that Bridget didn't open it right away. "You've been so homesick," she clucked, urging her to sit down and read the letter. But

Bridget wanted to save it until she had time to herself.

Like a little sprite, four-year-old Lillibet suddenly appeared beside her. Lillibet was her shadow and knew just when to try to cheer her up. She tugged at Bridget's apron. "Are you sad, Bridget?"

"Just homesick, I think."

"Do you miss your mama and papa?"

Bridget nodded. "And Daniel, and Moira. She's just about your age." Moira had been two when Bridget left Ireland, and she longed to hold her little sister. As if she could read Bridget's mind, Lillibet squirmed up on her lap. "Read me your letter."

"It's from my parents, as your mother thought. They've sold all their things and bought tickets for the four of them. We should look for them before Christmas."

"Goody," Lillibet said, bouncing. "Aren't you glad?"

"I am," Bridget said quietly.

"Then why aren't you smiling?"

How could Bridget explain it to her? Her loneliness had been a constant ache in her chest since she left Ireland. But at least she could always think of her family at home. Now there wasn't any home. No low stone hearth where her mother cooked over a smoky peat fire and her father warmed himself when the day was over, he and Daniel talking of the work they'd done.

With her family leaving for America, home was gone. There was just a shadowy someplace they would come to here. And that was assuming that everything went all right on the crossing and on the long journey up the river from New Orleans to Missouri.

But how could Bridget put all those feelings into language Lillibet could understand? She took a deep breath, ready to try. "If I were home, we'd be getting ready for Allhallows Eve. Hallowe'en. We'd be sitting around the fireplace and hollowing out a great turnip, for Jack's lantern. We'd be telling stories about banshees and goblins, and my mother would make us a special treat to eat."

"It sounds like fun."

"It is," Bridget said, feeling the tears start to come now that she was talking about it. "Go kiss your mama, Lillibet, and we'll tuck you into bed." She didn't want the little one to see her cry.

The vision of home in Ireland was wound so tightly around Bridget the next day that she was in a fog. She was surprised when Mrs. Breck called her after super. "Could you take this package to Mrs. Carpenter's for me, Bridget? It's some lace she ordered. She's already paid me for it."

Bridget gulped and nodded. Surely Mrs. Breck had lost her senses. What normal person asked someone to go out after dark on Allhallows Eve? She grasped the package, wrapped her shawl around herself, and left for the Carpenters' house, running.

She was glad it was only two streets over. The trees cast long shadows across her path, and scraped and tapped against the windows of the houses like a witch's bony fingers. "It's just old tales," Bridget said firmly to herself, as she hurried back through the darkness.

Her shoes clattered on the cobblestone street. Only a few more houses and she'd be at the Brecks' again. The cold October wind blew through her shawl, moaning like some unquiet thing. She lunged for the door, never so glad in all her life for the warmth and light inside.

"You look as though you've seen a ghost!" Mr. Breck exclaimed.

"Not exactly," Bridget gasped, still breathing hard. She noticed a large pumpkin sitting in the middle of the hearth. "What's this here for? Surely we're not going to start making pie at this time of night."

Albert grinned. "Lillibet said if we got a big one, you could do something with it. Can you?"

Lillibet smiled at Bridget. "There aren't any big turnips here. Can you use a pumpkin?"

Mrs. Breck handed Bridget a carving knife, and soon a grinning orange face stared at them from the hearth. Bridget slid a candle inside the hollow pumpkin. "Doesn't he look a fright?"

Lillibet giggled, and Mrs. Breck noticed the time. "Upstairs, miss. It's late as it is." Her mother scooped her up and carried her off to bed, Lillibet protesting all the way.

When Mrs. Breck came back to the fire, Albert said to Bridget, "Lillibet told us you know ghost stories. Tell us a scary one!" They all leaned forward, waiting for Bridget to begin.

Bridget looked at the pumpkin grinning on the hearth. "You've never heard the tale of Jack and his lantern, have you?"

Albert shook his head, and she launched into the story.

"... and St. Peter wouldn't let the old miser into heaven either, he was so mean. So he still wanders the earth, carrying his lantern. You can see him at night sometimes, over marshy ground, trying to lure some other poor soul into the bog with him," Bridget finished, almost whispering.

Just then, a sudden gust of wind blew down the chimney, snuffing out the light in their jack-o'-lantern. As Bridget and Albert jumped to their feet, a long, low shriek came from the corner. In the red glow from the fire, they saw a ghostly, oddly shaped figure drifting down the stairway. As they watched, rooted to the ground, the figure dipped low, gave a bounce, and tumbled down the last few stairs.

At the bottom of the stairway, the tumble sorted itself out into a small, blond figure wrapped in a bedsheet. "I was being Bridget's ghost. You said there was supposed to be one," Lillibet explained, looking up at Bridget and rubbing her knee where she had banged it. "But I fell down."

They all laughed, and Bridget pulled Lillibet onto her lap while Mr. Breck relit the pumpkin's candle. The wind drove tree branches against the window, but here inside they just made a scratchy, cozy sound. It was like that when you were home, Bridget decided, a warmth filling her as Lillibet pushed a sleepy head into her shoulder. Home wasn't a place far away. It was people who cared about you. It was coming into the light, out of the dark and the wind.

It was doing things for people, like finding them a pumpkin. Or finding them a new life, as she would have to do for her family when they came. When they came home, Bridget thought. Even in this near wilderness of America, anywhere they would be together would be home. Bridget smiled to herself, and the jack-o'-lantern grinned back, with a warm and flickering glow inside.

Children's book writer Margery Facklam has been known to write about extinction and the care of endangered species. Here is her article about birds that once may have faced "endangerment" but who now lead posh lives in a most unlikely nesting ground.

The Ravens of the Tower of London

by Margery Facklam
from Cricket

Every night at sunset, eight ravens flap and flutter to their roosts in the Tower of London. The Raven Master secures the latch on each cage as the ravens settle in to sleep.

Ravens look like their cousins the crows, but they are much larger. Many people think a raven is evil-looking with its beady black eyes, sleek black feathers, and long, thick, swordlike beak. But rather than a symbol of evil, the ravens who live at the Tower of London are thought to bring good luck.

In 1078 William the Conqueror built the Tower on the River Thames for use as a fortress. When it was finished, ravens flocked to it like pigeons to a park. Now, ravens are scavenger birds that feed on dead animals or fight over scraps from garbage. The Tower must have offered a wonderful new food supply: grain from the king's stables and bakeries, and garbage from the huge kitchens that fed the royal household.

The Tower offered nesting spots as well. Ravens usually nest on ledges of high rocky cliffs, but they quickly found safe places to raise their young on high window sills and in the openings built for the king's archers.

For centuries, no one seemed to mind having the ravens around. Then, in 1672 the king appointed the first Astronomer Royal. When John Flamsteed set up his new telescopes on the roof of the Tower, the constant screeching and *wonk-wonk* cries of the ravens annoyed him. Since ravens are messy birds, Flamsteed probably didn't like them sailing and swooping over his head, either. He wanted them gone!

Now, that was a problem for the king to think about. During the six hundred years that ravens had roosted in the Tower, an unusual superstition had grown and spread. People had come to believe that as long as there were ravens at the Tower of London, England and all its colonies would be safe. But if the ravens left, England would fall. Why would anyone want to take a chance and shoo away the ravens?

Finally, the king agreed that the ravens must not be allowed to annoy Flamsteed. He decided that six birds could stay at the Tower, with two extras in case something happened to one of the regulars. The others were driven out.

Today, there are still six official ravens at the Tower of London. Their wings have been clipped so they can't fly far, but they live royally. They have their own Yeoman Warder, called the Raven Master, who feeds them and cleans their cages. During the day the ravens preen, strut, and scream at tourists who come to take their pictures. And then, as dusk falls, the Raven Master checks Merry, Hectora, Garvey, Kala 2, Grog, Brorai, and the two guests, Larry and George, into their cages. England is safe for another night.

Haunted House Maze

by Maria Cristina Brusca

from Cricket

START

FINISH

© 1990 by Maria Cristina Brusca

The biospherians finally locked themselves inside their massive, man-made earth-type space in September 1991, but the talk about their adventure had been going on for months. If you were going off for two years to such a place, what would you take with you?

Biosphere II: Scientists Make Home in a Dome

by Hugh Westrup
from Current Science
accompanied by artwork by Laura Cornell from U*S* Kids

Imagine living in outer space and still feeling as if you never left Earth. You watch the planet Saturn float by your spacecraft's picture window as you enjoy a refreshing dip in the ocean. Or you gaze out on the cold, grim landscape of the moon from the comfort of a warm, tropical forest.

Life in space might be just like that one day, thanks to the pioneering efforts of a band of visionaries stationed in the Arizona desert. Later this year, eight members of this group—four men and four women—will enter a $30-million superstructure called Biosphere II and live inside it for the next two years with almost no help from the outside.

Covering 2½ acres (1 hectare), Biosphere II resembles a giant greenhouse. Under its glass-and-steel roof are five sepa-

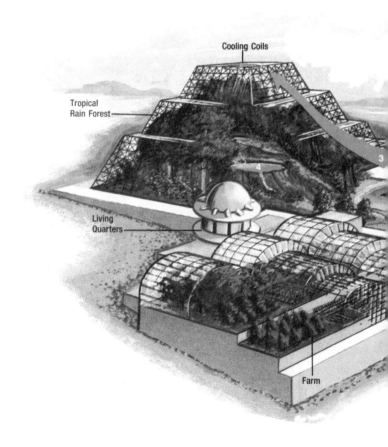

rate biological environments, or *biomes:* a patch of desert, a marsh, a *savannah* (a tree-shaded grassland), a 1-million-gallon (3.8-million-liter) ocean, and a tropical rain forest with a waterfall. The eight scientists, or *biospherians,* will eat and sleep in a two-story office-apartment complex located next to a barnyard with chickens, goats, and pigs and a farm where fruits, vegetables, and grains are grown.

Home Sweet Biome

Biosphere II is a radical experiment in ecology. Its designers haven't just tossed a bunch of plants and animals together and hoped for the best. They know that animals and plants live in complex arrangements with one another and their physical surroundings, called *ecosystems.* Biosphere II's goal is to find the right mixture of plants and animals for an artificial, self-sustaining ecosystem.

Biosphere II's designers know, for example, that insects are essential ingredients in any ecosystem because they help break down dead plant and animal matter. Consequently, Biosphere II is home to 200 species of bugs. But insect populations must be kept under control, so the five biomes are also home to bug-eating birds, lizards, toads, and bats.

Every detail in Biosphere II is part of a grand ecological design. The leaf litter that falls from trees and drifts into streams provides fish with shade and food. Tortoises in the desert walk on soft, windblown sand that doesn't cut their feet. Flowering plants offer their nectar to the local bees, and the bees return the favor by pollinating the plants.

Once the biospherians are locked up tight inside the huge greenhouse, the only things they'll receive from the outside world are sunlight, electricity, and electronic communications (TV and radio reception and computer mail). Everything else—water, air, food—must be recycled again and again, as it is in nature. A dire

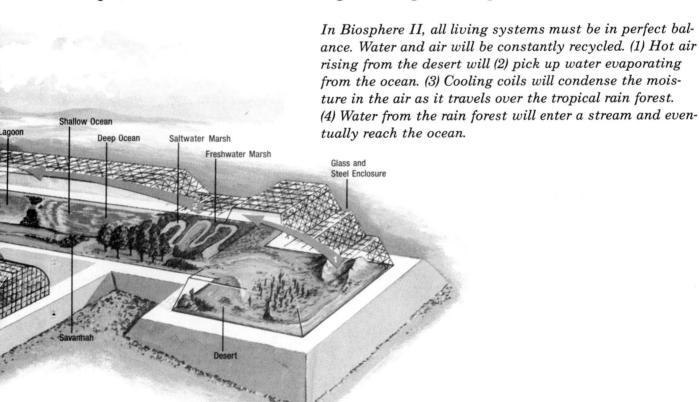

In Biosphere II, all living systems must be in perfect balance. Water and air will be constantly recycled. (1) Hot air rising from the desert will (2) pick up water evaporating from the ocean. (3) Cooling coils will condense the moisture in the air as it travels over the tropical rain forest. (4) Water from the rain forest will enter a stream and eventually reach the ocean.

Lagoon

Shallow Ocean

Deep Ocean

Saltwater Marsh

Freshwater Marsh

Glass and Steel Enclosure

Savannah

Desert

emergency, such as a serious illness, will be a biospherian's only excuse for leaving.

Visit to a Small Planet

Biosphere II's designers hope that the lessons learned from this experiment will lay the groundwork for future off-world habitats, such as space stations and colonies on other planets. They also hope to improve science's understanding of phenomena such as the greenhouse effect here on Biosphere I (Earth). Many climatologists think that carbon dioxide pollution is warming up our planet, though they don't know by how much. Perhaps by experimenting with carbon dioxide levels in a closed environment like Biosphere II, the scientists will gain a clearer picture of global warming.

Of course, Biosphere II is not without critics, some of whom wonder about the fate of certain vital nutrients, such as nitrogen and phosphorous, that must circulate through any ecosystem. Plants absorb these nutrients from the soil and use them to build plant tissue. Animals eat the plants for energy and leave behind the nutrients in the form of manure and dead tissue. Bacteria and fungi break down the manure and tissue into component parts, which enter the soil, enabling the cycle to begin anew. Critics say that the nutrients in an artificial environment may get stuck somewhere in the cycle, exhausting the soil and its ability to nourish plants.

Concerns also exist about carbon dioxide depletion. On Earth, plants take in CO_2 from the air and expel oxygen. Animals breathe in that oxygen and release CO_2. Skeptics doubt that the animals in Biosphere II can provide enough CO_2 to sustain its diversity of plant life. A food shortage could then follow.

But skepticism is one of the motors of scientific progress, and the biospherians are eager to put their glass-enclosed mini-planet to the test. "This is not just a Disneyland for eight people," says Biosphere II botanist Linda Leigh. "I think the benefits that are going to come out of it are going to be phenomenal."

One thing the biospherians may experience is a new brand of home-sickness. Laura Cornell's illustration, "Missing Mom and Dad," implies the essential point that "home" is more than the sum of its parts—something to do with "family" and all its entanglements.

Some of the same principles of clean living, at the "Dome" (see the article about Biosphere II in this section) or elsewhere, apply to your own house. If you want to take charge, be a member of the environmental detective force, or score a giant step for mankind, start here. Related wisdom: The journey into the distant future begins with a single step.

Don't Houseclean ... Airclean!

from National Geographic World

List of plants that fight pollution from Humpty Dumpty

Plant a Green Cleaning Machine

Grow houseplants. Scientists at NASA, the National Aeronautics and Space Administration, tested ways to keep the space station air fresh. They found that leaves, roots, and bacteria in the soil of some plants "eat" harmful chemicals such as benzene, taking them from the air. Peace lilies, spider plants, Chinese evergreen, some philodendron, English ivy, and mother-in-law's tongue are examples. About 20 such plants in 10-inch pots may clean the air in a 1,800-square-foot house.

Air It Out and Dry It Up

When using aerosol sprays, paint, or strong cleaners, open the windows so fumes can escape. Fans in the attic, bathroom, kitchen, and in windows help keep indoor air fresh. Make sure the fireplace, chimney, and furnace are cleaned yearly.

Bacteria, fungi, mold, and mildew grow fast in damp places. Released into the air, they can make some people sick or set off

allergic reactions. The best way to control them is to control moisture. Clean small humidifiers daily. Drain water from a de-humidifier frequently. Dry wet carpeting quickly.

Consider Careful Storage

If your parents must use a home product that gives off harmful fumes, ask them to buy only small amounts at a time. Store leftovers outside the house, in a garage or a shed. If that is impossible, call your local waste management office for information on proper disposal. Have you ever noticed that paint thinner evaporates from a container that is stored for a long time? The vapor that escapes contains the same hazardous chemicals that are in the liquid.

Shop Smart

Some companies sell products that cause less indoor air pollution. Ask your parents to look for building products and

carpeting with as little formaldehyde as possible. Encourage your family to use fewer aerosol sprays such as air fresheners, hair sprays, and insect repellents. Aerosols in the U.S. no longer contain the chemicals blamed for harming the earth's upper atmosphere. But they do have chemicals that, when inhaled for a long time, may make some people sick.

Use Safe Stand-Ins

Make substitutes for products that contain harmful chemicals. A paste of baking soda and hot water applied with a rough-sided sponge is a safe oven cleaner. A barely damp cloth makes wood furniture dust-free, and a mixture of vegetable oil and lemon oil shines unwaxed wood. A combination of 1/2 cup of borax and one gallon of water killed germs well enough to satisfy a hospital that used the combination as a disinfectant.

Healthful Home Work

Certain chemicals in the house may set off allergic reactions or, over time, cause illnesses. Below are safe and effective substitutes.

1. **Cleansers:** Some release chemicals that can cause respiratory problems. Follow the directions on the label. Never mix solutions. While cleaning, keep windows open.

2. **Moth repellents:** Store them with wool clothes in an airtight trunk, or don't use them. Put clothes in plastic bags with cedar shavings or lavender.

3. **Dry-cleaned clothes:** An odor means they are releasing perchlorethylene fumes. Dry cleaners should be able to remove most of the chemical. Your parents may ask to have it done.

4. Air-conditioning units: Rid them of mold and bacteria that grow in their drip pans by emptying and cleaning the pans often.

5. Gas stoves: The carbon monoxide and nitrogen dioxide their flames release should be directed outside by an exhaust fan. Remind your parents to have your stove serviced regularly.

6. Insect sprays: For insect-free plants, spray on soapy water. Try to avoid attracting insects in the house by removing trash and standing water and by keeping food covered.

7. Formaldehyde products: To reduce formaldehyde fumes, grow houseplants such as English ivy. They "eat" the harmful chemical out of the air.

8. Tobacco smoke: To avoid the many harmful chemicals in its vapors, ask your parents to set a rule: No smoking indoors!

9. House paints: While painting, open the windows. For 24 hours after finishing, leave them open and stay out of the room.

Houseplants That Fight Interior Air Pollution

- bamboo palm
- English ivy
- gerbera daisy**
- marginata
- mother-in-law's tongue
- potted mum**
- philodendron*
- spider plant*
- Chinese evergreen*
- ficus
- Janet Craig
- mass cane/corn cane
- Peace Lily
- warneckei
- golden pothos*
- dragon plants (dracaena)

*Rated the most effective in removing formaldehyde. The spider plant is also superior in removing carbon monoxide from the air in closed chambers.
**Rated superior in removing benzene.

4. Kids In Charge

Parents can't help it — they worry. So when you're on your own, observe a few rules for safety, and they'll cut you loose more often. And maybe you'll even have some tips to pass on to them.

How Not to Be Bitten by a Dog

by Ann Elliot, illustration by Bron Smith

from Humpty Dumpty

Most dogs like people as much as most people like dogs. They are wonderful friends and the best of pets. But a few dogs are mean.

You will not be afraid when you meet a mean dog if you have a plan. If you are not afraid, you are much less likely to be bitten. A dog knows when you are afraid. He thinks, "Something around here must be scary!" and then he may behave foolishly.

An animal doctor has made up three rules to tell you what to do when you meet a strange or frightening dog. Here they are:

1. DON'T TALK TO STRANGERS.
2. BE A TREE.
3. BE A LOG.

This is what they mean:

1. *DON'T TALK TO STRANGERS*

You've heard that before. It means don't talk to strange people. It also means don't talk to strange dogs. If you see a dog you don't know — **leave him alone!**

Don't try to pat him or call him. Tell a grown-up about him. It's unsafe for the dog to be alone. He could get lost or hit by a car. The police or animal wardens can help him find his owner.

2. *BE A TREE*

Suppose a strange dog, or a dog that looks mean, is running toward you. What should you do?

Stand still. Never, ever run!

If even the kindest dog sees a rabbit running, he thinks, "This is exciting!" and hurtles after it. If the rabbit's smart, it stays still and the dog often walks right by. You are smarter than a rabbit. So, put your elbows tight against your chest and your fists under your chin. Pretend you are a tree, but without branches. If you put your hands in the air like branches, the dog may think you are holding something and may jump up to discover what.

Talk quietly to the dog. You might say, "Hi, pooch!" or something funny like, "Would you like a watermelon?" This helps him know you are not mean.

Try not to stare at him because that makes him uncomfortable. If he's uncomfortable, he may get scared. Remember, if he's scared, he may get mean.

Chances are, if you stand like a tree

without branches, he'll just sniff you. Don't let that bother you. It's how a dog gets acquainted.

3. BE A LOG

Suppose you are sitting or lying on the ground and a dog rushes toward you. Or suppose you are taken by surprise and he knocks you down. Now what?

It would be a bad idea to jump up and be a tree. The dog would be most surprised! The best thing is to be a log. Roll onto your tummy, keep your legs together, and put your fists behind your neck so that your arms cover your ears.

Lie still!

A dog won't bite a log. He may poke you with his paw or nose, but that's checking the "log" out. He'll soon be bored. Don't get up until he has gone away. Then go tell a grown-up what has happened.

These rules are not just for kids. They are good for grown-ups too.

While thinking about safety around dogs, remember two extra tips:

Never bother a dog when he's eating. Even your own dog wants to be private when eating.

Never enter a dog's territory if he growls. His territory is his yard, his house, or his car. If he growls, he's warning you away. Guarding territory is his job. Wait for his owner to help.

Adapted from Animal Bite Prevention Program, by J. Michael Cornwall, DVM. For more information write to Glencoe Animal Hospital, 3712 N. High Street, Columbus, OH 43214.

Bulletproof School Kids

from Current Events

There's a new fashion statement for kids in New York City—bulletproof clothing. After a summer of violence, a number of parents are sending their kids to school wearing jackets lined with Kevlar—a thin bullet-resistant material. Kevlar is five times stronger than steel. It is widely used in bulletproof vests for police and in armor for vehicles.

Risks of injury aren't so great inside school as they are going to school. In one week in August, four New York City children were shot dead by stray bullets. New York Mayor David Dinkins complained that guns were now as easy to obtain as candy.

Guardian Group International Corp, a major manufacturer of Kevlar, says bulletproof schoolbags and clipboards are also selling well.

One eight-year-old boy said he liked the feel of his denim jacket lined with Kevlar. "It feels like you have good protection and nobody even knows you have it on," he said.

Just when you think it's safe to go to school, something comes along that nearly ruins your day...

My Dog Ate My Homework

by Susan Mitsch, illustration by Mark A. Hicks
from Child Life

My dog Barker ate my homework! That's why I couldn't turn it in today.

Oh, I know what you're thinking. But, really, my dog *did* eat my homework! Just let me explain.

First, you have to know my teacher, Ms. Bear. Her name isn't Ms. Bear for nothing. She's a real man-eater. They say that once, long ago, a student of hers didn't turn in his homework—and he was never seen again. He just disappeared. But everyone knows what *really* happened to him. So the kids in my class *always* bring in their homework. Or else.

Well, this morning was a very, very windy morning. I opened my folder on the front porch just long enough to check for my milk money, when—*PUFF!*—a breeze blew my homework away!

I started to chase my homework down the street. I didn't even want to think about what Ms. Bear might do if I lost it. So I ran as fast as I could.

The wind tossed my homework right over a high fence. I peeked through a hole in the fence and saw hundreds of workers building a skyscraper. And there, on top of a pile of pipes, was my homework!

I squeezed under the fence just in time to see a crane lifting the pipes—and my homework—all the way up to the thirteenth floor! I ran to the elevator.

"Hurry!" I yelled to a workman. "I have to get to the thirteenth floor!"

"Now, sonny," the worker said, "kids aren't allowed around here."

"But you don't understand!" I shouted. "My homework blew up there! My teacher is Ms. Bear, and if I—"

The man stopped dead in his tracks. "Did you say 'Ms. Bear'? *The* Ms. Bear? I've heard of her! Here, sonny, take a hard hat. Hop on!"

Up, up, up we went to the thirteenth floor. We got there just in time to see another workman kick my homework off a beam! Down, down, down it floated, till it landed on a fruit stand far below. A bald man was loading fruit onto the stand.

"I've got to get down there!" I shouted,

45

and back down we went as fast as the elevator would go.

I ran as fast as I could to the fruit stand. Somewhere under it all was my homework! I started looking, throwing fruit left and right.

"Hey! Whatta ya doin' with my fruit, kid?" the bald man yelled, looking very angry.

"My homework's in here somewhere. If Ms. Bear finds out I lost it, I'll—"

"Ms. Bear?" the bald man said. "Why didn't you tell me that? Come on, kid, I'll help." And the two of us searched, throwing apples, oranges and bananas all over the sidewalk. And then I saw it!

One corner was stuck under a peach, but when I picked up the fruit to grab the paper—*WHOOSH!*—another gust of wind took it flying again. Away I went after it.

I watched the wind carry the paper across the street. The bridge over the river was up and traffic was stopped, so the paper blew right over the edge. It landed softly on a huge boat going by! Now I was in real trouble.

A policeman who had been directing traffic was standing nearby. "Please, help me! Help me!" I begged, out of breath. "My homework . . . the boat . . . Ms. Bear!"

"Ms. Bear?" the policeman shouted. "Jumpin' catfish! Hold on, I'll help!" He blew and blew so hard on his whistle that the boat stopped right in the water.

"Thanks!" I cried, running to the edge of the river. There I borrowed a rowboat and row-row-rowed out to the big boat.

"Captain," I said to the tall man on board, "I lost my homework somewhere on this ship and if I don't get it back, Ms. Bear is gonna—"

"Ms. Bear? Yikes! Let's get going!" said the captain. But before we could even start, pirates came on board!

"We're going to take over this here ship, matey!" growled the head pirate, an ugly man with one wooden leg.

"Not before I find my homework, you're not!" I yelled. "My teacher is Ms. Bear!"

"Sharks alive!" cried the pirate. "Is she here?" All the pirates were so afraid of her that they found the ship's jail, jumped into it and locked the door tight behind them.

Suddenly, a loud *POW!* sounded. My homework blew out of the smokestack high into the air and settled slowly over the water. A blue whale jumped out of the water and grabbed it. I put on a life jacket and dove in after him.

The whale was swimming fast, but I caught up with him. Nothing was going to stop me from getting my homework! I wrestled that whale and he wrestled me. It was a terrible fight.

"You'll give me my homework or I'll . . . I'll . . ."

"You'll what?" asked the whale.

"I'll tell Ms. Bear you wouldn't let me have it!"

"Ms. Bear! Oh, no!" he cried, and with that he spouted my homework right into the air. But just my luck, a seagull snatched it before I could get it!

I swam back to the ship, sadly. Now I would never get my homework. But the captain said, "Here, son, you can borrow our helicopter."

Another chance!

I hopped in and tried to follow the bird, but I couldn't see it anywhere. Then, up ahead, I saw a real Martian spaceship! The Martians were taking samples of Earth's animal life and guess what? They wanted a seagull! They grabbed the seagull, my homework and all, and flew off—*ZIP!*—straight to Mars.

I could do nothing now. I gave the helicopter back to the captain and headed to-

ward school, depressed and tired. *Ms. Bear is going to eat me alive and no one will ever see me again,* I thought.

On the way, I had to pass my house. I thought I'd stop in for a quick, cool glass of water—probably my last! I went out into my backyard to say goodbye to my dog and there, right on my own lawn, was my *homework!* The Martians must have seen my name on it and realized that it was a paper for Ms. Bear and dropped it off for me here so I wouldn't get in trouble. I was overjoyed!

I ran out to grab the paper—but so did my dog Barker! He thought I wanted to play. He chewed it and shook it and stepped on it and chewed it some more.

"No, Barker, no!" I cried. "That's my homework! Bad dog! Put it down!"

But Barker didn't understand. He jumped and tore it until he had bitten my homework into tiny little bits. He dog-laughed and wagged his tail. He thought we were playing a game.

So now I'm on my way to school. I'm five hours late, and I don't have my homework. I guess I'll just have to tell Ms. Bear the truth—my dog ate my homework.

Do you think she'll believe me?

We're saying here that being in charge can also mean having to understand how things work, the way they are put together, what makes them function as they are supposed to. Now, don't be too encouraged to take matters into your own hands, and don't take anything apart unless you're certain that you can put it back together again . . .

Pencil Sharpener
&
Clocks and Watches

from Scienceland

Pencil Sharpener

A pencil sharpener is named for what it does, sharpen pencils. It comes in different shapes and sizes. Some are little pocket knives, others are so small they can be held in the palm of your hand. There are also electric pencil sharpeners. The cutaway pencil sharpener below is seen in schools and homes. The inside is not as simple as it looks on the outside.

Tapering cutters with many blades shave off the wood on the pencil. They continue to go around and around until the pencil tip is shaved to a sharp point. The shavings drop into a container that can be taken out and emptied. More and more people are using electric sharpeners because they are faster. However, they can be more difficult to repair. Furthermore, they cannot be used where there is no electricity. Except for speed, the manual or hand-wound sharpener might be a better choice. What do you think?

How a Pencil Is Made*

Did you know that a pencil is made out of two pieces of wood joined together with glue? After the graphite stick is placed into the trough of one piece of wood, it is covered by the other half. Then, after the two wood pieces are glued, the pencil is tightly pressed together.

*Still called "lead pencil" today because pencils began with the use of lead to write on thin leather called parchment *pärch'mənt*. Graphite *gra'fīt* softened with clay is used today.

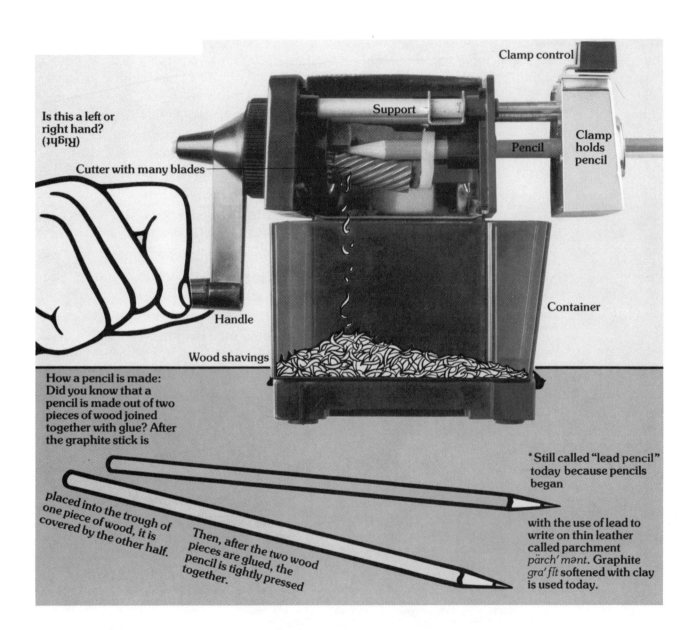

Clamp control

Is this a left or
right hand?
(Right)

Support

Pencil

Clamp
holds
pencil

Cutter with many blades

Handle

Container

Wood shavings

How a pencil is made:
Did you know that a
pencil is made out of two
pieces of wood joined
together with glue? After
the graphite stick is

placed into the trough of
one piece of wood, it is
covered by the other half.

Then, after the two wood
pieces are glued, the
pencil is tightly pressed
together.

*Still called "lead pencil"
today because pencils
began

with the use of lead to
write on thin leather
called parchment
pärch′ mənt. Graphite
grȧ′ fit softened with clay
is used today.

Clocks and Watches

Clocks and watches keep time. Since both keep time, is there a difference between clocks and watches? They look the same on the outside. Clocks usually are timepieces that are too large to carry. They hang on walls or sit on tables and dressers. Watches are smaller. They are worn (wristwatch) or carried in pockets (pocketwatch). Some are in lockets or brooches worn by women.

How do clocks and watches differ on the inside? Some run on springs wound by hand or by moving weights (self-winding). Most, today, run on batteries or electricity. They are more accurate and easier to use.

Here is an alarm clock. It runs on springs wound by hand or manually. There is a hammer in the middle at the top. It strikes both bells to sound a loud alarm. The alarm goes off at the time it is set to ring. It must be turned off and the spring rewound. Otherwise, it will not go off the next time it is set.

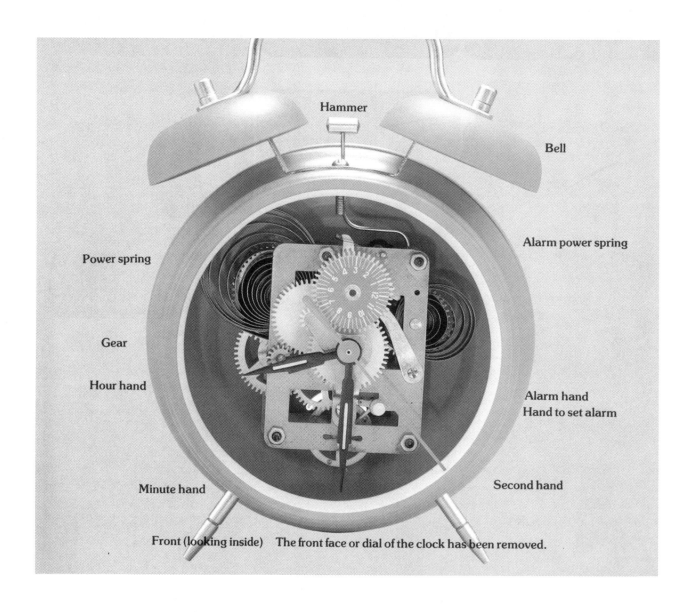

Hammer

Bell

Power spring

Alarm power spring

Gear

Hour hand

Alarm hand
Hand to set alarm

Minute hand

Second hand

Front (looking inside)   The front face or dial of the clock has been removed.

Here is the inside of the back of a quartz crystal watch. Electricity from the battery is sent through the crystal. This makes the watch keep time very accurately, far better than a watch that keeps time with a spring.

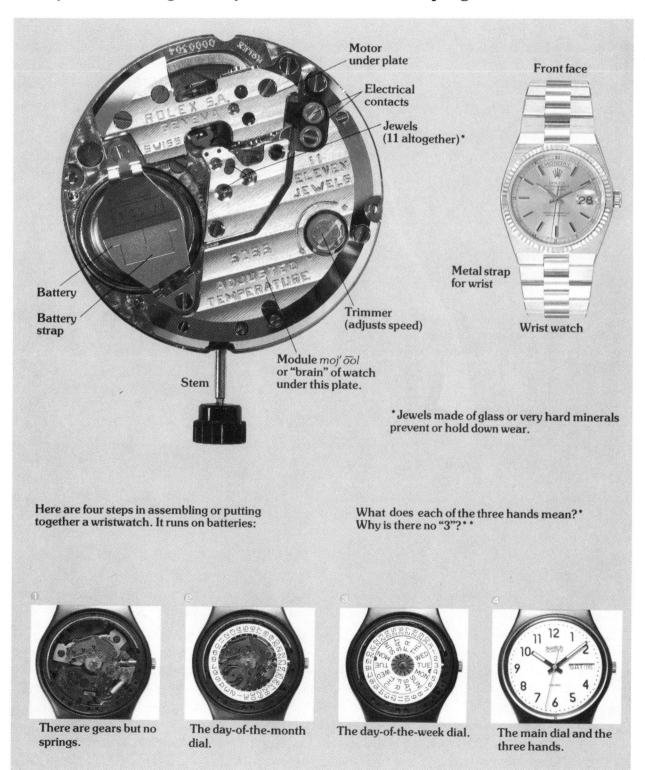

Motor under plate

Electrical contacts

Jewels (11 altogether)*

Front face

Battery

Battery strap

Stem

Trimmer (adjusts speed)

Module *moj′ ōol* or "brain" of watch under this plate.

Metal strap for wrist

Wrist watch

*Jewels made of glass or very hard minerals prevent or hold down wear.

Here are four steps in assembling or putting together a wristwatch. It runs on batteries:

What does each of the three hands mean?*
Why is there no "3"?**

There are gears but no springs.

The day-of-the-month dial.

The day-of-the-week dial.

The main dial and the three hands.

*Short hand (hour), long hand (minute), red hand (seconds)

**Because the date window must be there.

The photo that accompanies this article first appeared in National Geographic World; *it shows the way in which these children are launching themselves into their futures. You can see the chronicles of homeless children in a new book,* Shooting Back.

Shooting for a Dream

from National Geographic World

"I love taking pictures," says Dion Johnson, 13. "When I finish school I want to become a professional photographer." Dion, who lives in Washington, D.C., may do just that. Not long ago, though, Dion's goal might have seemed impossible. For two long years his family had no place to call home. He lived in a city homeless shelter with his mother, two brothers, and sister.

Now the family has moved to their own home. Dion's pictures line the living room walls. He shoots and develops them with the help of professional photographers, many from newspapers and magazines. They volunteer in a program called "Shooting Back." The program offers photography workshops to homeless children. "Dion was the first child I worked with," says Jim Hubbard, a photo-journalist and founder of the program. "I wanted to give talented youngsters like him a chance to learn photography as a possible career. And I wanted them to have a creative way to 'shoot back' nonviolently at the violence

they see on the streets." Since March 1989 more than 150 homeless and formerly homeless children have taken part in the workshops in black-and-white photography. Fifty photographers taught them.

"Jim came to my shelter every Saturday," Dion recalls. "He gave me a camera and showed me how to use it. I had fun taking pictures of my family, friends, and school."

Dion also photographed less happy scenes. His pictures recorded the tragedy of a fire that swept through his shelter. "It was sad," says Dion. "At first I didn't want to take pictures of where it had burned. But then I did. Sometimes it's like a news story. Your pictures tell people what happened, what it was like. That's important."

Through the program Dion has learned to develop and print his own pictures. For him that's the best part of photography. Someday he hopes to go to work for a newspaper or a magazine. And he has a special ambition: "I want to teach photography to kids," he says. "I'd like to teach

Columbia Thomas, 12, caught the action when a boy decided to cool off in a fountain.

them what I learned, how to do it." He has this advice for would-be photographers: "Get to know your subject and learn how the camera works."

The program now has a permanent media center with a darkroom and a classroom, where homeless children can take classes in photography and in other forms of journalism. Many photographs from the program have been exhibited at the Washington Project for the Arts gallery. Dion's pictures were among those selected. "I like having people admire my pictures," he says. "It makes me feel proud, knowing that I took them."

Here's more on kids in charge—and some of them are turning a profit! Stuff away those handmade signs for your lemonade stand—these kids mean business. And don't miss "The Pride of Parrott" or "They're in Clover." You'll want to see how big a difference other people your age can make.

Sweet Jobs: Kids in Business

from National Geographic World

Making Dough with Cookies

Whether it's making cookies or making change, Tardkeith McBride and Maurice Cobb learn how to handle dough at Champ Cookies & Things in Washington, D.C. Tardkeith, 14, and Maurice, 15, are among more than 65 young people who operate the factory.

Ali Khan, a former teacher and school guidance counselor, started Champ Cookies four years ago with three friends. Their idea was to help keep youngsters out of the crime and drug world. "We teach them how a business runs and encourage them to take pride in their work," Khan says.

Working for a few hours after school each day, the students learn every step of the business. "They buy the supplies, measure the ingredients, operate the equipment, bake the cookies, package and sell them," says Khan.

President Bush has invited Champ's top four cookie sellers to the White House for lunch. But it doesn't take a trip to the White House to make the "champs" feel proud. At Champ Cookies everyone's tops. William Brooks, one of the teenage workers, sums it up best: "Champ Cookies is a team kind of thing."

In Business with Birds

Nikky Hoyne will never get caught with all her eggs in one basket. They wouldn't fit. Nikky, 9, of Hinsdale, Illinois, sells as many as seven dozen eggs a day. When she began keeping chickens as pets four years ago, she gave the eggs away. Now Nikky has about 25 customers who buy them on a regular basis. "People like my eggs because they are so good and so fresh," she says. Nikky spends several hours a day caring for chicks and feeding, cleaning, and playing with her hens. For Nikky it's a labor of love. "My chickens are my friends," she explains.

"Beeing" Sisters

The Tarrant sisters of Hunt, Texas, make it their business to help spellers

© STEVEN PUMPHREY

The Tarrants: Natalie, at left, Huntley, and Valerie.

"bee" prepared. Natalie, 15, Huntley, 11, and Valerie, 17, visit Hunt Elementary School. Each of the three girls has won a first round of the Scripps-Howard National Spelling Bee.

As top bee competitors they have used their experiences to develop three spelling study aids. In 1983, for example, Valerie published the first edition of *Valerie's Spelling Bee Supplement*. It contains the meanings and pronunciations of 3,000 practice words she had looked up to prepare for the regional bee.

Each year the girls work with their parents and a small staff to update their products and to fill orders. The earnings go into savings for their college educations.

Profits aren't their only reward. Last year 30 of the National Spelling Bee finalists, including the winner, used Valerie's supplement to prepare for competition.

"Being able to help other spellers means the most to me," says Valerie.

Already a Vice President

Mary Rodas knows what kind of toys kids enjoy. That's why Catco, a toy company in New York City, depends on Mary's help in developing new products—the cloth-covered balloons on her desk, for example. "I helped pick the patterns and colors for the balloon balls," says Mary, 15, who lives in Union City, New Jersey.

Mary's career began when she was only four years old. A neighbor who invents toys noticed Mary's ability to figure out how things are made. Later, when he started Catco, he began to ask her for advice about the company's products. Now Mary is a vice president.

Mary's job doesn't interfere with her schoolwork or her social life. She still makes good grades and stays in touch with friends. After all, she says, "My job is to know what kids like."

Nice Arrangement

Brandon Bozek is a budding businessman. Brandon has been running Bloomin' Express, his flower delivery service, for more than a year. "I sell flower arrangements the way other people sell magazines—by subscription," explains Brandon, 11, of Miami, Florida. "I like telling my customers about the flowers and then delivering them."

Brandon claims that Bloomin' Express flowers last longer than arrangements from supermarkets. "They're fresher," he explains.

Each week Brandon finds out what his nine subscribers want, phones in the orders to the supplier, and—with his father's help—makes deliveries.

Sometimes Brandon's mother lends a hand, too. "My mom is great about helping me figure taxes and keep records—things I haven't learned to do yet," Brandon says.

Brandon hopes to increase his customers to about 15. "Finding new subscribers is the hardest part of my business," he says. For now most of Brandon's customers are friends of people he knows.

Whether you're talking about a boy putting a city on the map, three girls protecting an endangered species, or schoolchildren saving a piece of the rainforest, these kids are proof that you don't have to be an all-knowing adult to make a difference.

The Pride of Parrott

from Kid City

Everyone likes to point to their hometown on a map. But what if your hometown isn't there? For years the people who lived in Parrott, Virginia complained that their town wasn't listed on maps. "It made us feel like we didn't count," said the town's postmaster, Barry Albert.

Ten-year-old Chris Muncy changed all that. He wrote a letter to the people who publish the *Rand McNally Road Atlas.* "I

want you to add the town where my grandpa, grandma and uncle live. It's called Parrott, Virginia."

The people who work for Rand McNally agreed with Chris. They added the town of Parrott to their 1991 road atlas.

How did the folks who live in Parrott feel about this? They were thrilled! They even threw a parade and Chris was the guest of honor. All the people who lived in Parrott showed up for the parade. All 800 of them!

Kids Saved It!

by Chris Wille
from Ranger Rick

The roar of a howler monkey boomed through the treetops. Down below, four kids stopped walking and looked up. But the jungle was too dark and thick with leaves for them to see anything. Henri

tried to copy the monkey's call. But his yell sounded more like a small hoot than a howl.

"No question who's king of *this* jungle," Cynthia said with a little chuckle.

Henri, Cynthia, Kevin, and Evelyn were exploring a tropical rainforest. They were in the mountains of Costa Rica, a small country in Central America. The kids weren't afraid of getting lost. The trail they were on was easy to follow, and they knew this forest like their own backyard. In fact, it *was* their backyard. They lived in Monteverde (MON-tay-VAIR-day), a small village surrounded by deep rainforest.

The four kids moved on down the trail, looking here and there for the next discovery. They were glad to live in a place so full of incredible plants and animals.

There were so many sights, sounds, and smells in the forest that the four kids never got bored. There was always a new adventure, always a new surprise. But this rainforest was special in another way — it had been saved forever by kids just like themselves!

A Gift from the Children

In 1987, a scientist who studies rainforests visited a school in Sweden. She told the kids that the forests were being cut down — to make lumber and to clear the land for farms and ranches. She also told them that rainforests are the homes of millions of kinds of plants and animals. (So many different kinds live there that we may never discover and name them all.)

One of the kids, nine-year-old Roland Tiensuu, cared very much about wildlife. So he wondered what he could do to help save it. Then he had a great idea. "Why can't we earn money to help buy a rainforest park?" he asked. The scientist answered, "You can." And his teacher and classmates said, "Let's do it!"

By putting on plays, recycling, working at small jobs, making and selling T-shirts, saving allowances, and asking people for donations, the Swedish kids raised a lot of money. They sent it to a group of scientists in Costa Rica, who bought 15 acres (6 ha) of rainforest. (One acre is about the size of a football field.)

Soon, kids from all over Sweden began raising money to buy more rainforest. The idea spread to the United States, Canada, England, and Japan. So far, thousands of kids have raised more than a million dollars!

The money is used to buy parts of the rainforest around Monteverde. A special preserve there has been named the International Children's Rainforest. More than 140,000 acres have already been saved. And the monkeys, birds, and other things living there are now protected.

The Search for a Golden Toad

Henri, Cynthia, Kevin, and Evelyn moved along slowly, watching for birds and other animals. But they were looking especially for a famous creature called the golden toad. They wanted to show one to a group of kids from the United States. These kids had helped raise money for the forest, and now they were coming to visit.

Golden toads live only in the forests around Monteverde. And what makes them so special is that the male is completely orange. But the toads are so rare that they are very hard to find. If the kids found one today, they'd know where to look for more when their visitors were there.

"Let's check down by the creek," Kevin suggested. They scrambled down the trail to a small jungle stream. The Children's Rainforest has lots of creeks because it rains there almost every day. Around 118 inches (3 m) of rain fall every year. (A forest in the eastern United States gets around 45 inches, so you can see why a rainforest is so wet!)

Suddenly Evelyn let out a whistle. "Look!" she said. The others followed Evelyn's finger as she pointed into the tree-tops. Peeking down at the kids were two furry mammals—an olingo (OL-ing-go) and a tamandua (TUH-mun-DWA).

But then the kids saw something else. It was a quetzal (ket-SUL)—one of the most beautiful birds in the world. The quetzal's back is as green as an emerald. Its belly is as red as a ruby. And a male's tail feathers may be three feet (1 m) long. In ancient times, Mayan Indians used quetzal tail feathers to decorate the crowns of their kings.

Henri was now leading the others along the stream bank. Suddenly Cynthia whispered, "Careful of that salamander!" Just ahead of Henri's foot was a sleek, long-tailed creature. It blinked its eyes once, then scurried away under some dead leaves. Henri popped his hands down over the leaves and came up with his wiggling prize. The other kids checked out the salamander before Henri let it go.

After walking a little bit farther, Kevin stopped suddenly. "Wow, look!" he shouted. Everyone peered at what seemed to be a gleaming gold nugget lying on the ground. "Can you believe it? A gold beetle!" Gold beetles are one of the most beautiful insects on earth. And they are so rare that scientists know very little about them.

On a Tapir's Trail

The kids watched the beetle until it scurried out of sight. Then Cynthia no-

© MICHAEL AND PATRICIA FOGDEN

ticed something on the muddy ground in front of Henri. It was a weird, three-toed track. A big track. Something with feet as big as a horse's had been there. All four kids knew what it had to be—a tapir (TAY-pur).

The tapir is the biggest animal in this forest. Its closest cousins are rhinoceroses and horses. But it looks more like a huge, dark brown pig with an extra-long snout. Tapirs live deep in the forest. At night they roam along streams and wander into forest clearings to feed. The Children's Rainforest is one of the few places left in Central America where tapirs can be found.

Now it was time for the kids to think about going home. "Well," said Evelyn, "we didn't find a golden toad."

"No, but maybe we'll get real lucky and find one when our visitors are here," said Henri. "Anyway, we *did* find a gold beetle,

so we'll know where to look later. And there will always be lots of other neat things for our visitors to see. That's what's so special about a rainforest—you may not find what you're looking for, but what you *do* find is just as good."

The four young explorers headed back to get ready for their guests. All around them, the insects buzzed, the frogs croaked, and the birds chirped and screeched. High overhead a howler monkey roared. Henri tried again to copy the monkey's call. And this time it answered back.

The kids looked at each other and grinned. To them, the monkey and all the other creatures of the forest were like friends. But even more than that, the animals were living proof of what kids can do to help save the world.

They're in Clover

from National Geographic World

Many people think it's good luck to find a four-leaf clover. Girl Scouts of Troop 189 in Windom, Minnesota, feel lucky when they find prairie bush clover. It's a rare plant classified as threatened. The Scouts helped protect the clover in a state park in Minnesota. To give the plant the sunlight it needs, the girls cleared away trees and shrubs from a section of prairie. For their hard work they received an award from the U.S. Fish and Wildlife Service, the agency that protects endangered and threatened species.

You may know other stories by E. Nesbit (some of her books are considered classics in children's literature) — this one is from The Railway Children, *but she also wrote* Five Children and It. *This is another version of "Kids Saved It!" (see previous article), but in this case, the lives they rescued were human ones.*

Saviors of the Train

by E. Nesbit
from Cricket

One morning Peter, Phyllis, and Bobbie decided to pick wild cherries. The cherry trees grew along the rocky face of the cliff out of which the mouth of the railway tunnel opened.

When the children got to the cutting, they leaned over the fence and looked down at what Phyllis said was exactly like a mountain gorge. "If it wasn't for the railway at the bottom, it would be as though the foot of man had never been there."

The sides of the cutting were of gray stone, roughly hewn. Among the rocks, grass and flowers grew, and seeds dropped by birds had taken root and grown into bushes and trees. A flight of steps led down to the railway line.

"The cherries will be easy to get at from the steps," said Peter. They went along the fence toward the little swing gate at the top.

Suddenly Bobbie said, "Hush. What's that?"

"That" was a very odd noise indeed — a soft noise, but plainly to be heard through the sound of the wind in the branches. It was a rustling, whispering sound. As they listened, it stopped and then began again.

This time it grew louder and more rustling and rumbling.

"Look," cried Peter. "The tree over there!"

The tree he pointed at was moving — not the way trees ought to move when the wind blows through them, but all in one piece, as though it were a live creature walking down the side of the cutting.

"It's moving!" cried Bobbie. "Oh, look! And so are the others."

"It's magic," said Phyllis breathlessly.

It really did seem like magic. All the trees appeared to be slowly walking down toward the railway line, a tree with gray leaves bringing up the rear like some old shepherd driving a flock of green sheep. Stones and loose earth fell down and rattled on the railway metals far below.

"It's *all* coming down," said Peter. And just as he spoke, the great rock underneath the walking trees leaned slowly forward. The trees stood still and shivered. They seemed to hesitate a moment, and then rock and trees and grass and bushes slipped away from the face of the cutting and fell on the line with a crash that could have been heard half a mile off. A cloud of dust rose up.

"Oh," said Peter, awe-struck.

"Look what a great mound it's made!" said Bobbie.

"Yes, it's right across the line," said Phyllis.

"That'll take some sweeping up," said Bobbie.

"Yes," said Peter slowly, leaning on the fence. Then he stood upright. "The 11:29 hasn't gone by yet. We must let them know at the station, or there'll be a frightful accident."

"Let's run," said Bobbie, and began.

But Peter cried, "Come back!" His face looked whiter than they had ever seen it.

"No time," he said. "It's ten miles away and it's past eleven. If we only had something red, we could go round the corner and wave to the train."

"We might wave anyway."

"They'd only think it was just *us,* as usual. We've waved so often before. Anyway, let's get down."

They went down the steep stairs. Bobbie was pale and shivering. Peter's face looked thinner than usual. Phyllis was red-faced and damp with anxiety.

"Oh, how hot I am!" she said. "I wish we hadn't put on our—" She stopped short and ended in quite a different tone, "—our flannel petticoats."

Bobbie turned at the bottom of the stairs.

"Oh yes," she cried, "*they're* red! Let's take them off."

With the petticoats rolled up under their arms, they ran along the railway, skirting the newly fallen mound of stones and rock and earth and bent, crushed, twisted trees. They reached the corner that hid the mound from the straight line of railway that ran half a mile without curve or corner.

"Now," said Peter, taking hold of the larger flannel petticoat.

"You're not—," Phyllis faltered, "you're not going to *tear* them?"

"Oh yes," said Bobbie, "tear them into little bits. Don't you see, Phil, if we can't stop the train, there'll be a real live accident, with people *killed.*"

Peter divided each petticoat into three pieces. "There! Now we've got six flags." He looked at his watch. "And we've got seven minutes. We must have flagstaffs."

The knives given to boys are, for some odd reason, seldom of the kind of steel that keeps sharp. The young saplings had to be broken off. Two came up by the roots. The leaves were stripped from them.

"We must cut holes in the flags and run the sticks through the holes," said Peter. The knife was sharp enough to cut flannel. Two of the flags were set up in heaps of loose stones beneath the sleepers of the line. Then Phyllis and Bobbie each took a flag and stood ready to wave it as soon as the train came in sight.

"I shall have the other two myself," said Peter, "because it was my idea to wave something red."

"They're our petticoats," Phyllis was beginning, but Bobbie interrupted.

"Oh, what does it matter who waves what, if we can only save the train?"

Perhaps Peter had not rightly calculated the number of minutes it would take the 11:29 to get from the station to the place where they were, or perhaps the train was late. Anyway, it seemed a very long time that they waited.

Phyllis grew impatient. Peter relaxed his heroic attitude, and Bobbie began to feel sick with suspense.

It seemed to her that they had been standing there for hours, holding those silly little red flannel flags that no one would ever notice. The train would go rushing by them and tear round the corner and into that awful mound. And everyone would be killed. Her hands trembled so that she could hardly hold the flag. And then came the distant rumble and hum of the metals, and a puff of white steam showed far away along the stretch of line.

"Wave like mad!" said Peter. "When it gets to that big bush, step back, but go on waving! Don't stand *on* the line, Bobbie!"

The train came rattling along very, very fast.

"They don't see us! It's no good!" cried Bobbie.

The two little flags on the line swayed as the nearing train shook and loosened the heaps of stones that held them up. One slowly leaned over and fell. Bobbie jumped forward and caught it up and waved it; her hands did not tremble now.

"Keep off the line, you silly cuckoo!" said Peter fiercely. "Stand back!"

But Bobbie cried, "Not yet, not yet!" and waved her two flags right over the line. The front of the engine looked black and enormous.

"Oh, stop, stop, stop!" she cried. The oncoming rush of the train covered the sound of her voice. But afterward she wondered whether the engine itself had not heard her—for it slackened swiftly and stopped not twenty yards from the place where Bobbie's two flags waved over the line. She saw the great black engine stop dead, but somehow she could not stop waving the flags. And when the driver and the fireman had got off the engine and Peter and Phyllis had gone to meet them, Bobbie still waved the flags but more and more feebly and jerkily.

When the others turned toward her, she was lying across the line, still gripping the sticks of the little red flannel flags.

The engine driver picked her up, carried her to the train, and laid her on the cushions of a first-class carriage.

"Gone off in a faint," he said.

It was so horrible to see Bobbie lying so white and quiet.

"I believe that's what people look like when they're dead," whispered Phyllis.

"*Don't!*" said Peter sharply.

They sat by Bobbie on the blue cushions, and the train ran back. Before it reached their station, Bobbie sighed, opened her eyes, and began to cry. This cheered the others wonderfully. They had not known what to do when she was fainting, but now she was only crying, they could thump her on the back and tell her not to, just as they always did.

When the station was reached, the three were heroes. The praises they got were enough to turn anybody's head. Phyllis enjoyed herself thoroughly. Peter's ears got very red. Yet he, too, enjoyed himself. Only Bobbie wished they all wouldn't. She pulled at Peter's jacket. "Oh, come away! I want to go home," she said.

So they went. And as they went, station master and porter and guards and driver and fireman and passengers sent up a cheer.

"Oh, listen," cried Phyllis, "that's for *us!*"

"Yes," said Peter. "I'm glad I thought about waving something red."

"How lucky we put on our flannel petticoats!" said Phyllis.

Bobbie said nothing. She was thinking of the horrible mound and the trustful train rushing toward it.

"How dreadful if they had all been killed!" said Phyllis. "Wouldn't it, Bobbie?"

"We never got any cherries, after all," said Bobbie.

The others thought her rather heartless.

The next four articles are brought to you courtesy of Consumer Reports, the agency that protects any of us who will listen from making stupid mistakes when we spend money—its magazine, Zillions, certain to be of ever-increasing value well into the future, is a source of eye-opening surprises. Whether you are dealing with an allowance, or earnings from helping around the house, read on to make sure you're getting the best mileage for your money.

The Sneaky Sell

from Zillions

"Is *Zillions* getting lazy?" you ask. Couldn't we think up some fun and games of our own? We're happy to report that you'll never see any action-packed pages quite like these in *Zillions*. No, we don't have anything against good, clean fun. But that's not what you're looking at. These are *advertorials*—ads dressed up to look like just another part of the magazine around them. And that earns them a good, solid spot in our Sneaky Sell Hall of Shame.

Advertisers may be sneaky, but they're not stupid. They know that the more familiar kids are with their products, the more likely they are to buy them. That means slapping their commercials onto TV screens, slipping their products into movies, and plastering those brand names all over magazines kids love to read. But advertisers also realize that too much obvious product pushing may turn kids off. So what's an advertiser to do? Reach kids with advertising kids won't recognize as advertising. The perfect solution! For *them* maybe, but not for *you*.

What's wrong with making ads fun and interesting? Nothing, as long as the ad is clearly an ad. Just think of how your brain cells work when you curl up with a favorite magazine. You dive into articles with an open mind, ready to learn or laugh at all those juicy tidbits the magazine has to offer.

But what happens when you stumble across an ad for Buffalo Billy's Super-Delicious, Can't-Live-Without-'Em Banana Cream Donuts? In a flash, your open mind probably closes a bit, as a little red light goes off in your head: Ad alert! Ad Alert! Then come the big questions. Are Buffalo Billy's donuts really as tasty as they say? Are they really as tempting as they look? Do I really need them to live a long and happy life? You're *right* to question the ad. When advertisers are urging you to do what *they* want (buy, buy, buy), it's always important to judge what's true and best for *you*.

But advertorials sneak up on the reader disguised as non-advertising. Kids are more likely to read them and *less* likely to question their underlying message. And

no matter how clever or colorful the disguise, that message is always the same: BUY THIS PRODUCT.

What's a kid to do? Keep your eyes peeled for tiny print that says "Advertisement" (a sure sign that you've run across a sneaky sell). But some of the sneakiest sells don't offer that warning. So whenever you see a brand-name product on a printed page, make sure that little red ad-alert light in your head starts blinking. Better safe than sneaked.

Secrets of the Gap

from Zillions

You need a white shirt. You want to pay $15, tops. But you stagger out of the Gap with a bulging bag and 35 fewer dollars in

your wallet. Sound familiar? Maybe you've been snared by the "secret" selling strategies used by many stores.

Secret 1: "Sale" Racks

The Gap places its "sale" racks in two key locations: at the front and rear of the store. Ever wonder why? A "sale" sign near the door is designed to pull you into the store—even if you didn't intend to shop there. This strategy has snagged Margo, one *Zillions* reader who admits to being drawn to "sale" racks at store entrances. Nikki also has trouble resisting a "sale" come-on. "The signs are really large and eye-catching," she says.

Why put "sale" racks at the *back* of the store? So bargain hunters have to walk past all the exciting new styles to get to the cheaper goods. Stores realize that the more you see, the more you'll be tempted to stop and buy. "They want you to look at the higher priced clothes *first*," says Lauren, "because stores make more money on them."

Secret 2: Accessory Spotting

Where do you find accessories like socks, backpacks, and hats? Near the cash register, where every buyer winds up. "After I pick out an outfit, I'll see the matching headband as I'm standing on line," says Margo, "so I buy that, too." Waiting to pay doesn't just waste Margo's time—it costs her cash.

Accessories are also placed near basic clothing. When Lauren is choosing, she often "sees something else appealing nearby." She admits to buying socks she doesn't need "on impulse," to match an outfit.

Secret 3: Color Changes

The Gap changes its basic colors every six weeks. On one shopping trip you'll see lots of cobalt blue and mustard. Two months later it's hot pink with neon green. Why all the changes? The store wants to keep buyers coming back to check out new colors—and buy more. Margo has fallen for the "hot new color" strategy more than once. Her closet is packed with her favorite styles—in trendy tones she no longer wears.

Shopper's Secret: I Do Not Buy What I Do Not Need

It's really just a game. Stores like the Gap use these strategies to put you in a spending mood. *You* know it's smart shopping to understand what the stores are up to—and to resist the temptations. On your next shopping trip, will you leave the store with nothing more than you really need? Or will the *store* win the sales game?

TV Trouble at North High

from Zillions

TV came into North High, and the students walked out. In September 1990, most students refused to sit in class to watch a TV show. What was going on?

TV Goes to School

When North High students showed up for classes last September in Fargo, North Dakota, they discovered a new rule. They would be required to watch a TV show called Channel One every day. Two minutes of the daily 12-minute program is national news. Another two minutes is ads. The other eight minutes is devoted to feature stories on anything from new haircuts to new cars. The fast-paced show has young announcers and rock music.

To make time for Channel One, a special 20-minute homeroom class was added to North High's busy schedule. Attendance was taken, and the viewing was followed by a discussion. Students were graded on their participation.

"I was looking forward to the program, until I actually saw it," said Leslie Doran, a senior. "But the news lacks any kind of depth." Erika Hovland, the student-body president, agreed: "The show is at a lower grade level and is mostly entertainment."

Many other kids also objected to Channel One. "How can we be graded on a show too shallow to discuss?" one asked. Others were unhappy that the extra homeroom cut into their lunch period. "Now we only have 17 minutes to eat," complained a senior.

One student wondered: "Why did they ever agree to a TV show in school to begin with?"

Free TV

North High had its reasons. The school made a deal with a company called Whittle Communications. North High got a TV satellite dish, two video cassette recorders, and 37 TV sets—all for free. In exchange, the students would be required to watch Whittle's Channel One program every day. Whittle made agreements like this with many schools around the country.

Why was Whittle so generous? The company had *its* reason—making money. Each Channel One program has two minutes of ads. Advertisers pay Whittle $150,000 for every 30-second commercial on the show.

Some parents of North High students didn't think school was a place for ads. Many kids were more upset over the lack of choice. "We don't feel corrupted by watching commercials," one said. "But we think we should have the choice of watching or turning them off."

Tuning Out TV

When a history teacher encouraged the students to take a stand, a protest was planned. The students' demand: Drop Channel One. The method of protest? Skip homeroom. On the first day of the homeroom boycott, 250 kids refused to watch Channel One. By the second day, 600 of the 850 North High students cut out. Even the principal was impressed.

But he thought the boycott had made its point. He told the students to go back to class or face a three-day suspension. If they returned, the students would get to present their opinions to the school board. The students agreed. "We thought that if we cooperated, the administration would respect what we had to say," said Erika.

"I was pleased with the kids," said principal Ed Raymond. "If they could learn how to handle this protest, it would teach them something about a democratic society."

Talking TV

One week later, four North High students and many friends crammed into a tiny room to talk to the school board.

The kids had lots to say. As student-body president, Erika began: "Channel One has no educational value. The school gets $50,000 in free equipment, but the students gain nothing." Leslie continued: "If Whittle is truly interested in education, it would provide the equipment with no conditions."

Jared Eide suggested alternatives to Channel One, such as CNN or the Cable Alliance for Education, which emphasize real news. Jared said students would be willing to raise money to pay for TV equipment. Aimee Jagula felt that forcing students to watch Channel One was a violation of their freedom of choice.

A parent said the "school district has sold the students to Whittle for two minutes a day." He pointed out that a North High senior would have seen 24 hours of commercials over four years of watching Channel One.

The next day, a local newspaper wrote: "This time, the kids have it right." *USA Today* and TV news shows also covered the story, supporting the students' action. "We got pretty used to interviews," said Erika.

Chopping Channel One

Despite all the publicity, the North High school board hasn't moved very fast. A committee (with no student members) is still studying the situation. For now, Channel One is still on the air at North High.

But the protesters did win on some points. The extra homeroom period is gone. Channel One is now viewed during the last period, when many students have already left school. And the graded discussion is a thing of the past. In Erika's opinion, "It's a positive change, but our main goal is still to get rid of Channel One."

Are things any different at North High? According to one teacher, "This boycott brought the school together. School spirit has never been better." If the school board decides to stick with Channel One, the students claim they'll keep protesting. Leslie says they learned one important lesson from boycotting Channel One: "When you believe in something, you take a stand."

What's Your Bag? An Inside Look at Backpacks and Book Bags

from Zillions

You'll need *something* to lug that ton of schoolbooks, as well as a binder, notebooks, pads, pens, pencils, and a pair of sneakers—all without squishing your lunch. It has to be strong, lightweight, and goodlooking. A shopping bag will rip. A suitcase is overdoing it. And your kid brother's little red wagon is definitely out. Unless you're allowed to hitch up a mule in the school yard, you're probably planning to get a new backpack or book bag.

We asked 600 *Zillions* readers to tell us what's on their minds when it comes to what they carry on their backs. They complained about zippers that rip, straps that tear, bottoms that fail, and bags that disappoint. Most said their book packs don't last a year. With so much riding on your book pack—and *in* it—we asked kids and experts to test 10 of them.

Torture Tests

First, we had to figure out how kids use—and sometimes misuse—their book packs. They get thrown on the floor, dragged on the ground, stepped on, sat upon, kicked around, flung, chucked, smashed, and jammed into lockers. So we treated the test bags the same way. We designed torture tests to find out which bags would hold up *best* under the *worst* conditions.

To test the strength of the fabric, seams, and straps, we bashed loaded-up book packs against a concrete floor. Then we jerked them up and down by one strap. We bashed and jerked them thousands of times.

To separate bags that resist rain and keep the contents dry from ones that are all wet, we set each bag under the sprinkler for two hours.

Torture-Test Losers

No wonder so many kids were ripping mad about their book packs. Several bags failed our tests.

• The fabric tore in four bags: the *Esprit, Nike, J.C. Penney,* and *Eastpak* Day Pakv, R. The *Esprit* is made of cotton cloth. The three others are made of a thin nylon.

• The outside pocket on the *Eastpak* leather-bottom bag shredded into pieces.

• The straps on the *Esprit* and *Lands' End* bags pulled loose.

• The *Nike* and *Esprit* bags let in so much water they would have to be characterized as water-*poof,* not waterproof.

Torture-Test Winners

The *Caribou* Super Dealer and *Jan-Sport* Santa Fe passed our back(pack)-breaking torture tests with excellent marks. Some of their features helped them survive the torture tests with flying colors:

• **Heavy, tightly woven fabric.** The *Jan-Sport* Santa Fe is sturdy because it's made

out of leather—but this also makes the bag expensive. Some synthetic fabrics, such as the thick, rough nylon used to make the *Caribou* briefcase, are nearly as strong and cost much less.

• **A ¼-inch band of material sewn over the seams.** This extra material helps prevent the seams from splitting or unravelling.

• **Double-stitched straps.** Straps are held in place by a nylon strip, leather patch, or rivets.

• **A reinforced bottom.** Extra layers or padding add support and protect the bottom from being scraped through. You wouldn't want your homework to drop out on your way to school.

Two more bags, the *JanSport* Collegian and *L.L. Bean*, should also graduate with you in June. The six other bags that flunked our torture tests may also survive if you take proper care of them. (So play tug-of-war with your dog with something else.)

Comfort Test

You and your book pack are destined to cover plenty of territory together. So how a bag feels may wind up as your top consideration. By the end of the day, you don't want your bag to be the straw that breaks the camel's back (especially since you're the camel).

Five junior high testers packed each test bag with two heavy textbooks, a binder, a notebook, a paperback, and a sweater, then slipped it on and adjusted the straps. They trudged halfway around a school track, took the bag off, then rated it. After each tester tried all 10 book packs, we bagged the test and tallied the results.

• Seven bags were rated "Easy" or "Very Easy" to load and unload. But three didn't measure up. Testers had trouble fitting books into the *JanSport* Collegian. They struggled to zip up the stiff leather *JanSport* Santa Fe. The *Eastpak* leather-bottom was also hard to close. "It really can't hold a lot," said Michelle. (Zipper failure is often caused by overstuffing the bag, then trying to force the zipper shut. Be sure to find a bag big enough to hold your book load.)

• The *Esprit* bag looked cool, but everyone complained about the uncomfortable rope strap. "It hurt when it dug into my shoulder," said one tester. Fortunately, most of the other bags landed in the comfort zone.

• Do you sling your backpack over one shoulder? Then you'll appreciate the padded straps on *Lands' End, L.L. Bean,* and both *JanSport* and *Eastpak* models.

• Are you a two-shouldered bagger? The padded back of the *Lands' End,* leather *JanSport,* and leather-bottom *Eastpak* gives added comfort.

Making the Grade

The final test results are posted in the chart below. The *JanSport* Santa Fe nudged out the nylon *Eastpak* and *L.L. Bean* backpack for best combined score. But the all-leather *JanSport* costs a hefty $50.

Price isn't the only thing about the *Jan-Sport* that's heavy. It weighs three times more than the nylon *Eastpak.*

The other *JanSport* model, the Collegian, also passed both tests, and is half the price ($25). The Santa Fe has one inside pocket, but the Collegian has two, plus organizer compartments for smaller items.

The *L.L. Bean* bag has one large pocket, a deep compartment, and a zippered pouch on the inside. It also has two roomy exterior pockets, which many kids liked. Outside pockets are easier to get at when you're in a hurry.

One of these bags may be what you're looking for. Just don't fret if you can't find the *L.L. Bean* or *Lands' End* book packs in a store. These mail-order catalogue items are a phone call away from being sent directly to your home. And you can return your purchase if you aren't satisfied.

Bags are listed in order of quality. Ratings scale is from five stars (better than most) to one star (worse than most). Three stars is the minimum passing grade for each test. These are the prices we paid. Prices may differ at your local stores.

Book Pack	Torture Test	Comfort Test
JanSport Santa Fe ($50, leather)	☆☆☆☆☆	☆☆☆
Eastpak Day Pakv R III ($20, nylon)	☆☆☆	☆☆☆☆
L.L. Bean Book Pack ($25)*	☆☆☆	☆☆☆☆
JanSport Collegian ($25)	☆☆☆	☆☆☆
Lands' End Bookpack (large) ($20)*	☆☆	☆☆☆☆☆
Caribou Super Dealer Briefcase ($40)	☆☆☆☆☆	☆☆
J.C. Penney Sport ($15)	☆☆	☆☆☆
Nike Elite Gear Bag ($35)	☆☆	☆☆☆
Eastpak X-Country Pak' R II ($38, leather bottom)	☆☆	☆☆
Esprit Big String ($26)	☆	☆

*Available through mail-order or by phone order: L.L. Bean (800-221-4221); Lands' End (800-356-4444).

Part II

REACHING OUT!

When you've had your fill of *you:* a catalog of *communication* unfolds in this part of the volume—the bridges between you and everyone (and everything) else.

Critter Crackups

by Anthony Taber

from Ranger Rick

To enhance our ever-needed powers of communication, coming soon, to a telephone near you . . .

Touch-Tone Translation

accompanied by Fiddle Faddle photograph
from National Geographic World

Language barriers may tumble thanks to a translating computer being developed in Japan. In a flash it will translate a telephone conversation from the language of the speaker into the language of the listener. If your telephone were equipped with such a computer, you could hold a conference call with people who speak many different languages and still understand everyone! By the start of the next century experts hope computerized translators will link people all over the world by phone. If that happens, kids of the 21st century may have phone pals as well as pen pals.

This *is a fiddle? Surprise! It's a phone booth. Disguised as a double bass (BASE), it stands outdoors near a concert hall in Takasaki, in Japan. A musician is making a phone call (left). In this booth she can also press buttons to play recorded music. Phone company officials say the booth was expensive to build. But, they add, it attracts a lot of callers!*

If you've ever played a game called "Telephone," you'll know just how mouth-to-mouth information can be "modified" beyond recognition. We're presenting you with what is otherwise known as just the facts, please.

Pssst ..., Here's the Truth About Rumors: They're False!

by Russell Ginns, illustrations by Denise Brunkus
from 3-2-1 Contact

Have you heard that there are alligators in the sewers beneath New York City? That some brands of candies contain spider eggs or mind-control drugs? That if you swallow a piece of gum, it stays in your stomach for seven years?

Well, hold on a minute! Those stories are false. They are just rumors—phony tales that travel from person to person around the country. They tell of funny events, hidden dangers or mention false facts that are just plain weird. Usually, rumors are fun to pass along. But sometimes, when they run wild, rumors zigzag across the country, causing serious harm to people or even to big corporations.

Friend of a Friend of a Friend . . .

"A hot rumor can wind up being told all around the country at the same time," says Jan Brunvand, a professor at the University of Utah, who is an expert at tracking down rumors. He has written several books about unusual stories that people tell. Although the stories almost always turn out to be false, the teller always swears that it happened to "someone they know."

"I call these stories FOAFs—friend of a friend," Professor Brunvand told *Contact.* "If you try to find the actual person in the story, you'll discovery an endless chain of people, until the trail disappears."

Sometimes, a rumor turns out to be a spiced-up version of something that really happened. More often, the trail of story-

78

tellers goes on forever. The source of the rumor can't be found.

If people don't really know that a story is true, why are they so eager to pass it along?

"Rumors make people feel special," says Dr. Lawrence Balter, a psychology professor at New York University. "It's as if you've been let in on a secret. You feel like an insider."

This could explain why people spend so much time searching for "secret messages" on record labels—sometimes even playing the albums backwards. Or why some people look for "hidden" pictures in magazine ads.

For years, kids have peeled away the outside layers of golf balls. Many people believe that there is a high-explosive liquid in the center. It's exciting to have an "in" on this neat—but completely false—bit of information.

This would also explain why people like to pass along wild stories about famous people. If you know a secret about a movie star or a great athlete, it's almost as if you are closer to that celebrity than other people are.

Filling in the Blanks

Several years ago, some psychologists conducted an experiment. They showed a picture of an unfinished triangle (*Drawing A*) to a group of people, and then asked them to draw what they thought they saw.

[DRAWING A]

Almost everyone copied the picture exactly.

Then, they tried it again with a different group, but the scientists waited one month before they asked everyone to draw the figure. That time, many people drew the lines in the lower right corner much closer together (*Drawing B*).

[DRAWING B]

"Hey, there's a speck on this candy."

"Squiggies Candies have dirt in them."

Finally, when researchers showed the picture to a third group and waited three months before asking everyone to draw what they remembered, many people drew a perfect triangle (*Drawing C*). Without realizing it, the subjects added extra information to complete the picture.

[DRAWING C]

Many experts believe that the same thing happens when rumors spread.

"When people only have some of the information, they fill in the blanks," Dr. Balter told *Contact*. "Sometimes, you have a couple of different facts and you blend them together to fit your own beliefs."

It's a lot like the game "Telephone." A story passes from person to person and changes as people fill in missing pieces of information with what they think is correct.

Professor Brunvand adds: "If you've heard part of a story about someone who finds a bit of dirt in a piece of candy, you might forget about it. But what if it was a spider egg? After all, spiders seem like the kind of creatures that infest things." Maybe you'll mention that as a possibility.

Then, the next person might tell the story and swear that the candy was full of spiders.

"Suddenly, it's a much better story. It's grosser, so it's more interesting. More people will want to pass it along," says Brunvand.

Sometimes, people pass a story along because it helps to prove a point – even though it may not be true. Rumor has it that a famous blonde star is really bald. She dyed her hair so many times it all fell out. If you've heard this told about a movie star or a singer, don't worry. It's not true. Maybe this tale spread because some people don't approve of the way some celebrities dress or act. Since the rumor tells how the star has been punished for her actions, some people might pass it along as a warning not to imitate her.

Something for Nothing

Another reason that rumors spread is that people want their wishes to come true. Rumors sometimes falsely tell how you can get something for nothing.

Many people claim that if you find a Tootsie Pop wrapper with a complete picture of an Indian with a bow and arrow, the company will give you a crate of candy. But this isn't true. Tootsie Roll Industries

"There's something gross in Squiggies Candies. I bet it's bugs!"

"Hey!..."

"Ooh!"

"There are spider eggs in Squiggies candies."

swears that this offer was never made.

For years, people believed that if you found a 1943 copper penny and mailed it to a big auto company, they would send you a free car. Not so. Some people will tell you that if you grow your fingernails more than one inch long, a cosmetics company will buy them for 100 dollars. Nope. Across the country, people spread false stories about a "friend of a friend" who did a small favor for a movie star and was given a TV set, a diamond ring or a sports car. Unfortunately, these stories are usually phony, too.

No Laughing Matter

While many rumors may be fun to pass along, they can be very damaging to people, and even to entire companies. Several fast food chains say they lost millions of dollars in sales because of this false rumor: that their fried food is actually fried rats. In 1977, a candy company spent over $50,000 in advertising. Why? Because kids were spreading a rumor that the company's new brand of bubble gum contained bugs.

In 1985, a post office in Scotland almost had to shut down when it was flooded by postcards addressed to "Little Buddy." It turns out that a fake story had spread about a dying child whose last wish was to get into the *Guinness Book of World Records* for having received the most postcards.

More often, however, rumors just hurt people's feelings. So it's important to think twice before spreading the latest gossip.

"Use some critical thinking," says Dr. Balter. "A story could be harmful to someone's reputation, so protect other people's feelings. Think about where you heard the story, and whether or not it's really possible."

And what should you do if a rumor is being spread about you? According to psychologist Ron Taffel, one of the best ways to stop a rumor is to ignore it.

"Don't waste your time trying to deny a story that people might be spreading," Dr. Taffel told *Contact.* "When they ask you about it, just tell people the truth. Usually, people will realize that it's not really true, or that there's nothing new to say about it. In time, the rumor will die down."

"Don't eat those! The main ingredient is live spiders!"

"My friend found spiders in her Squiggies."

This article looks mystifying at first. But keep reading and it may change the way you feel about commas Capitalization and semicolons forever. Or, it may simply be something that has to do with clarity, *a concept that has something to do with good Communication.*

A Short History of Punctuation

by Polly M. Robertus, illustrations by Jan Adkins
from Cricket

EARLYGREEKSHADHARDLYANYPUNCTUATION
FONOITCERIDEHTDEGNAHCNEVEDNA
THEIRWRITINGATTHEENDOFEACHLINELATER
TAHTGNITIRWFOYAWAOTDEGNAHCYEHT
FAVOREDRIGHTHANDEDPEOPLEANDSHOWED
WHEREANEWPARAGRAPHBEGANBYUNDERLINING
THEFIRSTLINEOFIT<u>LATERTHEGREEKPLAYWRIGHT</u>
ARISTOPHANES•INVENTEDMARKSTOSHOW•WHERE
THEREADERSHOULDTAKEABREATH:
THE•ROMANS•MADE•WRITING•MUCH•EASIER•
TO•READ•BY•PUTTING•DOTS•BETWEEN•WORDS•
AND•BY•MOVING•THE•FIRST•LETTER•OF•A•
PARAGRAPH•INTO•THE•LEFT•MARGIN: THEY•
ADAPTED•SOME•OF•THE•GREEK•MARKS•SUCH•AS•
THE•COLON•MARK•TO•INDICATE•PHRASE•ENDINGS:

ROMAN WAX TABLET

STYLUS

CHISEL FOR LETTERS IN STONE

LEAD MALLET

JAN ADKINS DREW THESE PICTURES WITH A FELT TIP PEN

INTHEEARLYMIDDLEAGESTHISSYSTEMOFPUNCTUATION
BROKEDOWNBECAUSEVERYFEWPEOPLECOULDREAD
ANDWRITE   BUTWRITERSKEPTASPACEATTHEENDOF
ASENTENCEANDCONTINUEDTOMARKPARAGRAPHS
EVENTUALLY WORDS WERE SEPARATED AGAIN AND
NEW SENTENCES BEGAN WITH A LARGER LETTER

THE MIDDLE AGES WAS A PERIOD OF EUROPEAN HISTORY FROM ABOUT THE 500s TO THE 1300s.

THE RENAISSANCE WAS A GREAT REVIVAL OF ART, LITERATURE, AND LEARNING THAT TOOK PLACE IN EUROPE FROM THE 1300s TO THE 1500s.

The educational reforms of Charlemagne led to the invention of lowercase letters which could be written and read much faster /Phrases and sentence endings were indicated either by ∴ or by a slash /

As time went on writers looked for more ways to clarify meaning / In medieval music notation they found a way to indicate how a voice should rise or fall at the end of a sentence or phrase⋎ Can you hear your voice rise at the end of a question⸮ Our question mark came directly from medieval music notation⋎ When a long sentence broke in the middle > they put a new mark that became our semicolon and colon⋎ The hy= phen appeared as two lines instead of one⋎

Around A.D. 1500 the indented paragraph appeared, as did the comma and period as we know them. Printers of the Renaissance invented new marks like the exclamation point and quotation marks. By that time, people were commonly reading silently, and punctuation came to depend more on grammatical groups than breath groups. (Parentheses and dashes appeared with the advent of printing—these made text read more naturally to the inner ear.)

By the end of the seventeenth century, our punctuation system was in place for the most part, though sometimes details varied. Just think, though: After only a few lessons in school—and with lots of practice reading and writing— you can boast that you've mastered a system that took Westerners many centuries to develop!

LEAD TYPE

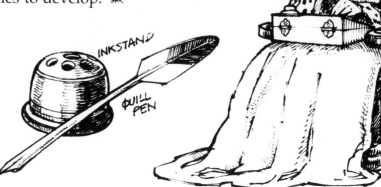

INKSTAND

QUILL PEN

There isn't a day that goes by that you aren't affected by the work of printers. Books, posters, magazines—even the TV Guide—all these rolled off a press at some point.

On a Roll: Printing Press Operators

by Karen Judson

from Career World

illustrations by Ann Neilsen
from Jack and Jill

Extra! Extra!
Read All About Career
Opportunities in Printing—
This Country's Fastest-Growing
Manufacturing Industry

Does this headline surprise you? Most people don't realize that over the last decade, according to the U.S. Bureau of Labor Statistics, the American printing industry has been number one in growth among all other manufacturing industries. It's also the fifth largest in terms of total employment. The U.S. Commerce Department states that it is the largest of all manufacturing industries in number of establishments and the sixth largest in sales.

Unlike most manufacturing jobs, the opportunities in printing are expected to continue to increase.

If you like to work with sophisticated electronic machinery, have a flair for organization, and take pride in seeing a project carefully through to completion, printing press operator could be an ideal career for you.

Roll the Presses

Printing press operators, in general, prepare and operate the printing presses that put images on paper for newspapers, books, magazines, business forms, catalogs, brochures, greeting cards, posters, and other printed material.

Presses can range from block-long pieces of machinery requiring a team of operators, to small presses operated by one person.

In some shops, duties of the press operator include oiling and cleaning the presses and making minor repairs. Increasingly, operators of larger printing presses must also learn to use computerized controls.

As a first press operator at Quad/

84

Graphics, a large printing company in Pewaukee, Wisconsin, where *Time, Newsweek, Architectural Digest, True Story,* and many other monthly magazines are printed, Keith Ewing uses computer controls to operate eight- to 10-unit presses. (The number of units indicates color-printing capacity.)

Ewing was promoted to his present position two years ago, and now supervises *helpers,* who install and ink the plates, *roll tenders,* who feed paper into the presses,

and *press operators,* who monitor and adjust color.

"As a supervisor, it's important that I know how to work with people," he says, "and it helps to be mechanically minded. Here at Quad/Graphics, press operators are also tested for good color vision before they are hired."

"A good press operator can make the colors shine," says Lyle Mum, who hires offset printing press operators for his commercial printing business in Fort Dodge,

Iowa. "They are creative in that they pay strict attention to detail, quality, and color-matching in a product. And an experienced press operator can hear if something goes wrong with the press."

Often press operators must make quick decisions when something happens to stop the presses, such as a paper jam or tear. "When the press isn't running, I lose money," says Mum, who bills $500,000 a year in printing orders.

"An employer looks for a strong math background since everything printed has to go on a certain size paper, with specific margins, and sometimes has to be centered, as well," stresses Linda Minahan, graphic arts coordinator at Iowa Western Community College (IWCC) in Council Bluffs, Iowa.

Running a printing press can be noisy work—press operators wear hearing protection devices—and when repair or maintenance work is required, they can be "up to their elbows in ink," says Minahan. "But the challenge of the job overrides the negatives," says Charles A. Alessendrini, president of the National Association of Printers and Lithographers (NAPL).

Deadlines are a fact of life for printing press operators (today's newspapers can't be delivered tomorrow). Individuals who can deal calmly with time constraints will probably perform better than those who cannot.

Chapter and Verse about Training

Several opportunities for training as a printing press operator include apprenticeship as well as vo-tech programs and on-job training. An apprenticeship, in which you get on-job training as well as related classroom instruction, usually takes about four years to complete.

Many vo-tech schools and community colleges offer one- to two-year programs in graphic arts (which includes printing press operation), awarding diplomas, certificates, or associate degrees.

Because the technology is changing so fast in the printing industry, programs for *retraining* and *skill updating* for experienced workers will take on greater importance.

Ewing was hired by Quad/Graphics with no printing experience and was trained by the company, a common practice in the industry due to the shortage of experienced press operators. The company's technical center also offers optional classes to workers interested in changing jobs or moving up.

"Many of the employers who call us are looking for someone with experience," says IWCC's Minahan. "Graphic arts students here get hands-on experience in our in-plant press. This can be listed on their resumes as work experience, since they help print about 90 percent of the college's printed material."

IWCC's graphic arts course takes 14 to 16 months to complete, and covers all aspects of printing, from typesetting to press and bindery work. "We teach the basics," says Minahan, "and when our students finish they can apply those basics to whatever situation they find in the workplace."

Hot off the Press: News about Wages and Hours

"Some people outside the industry think the hours are long and the work is hard," says Keith Ewing. "But I don't see that at all. The work is moderately physical, but most people can do the work. I work nights—most new managers here at Quad/Graphics work the nightshift—and I work 36 hours one week, 48 hours the next."

Press operators who work for daily newspapers must often work at night, to get the morning edition ready for early-morning distribution.

Variables that can affect wages include experience, education, union vs. non-union shops, and the type of press operated. Earnings are usually lowest for shops running smaller, less-complicated presses as opposed to larger, computerized ones.

The following shows the average estimated annual earnings for press operators for 1990–91 as compiled by NAPL. (Job titles are based on collective bargaining classifications and may differ in non-union shops. Also, salary figures vary depending on such things as press size and the number of ink colors.)

- Helper: Entry-level position $15,900–$24,500. According to the NAPL, graduates of a vo-tech program in graphic arts will generally begin at the higher salary level.

- 2nd Assistant Operator: $25,000–$33,000

- 1st Assistant Operator: $26,100–$33,400

- 2nd Press Operator: $27,400–$35,000

- 1st Lead Press Operator: $31,400–$37,000. Usually supervises positions listed above.

"These are average wages," stresses Jackie Pantaliano of the NAPL. "We know of press operators who earn $40,000 a year and up."

See It in Print

The world of print communication is expanding at a rapid rate, and technological advances continue to make printing presses more responsive to sophisticated needs. If you think the pressroom sounds like an exciting place to be, then operating a printing press could be just the right career slot for you. In that case, this headline may be in your future:

Graphic Arts Graduate Finds Dream Job in the Nation's Fastest-Growing Manufacturing Industry!

This isn't a conventional dictionary (if only they were all this short!), and maybe we should have put this sportspeak in the section on sports. But it makes a nice point without a lot of brass: dictionaries are a pretty convenient way to find out what other people are talking about—and how to talk back.

Dictionary for Dudes

from National Geographic World

"Snowboardese" includes expressions from other sports and from the inventive minds of snowboarders.

biff—fall
catch or *grab air*—jump
crail, fakie, method air, mute air, nose wheelie, rocket, sidekick, stale fish—freestyling tricks
freestyle—perform tricks
gnarly or *rad*—awesome
head plant or *invert*—face-first fall
pipe dogs—snowboarders who freestyle in half-pipes
rails—side edges of a snowboard
stick or *shred sled*—snowboard

No Swearing Allowed

from Current Events

illustration by Laura Cornell from U*S* Kids

Can a town ban the public use of swear words?

Town officials in Quincy, Mass. think it can. On December 17 the Quincy town council passed a law banning the use of "obscene language" in public. The law is designed to get tough with teen-agers who use abusive language. Violators can be fined $100.

But is the law legal? The American Civil Liberties Union (ACLU) has its doubts. The ACLU points out that the U.S. Supreme Court has struck down similar laws in other cities as viola-

Illustration by Laura Cornell

tions of the First Amendment, the part of the U.S. Constitution that guarantees freedom of speech.

Its supporters say the law has wide public support.

"We have to be concerned about the rights of families to come into downtown without being harassed by bad language," says Quincy's mayor.

How do you feel? Do you think the right to say what you want in public is more important than the right of others not to hear offensive language?

Nonsensical Nonsense

by Elroy Anderson, illustrated by Tom Yakutis
from Children's Digest

How far will you fall when you fall
    asleep?
Could you walk on the bridge of your nose?
Could you ever play the drums in your ears
Or drive the nails of your fingers and toes?

Could you play ball with the ball of your
    foot?
Could your blood vessels sail on the sea?
Do you ever feed the calf of your leg
Or try wearing the cap of your knee?

Could you walk under the arch of your
    foot?
Could you make your hair fat if it's thin?
If a king wanted the crown of your head—
Do you think you would give it to him?

Could your eyeteeth take the place of your
    eyes?
Could your shoulder blade be on a knife?
How would you shingle the roof of your
    mouth—
If you tried for the rest of your life?

When you read the number of complicated steps mentioned in this Boys' Life *article, the fact that the mail arrives at all seems something of a miracle. The nicest surprises come through the mails—birthday presents, magazines, letters from far-away friends. No wonder just seeing a postal worker with a bag brings, among other things, smiles to our faces.*

How the Mail Gets to Us

by Robert Bahr

from Boys' Life

accompanied by Postal Pickups photographs
from National Geographic World

In December 1989, Sue Michael, who lives near Memphis, Tenn., received a letter from her husband, Darwin. He had mailed it from Blythe, Calif.—on Aug. 16, *1943.*

Stories like that are rare. The United States Postal Service (USPS) is the largest, fastest and most reliable in the world.

Each day, six days a week, 535 million letters are delivered. Most deliveries take three days or less. How is it done? Some of the credit goes to a spectacular machine known as the "facer canceler."

This whiz of a gizmo does something very important: It determines whether an envelope has a stamp on it. That may not sound like much, but it is. Stamps pay the cost of making the Postal Service run. Letters without stamps are trying to get a free ride. The USPS can't allow that.

The facer canceler machine checks each envelope electronically for the presence of phosphorus, a mineral embedded in postage stamps. It then applies the postmark which cancels the stamp. If the phosphorus—and therefore the stamp—is missing, the letter is flipped into a reject pile to be returned to the sender.

Another impressive machine is the optical character reader (OCR). It doesn't look much like a person, but it can read a neatly printed address like one. Then it prints a bar code, or series of lines, along the bottom of the envelope. This bar contains a coded version of the destination ZIP code.

The OCR then passes the letter along to another device, the bar code sorting machine. This gadget works like the scanner at your supermarket that reads the bar code on your box of cereal. But instead of automatically ringing up a price, the machine at the post office automatically sorts envelopes by ZIP code.

The OCR and bar code sorting machine are big time savers for the post office. Letter-sorting machines operated by people process only 3,600 letters an hour, while the automatic sorting machine can handle up to 25,000 letters at a much lower cost.

While machines are important, human beings still get most of the credit for delivering the mail to us.

Early every morning, the "mailman" (who is often a woman) picks up the sack of mail that awaits him or her at the post office. He sits in front of a case divided into hundreds of slots, each representing an address on his route. For several hours he puts letters into their proper slots. Finally, he bundles them for delivery.

What about mail that goes to other cities? Most letter mail traveling 1,000 miles or farther goes by passenger airline. That's right. The same plane whisking you to your dream vacation in Honolulu is likely to be carrying first-class mail in the cargo hold. Commercial airlines earn millions of extra dollars this way. Out-of-town mail going shorter distances is moved by truck.

In the early 1800's, before postage stamps, mail carriers made their living by charging 2 cents for every letter they delivered. The person receiving the letter had to pay.

Mail carriers on country routes often picked up groceries for customers who couldn't get into town. They would take laundry to the cleaner's, and they even counted livestock for an agriculture survey. Today, in a program called Carrier Alert, a carrier will alert authorities when he notices that the mail hasn't been picked up for several days.

Since postal service began more than 200 years ago, dogs have been bad news for mail carriers. In 1990, 2,782 carriers were bitten by dogs.

Another carrier was bitten by a goose, and a third by a bantam rooster. A Texas carrier never said he was bitten, but insisted that he was chased from a house five times by a *rabbit,* a child's Easter gift.

Yet, letter carriers still strive to uphold the spirit behind the words carved into the facade of the General Post Office on Eighth Avenue in New York City:

"Neither snow nor rain nor heat nor gloom of night stays these couriers from the swift completion of their appointed rounds."

At the Moake home near Eldon, Washington, mail arrives by rail. The lunch box-shaped mailbox, in numerous sizes and disguises, has been standard on U.S. rural routes since 1915.

© RICH IWASAKI

Munching mail? That's what this huge head near St. Augustine, Florida, appears to be doing. Postal regulations permit any kind of mailbox base that is neat, supports the mailbox, and doesn't interfere with the mail carrier's vehicle.

Only an eagle could deliver airmail to this treetop-tall box in Hillard, Ohio. Human letter carriers use the lower box. The top one is just for fun.

©JOANNE KASH

AIR MAIL
5730

©TIM DANIEL

The naming of either a person or a place is a pretty important piece of work. The next two articles will surely make you think about memorable names you've known—last names and place names (or maybe, a name you have?). Perhaps the most fun thing about having an unusual name is that people aren't likely to forget it.

Unusual Place Names Across America

by Sheila Stagg
from Cricket

Nags Head, North Carolina; Rough and Ready, California; Santa Claus, Indiana; Odd, West Virginia—the list of unusual American place names is endless.

In the 1800s, when the United States was still a very young country, settlers established homes and formed new towns across the land. Many names were needed for the new settlements, but often settlers used the same name for several different towns. This caused a great problem for the U.S. Post Office.

When a settlement or township applied for a post office, its name had to be different from all the other place names in that state. If it already existed, the townspeople would have to get together and choose a new name or the Post Office would choose one for them.

Sometimes the townspeople showed a sense of humor in the names they selected. When Odd, West Virginia, was chosen, someone had suggested using an odd or unusual name. Wyoming settlers picked Bill as their town's name for the first name

of most of its male citizens. In an Indiana township, a settler dressed as Santa Claus happened into the December town meeting. The town has been called Santa Claus, Indiana, ever since. Twig, Minnesota, was so named because it was a "small branch" of the U.S. Post Office.

The railroad named dozens of towns when the West was being settled. Many of the stations had few inhabitants, so the railroad took the liberty of picking names for them.

For instance, in Wisconsin in 1870, a railroad crew was supposed to put up a sign "Cedarhurst." It was forty-seven degrees below zero, and one of the crew members remarked it was the "chilliest" place he'd ever been. So the men changed the sign to Chili, Wisconsin. Frogmore, Louisiana, was named by a member of the railroad surveying party who said that the area had more frogs than he had ever seen.

Many places were named after famous Americans or local townspeople. Rough and Ready, California, comes from the nickname of President Zachary Taylor. Mr. Snow and Mr. Flake provided the name Snowflake, Arizona.

Interesting stories are often behind unique place names. Nags Head, North Carolina, tracks the history of its name to pirates who hung a lantern on the neck of a nag, or horse, to lure ships close to the shore at night. When the ships foundered on the rocks, the pirates salvaged the goods left aboard. In Nevada, settlers claimed that visitor Mark Twain, on seeing steam rise from a local geyser, asked, "What is a steamboat doing out in this desert?" The location was dubbed Steamboat,

Nevada, at that moment.

Every state has places with unique and unusual names. The study of place names is called toponymy, from two Greek words, *topos* (place) and *onyma* (name). To learn about the toponymy in your area, check a state map, an atlas, or an encyclopedia to find a list of towns with unusual names. Write a letter to the Postmaster of each town to ask the town's history and how it was named. Address the letters to Postmaster, Name of Town, State, and Zip Code (available from your local Post Office).

What If Nobody Had a Last Name?

by Jean Peters Kinney
from Children's Digest

How many boys named "John" are in your class? If the teacher wanted to call on "Debbie" and there were two in the class, she would have to say "Debbie Ritter" or "Debbie DeAngelis."

Can you imagine what it would be like if nobody in your class, your school, or your entire town had a last name? Well, hundreds of years ago that was the case. Nobody had a family name (also known as a surname)—only a first name, or baptismal name, as it is often called.

Where did all our surnames come from? And when did they become necessary? When only ten families lived in one place, each person knew everyone else. No one

needed a family name. In Europe, this situation lasted until the 1100s.

Too many people with the same first name living in the same area began to cause confusion. Can you imagine a neighbor running to someone for help and begging: "Come quickly! Peter was thrown by a horse and cannot get up!"

"Which Peter?"

"Why, Peter, the blond one, son of Rudolph." Only then would the man know exactly who was injured.

Family names came into existence throughout Europe in several ways: by adding a word to describe the person, as in Armstrong and Swift, by adding the name of the father, or by describing the person's profession, as in Baker or Butcher.

English names such as Robertson, Johnson, or Williamson tell us that these names were first used for a child who was the "son of Robert," "son of John," or "son of William." A person of Scottish ancestry might have the name MacIsaac, MacDonald, MacNeil, or MacAndrew. These names originally meant the child of Isaac, Donald, Neil, or Andrew. In Gaelic, "fitz" means "son of," as in the common Irish names Fitzpatrick, Fitzgerald, Fitzwilliam, or Fitzhugh. The Russian names Romanovitch and Ivanovitch tell us that the first bearer of that name was the child of Roman or Ivan.

Another very important way to identify people was to use their types of work, or occupations. Alfred, the miller, who would later be called Alfred Miller, earned his living by producing flour from grain. Michael Cooper was at first Michael, the cooper or barrel-maker. Theodore Smith was originally Theodore, the blacksmith who forged tools and shoed horses. The importance of this job is evident from the huge number of families with the name Smith. The names Weaver, Carpenter, and Taylor should need no explanation. There were identical surnames in other languages. For example, in German, Schneider is the word for "tailor."

China had the most unusual way of adopting surnames. A royal decree required all Chinese families to take a last name from a sacred poem called *"Po-Chia-Hsing."* This limited the choices, and almost twenty-five percent selected Chang, meaning "drawn bow," Wang, meaning "prince," and Li, meaning "plum."

Today, a first name *and* a family name help identify each individual. If your name is not mentioned here, why not try a little detective work? Dozens of volumes have been written about the origin of thousands of surnames. Perhaps there is one on the shelf of your local library. Where did your family name come from?

Here's the evolution of a road, from its earliest beginnings before the American Revolution, to the time it's bypassed by a modern interstate highway.

Time on the Road

by Vicki Burton

from Cobblestone

1751 The Ohio Company sends Thomas Cresap to blaze a trail from Cumberland, Maryland, to report on land values in the Ohio country.

1755 General Braddock constructs a military road along the path Cresap has marked with a Delaware Indian named Nemacolin.

1796 Colonel Ebenezer Zane receives permission from Congress to open a trail from Wheeling to Limestone, Kentucky.

1806 President Thomas Jefferson signs the act establishing a national highway from Cumberland, Maryland, to the Ohio River.

1811 Construction begins on the National Road west of Cumberland.

1818 The road is completed to Wheeling. Mail can be carried to Wheeling by stagecoach from Washington, D.C. Pioneers and freight wagons fill the road.

1825 President Monroe appropriates the money to build the National Road from Wheeling to the capital of Missouri. Ground is broken on July 4 in front of the courthouse in St. Clairsville, Ohio.

1830s Congress turns maintenance of the National Road over to the states it crosses. The states erect tollgates to fund repairs.

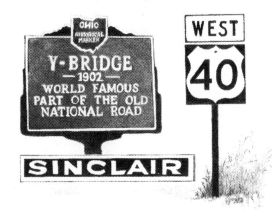

1839 The National Road reaches Vandalia, Illinois, where construction stops.

1853 The Baltimore and Ohio Railroad reaches Wheeling. The National Road grows quiet.

1880 The safety bicycle is developed, and the League of American Wheelmen is organized to reform America's road system.

1912 The auto age is born. Congress approves half a million dollars for the improvement of mail routes. New paved surfaces on sections of the National Road are planned in all six states. Automobile travelers and truckers take to the road. The National Road is designated a part of the National Old Trails Road.

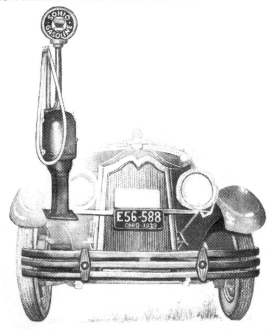

1914 Increased automobile traffic brings the need for sturdier road surfaces. Water-bound macadam, brick, and concrete are used for the first time on the road in Ohio.

1925 The Joint Board on Interstate Highways recommends a grid system for numbering roads.

1926 The National Road becomes part of U.S. Route 40, a highway that runs coast to coast.

1960s Route 40 is bypassed by Interstate 70.

Buckle Up! Illustration by Laura Cornell from U*S* Kids

Countries and cultures have been joined by trade, by marriages between heads of state, even by conquerors. Here, they will be joined by an underwater structure some call the Chunnel. The world is getting smaller all the time.

Tunnel Links England and France

from Current Science

People can now walk between England and France without getting their feet wet.

In one of the major engineering feats of the 20th century, French and British drillers recently fulfilled a nearly two-centuries-old dream by completing drilling of the first of three tunnels that will link England and France. While French workers yelled "God Save the Queen" and British workers cheered "Vive la France," a French worker and a British worker shook hands 162 feet (50 meters) beneath the seabed of the English Channel. The two sides met after separate tunnels were drilled from opposite sides of the channel.

Two of the tunnels will be used to whisk passengers in trains beneath the 23.6-mile- (39-kilometer-) wide channel. The train trip will take 35 minutes, whereas ferries now take 90 minutes. A third tunnel, the one that was just completed, will be used as a service tunnel.

The tunnel complex has been called Eurotunnel, Channel Tunnel, and Chunnel. To drill the first tunnel, large drilling machines bored through a soft rock known as blue chalk. The chalk, which formed from the remains of countless billions of marine organisms, is soft enough to scratch with a fingernail.

As a 27-foot- (8-meter-) wide drill cut into the soft rock at a rate of about three revolutions a minute, pieces of chalk chipped from the layer were sent by conveyor belt to wagons that hauled the material out of the tunnel.

A laser measuring device was used to make sure the drills headed in the right direction. The drilling of the first tunnel was so accurate that French and British sections of the tunnel were only 20 inches (50 centimeters) off when the two sides connected. The total length of the tunnel is 31 miles (50 kilometers).

The two rail tunnels are scheduled to be completed by the middle of the year. By the time the first trains start operating beneath channel waters in 1993, the English Channel drilling project will have cost at least $17 billion.

There is such a thing as the joining of continents, of worlds, of time spans, or of myths. Here, it takes place on a narrow strait between Europe and Asia, and it's simply known as . . .

A Cow's Crossing

by Charles F. Baker
from Calliope

In the southwest corner of the Black Sea, a narrow channel joins the waters of this sea with those of the Sea of Marmara. This narrow strait, which divides the country of Turkey, also separates the continents of Europe and Asia. Its name, a combination of the Greek terms βós πορος (Bosporos), meaning "Cow Crossing," traces its history to the mythology of the ancient Greeks.[1]

"How beautiful she is!" mused the great Zeus, king of gods and men, as he glanced down from his palace on Mount Olympos[2] in northeastern Greece. Zeus had caught a glimpse of Io, the daughter of the river god Inachus and the granddaughter of Oceanus, the mighty god of the oceans. Zeus watched her idly singing and gathering flowers along the riverbank. His admi-

ration and desire to speak with her grew, but he feared his wife Hera's reaction. She was a very jealous goddess and treated any female Zeus admired or praised with great disdain. Hera often punished these women, sometimes cruelly. He had to think of a clever plan that would fool her.

Zeus pulled a large cloud to Mount Olympos and then calmly covered himself and his tracks with it. Slowly he approached the unsuspecting maiden. When Io noticed a gray cloud darkening the horizon, she stood still, for this cloud seemed different. It moved in only one direction—straight toward her. When she saw the majestic figure hidden within the gray mass, Io knew at once who her regal visitor was. She welcomed Zeus to her land and showed him the river sacred to her father. Zeus was enthralled. Io was even more captivating in person than she had appeared from atop Mount Olympos. Zeus and Io walked and talked for hours, protected, so they thought, by the massive cloud.

The cloud did conceal them, but nothing concealed the cloud, and Hera became suspicious when she noticed that only one rather small area seemed overcast. "Zeus is trying to trick me!" she raged. Determined

[1]This story of Io is a combination of the tales written by the Roman author Ovid (43 B.C.–A.D. 17) in *Metamorphoses* and by the Greek playwright Aeschylus (525/4–466/5 B.C.) in *Prometheus Bound.*
[2]Olympos is the Greek form; Olympus is the Latin/Roman form.

to know the truth, Hera boldly approached the cloud. With one commanding sweep of her arm, she lifted the gray covering and came face to face with her husband.

But Zeus's companion was not whom Hera expected. Zeus had heard Hera approaching and had changed Io into a cow to protect her from Hera's wrath. Hera was not fooled, however. "My dear husband, what a beautiful cow!" she said. "A gift for me?"

Zeus could only answer, "Yes, my dear, I was trying to keep it a surprise until just the right moment to give it to you."

Hera quickly took the cow's lead rope and headed for the cave of her servant Argos. This ugly creature had one hundred eyes, only two of which closed at any time. Hera commanded him to guard the cow and never lose sight of it.

Poor Io! Who could save her from this predicament? Sadly, she roamed the fields as far as the rope Argos had attached to her collar allowed. Io's father, Inachus, often passed by looking for his daughter. Io longed to tell him of her fate, but she could not speak. Then she thought of a way. One morning, as he searched the riverbank, she slowly lifted her right front hoof and scratched an I and an O in the dirt. Inachus saw the letters and understood, but he did not know what to do. Argos was too powerful for him to defeat.

Finally, Zeus resolved to act. He called his son Hermes, the messenger of the gods, and commanded him to destroy Argos.

First Hermes dressed himself as a shepherd. Then he took his lyre, slipped on his winged cap and winged sandals, and flew to Argos's cave. Argos carefully eyed the new arrival in his territory. Deceived by his guest's calm, unpretentious manner, Argos welcomed Hermes. After talking for a while, Hermes began to strum his lyre. It took hours, but finally all one hundred of

Argos's eyes were closed and the ugly creature was sound asleep. Hermes quickly unsheathed his hidden sword and slew the monster. He cut Io's rope, but he could not change her form.

Meanwhile, Hera had arrived to check on Io and Argos. When she saw Argos dead and decapitated on the ground, she gathered all one hundred of his eyes and placed each one at the end of a feather of her favorite bird, the peacock. Then she commanded a gadfly to bite and annoy the cow. Io could not swish her tail far enough or hard enough to swat the persistent fly.

In desperation, she began to run, hoping to elude the tiny creature. When she came to a broad expanse of water, she walked in and began to swim. The ancients named these waters to the west of Greece the Ionian Sea. Io traveled as far as the Black Sea and crossed the narrow strait that separates the continents of Europe and Asia. The ancients named this strait the Bosporus, or "Cow Crossing," in her honor.

Finally, Io reached Egypt and the Nile River. Zeus had watched Io's journey from Mount Olympos, and he knew he had to act. One afternoon he approached Hera and confessed that he had admired Io's beauty. Promising never to visit or speak with Io again, he asked, "My dear Hera, I beg you to have pity on young Io and change her into her true form." Hera thought for a moment and then agreed to do so.

Suddenly, on the banks of the Nile River, a wonderful transformation took place. Io rejoiced as her coarse hairs fell to the ground and her clumsy hoofs became hands and feet. Inachus wept tears of joy as he embraced his daughter. Io started to speak but stopped, fearful of the sounds her vocal cords would make. But Hera had kept her promise, and Io soon realized that all of her, even her voice, had been restored.

We weren't sure if this was about a bridge, or a tunnel. You decide.

Salamander Bridge

by Gloria Boudreau
from Dolphin Log

How do salamanders cross the road? Very carefully, unless they live in Amherst, Massachusetts, where two tunnels have been built to help them cross safely.

In winter, salamanders stay safe by hibernating under rocks, rotting tree stumps or damp burrows. When spring comes, the salamanders come out of hiding and begin journeying to their breeding ponds. But the journey may take them across busy roads. So the Massachusetts Audubon Society and the University of Massachusetts combined efforts to build two underground tunnels as part of a five-year research project. Low fences direct the salamanders into the tunnels, which lead from a hill on one side of the road to breeding ponds on the other.

The following is just one more communication story. Its gentle message is music to the ears of the inhabitants of one world but rings true, loud and clear, to ears far beyond. If you think the alarm clock that rousts you out of bed each morning is far too clanky, maybe you can move to Japan. There the sounds of feathered wildlife gently trill out over the airwaves, awaking sleepyheads.

Impresario of the Morning Chirp

by Lucille Craft

from International Wildlife

illustration by Charles Peale
from National Wildlife

One of the longest-running hits on Japanese radio is only five minutes long, ends before most people wake up and features one song. A bird song.

Since 1953, strains of the Peer Gynt Suite have ushered in *Asa No Kotori*, or Morning Bird Songs, a folksy monologue on the calls and behavior of the world's feathered fauna. A cheery female announcer, accompanied by bursts of chirping, narrates an encounter with the species of the day: "The bird to be discussed this morning is the *Iwa-Hibari*, or alpine accentor," she begins one morning's program. "The sun is rising gloriously over a sea of clouds, tinting the sky with gold. We can see the alpine accentor on the edge of a rock. It's a cute little bird."

The simple descriptions mask the encyclopedic knowledge of Morning Bird Songs' creator, 65-year-old Tsuruhiko Kabaya, a high-school graduate who has never taken an ornithology class. Scarcely 5 feet tall and bespectacled, he is perpetually chuckling over one bird foible or another. Perhaps "birdlike" is the best adjective for the gaunt, light-footed man who has stalked and recorded nearly 1,000 birds around the world.

Kabaya may have received early nudges toward his occupation: The "tsuru" part of his first name means crane. His earliest close encounter with birds came at age six when neighbors gave him a pigeon as a pet. Then fate intervened, in the form of a ravenous weasel. "I was so saddened by the sight," he recalls. "I decided it was better to look at birds in the wild than try to keep them at home."

Kabaya made dozens of bird-watching trips to Tokyo's parks and, at 13, became the youngest member of the Japan Wild Bird Society. That's when he spotted an article in the society's magazine about a

team of Cornell University professors recording bird sounds. Kabaya wanted to try, too.

Eleven years later, in 1951, he got his chance. With the help of his younger brother, an electronics student, Kabaya built a primitive tape recorder and amplifier. At 79 pounds, the crude device weighed only 9 pounds less than its designer. Kabaya had no battery pack and no car, so he had to haul the recorder through the woods on a wagon, never farther than the reach of a 328-foot-long power cord. The project would have been hopeless were it not for the local Shinto priests. They let the Kabaya brothers plug their recorder into an electrical outlet at the shrine at Mount Mitaka, a short train ride from Tokyo.

By then Kabaya had a job as a lowly clerk in a college administrative office, but his heart wasn't in his work. He yearned for the outdoors, and nothing matched the fascination of capturing bird songs on tape. "Birds are comparatively musical— and together with their appearance, they are very compelling subjects," he says.

Kabaya developed an obsession with having the best equipment, which threatened to bankrupt him, a fact he concealed from his fiancée. But when his debts reached $8,000, fate stepped in once again.

A bird-society colleague brought Kabaya's tapes to the attention of a Tokyo radio station, and the match proved perfect. The brand-new station needed low-budget programming. And Kabaya desperately needed a sponsor.

By 1954, fortified by an expense account and inspired by a new audience, Kabaya traded up to the latest battery-powered tape recorder by Tokyo Tsushin Kogyo, later to become Sony. An improvement over his homemade equipment, it still had to be cranked up. Also, it weighed 22 pounds and required incredible good luck in order to be useful. "The tapes were only three minutes long," he says. "By the time you found a nice bird, the tape had run out."

Scratchy, short tapes and jerry-built recorders now gather dust in Kabaya's attic. These days he carries a parabolic microphone effective up to 100 feet and, best of all, a 4-pound digital audio tape (DAT) recorder that runs tapes 120 minutes long. His system produces sound of such high quality that bush warblers and nuthatches seem to be right in his studio.

Sadly, not everything has improved in the world of bird recording. "Though the equipment is better today," Kabaya says, "it's harder to record pure sound because of all the noise pollution." And since he began recording, some bird species, such as the Japanese crested ibis, have disappeared from the islands.

In the 38 years Kabaya has been recording, he has yet to miss a single deadline. The show is broadcast in pre-recorded form every Saturday and Sunday at 5:05 A.M. Reminiscent of an explorer back from safari, he brims with tales of collecting the show's material, like the time he climbed a low tree in Malaysia, belatedly noticing a snake coiled in strike position above his head. "I dove, and my guide hit it away," says Kabaya, who seems to find the whole episode funny. "I've had a lot of close calls, but no bites."

Insects are a different story. No amount of repellent works when the sweat is rolling, and Kabaya must remain still for hours or risk ruining his recording. Perhaps the only time optimism deserted the otherwise unflappable bird-watcher was about 20 years ago, in Uganda. "I felt a sting on my hand and smashed at it to kill the bug so the hotel people could identify it." He calmly headed back to the hotel, where, to his horror, he was treated for a tsetse fly bite that had given him sleeping sickness. "Lying on my bed, I thought, 'What am I doing here in the middle of nowhere? What a place to die!'" In a month, however, he recovered enough to go home. He would never travel alone again.

Insects aren't the only menaces Kabaya has faced. The stringy bird-watcher was once approached at close range, and then abandoned, by a bear in northern Japan. "He probably decided I would not be very delicious," says Kabaya. Once, mesmerized by a flock of swans, he foolishly stepped onto an ice floe off the eastern coast of Hokkaido. Deep in concentration, he floated seaward until his frantic assistant finally caught his attention. Kabaya had to wade back to shore in near-freezing—but luckily only knee-deep—water.

In spite of these brushes with disaster, he maintains, "I'm very careful. Because of the show, I simply cannot get sick or injured. I'm not a daredevil."

He may have been lucky with his health but not with his equipment. He's replaced microphones most often—he lost one on a boat when a wave swept the equipment overboard; he placed another strategically in an eagle's nest, only to have the whole device plucked out by the occupant, which flew away with it. Sometimes Kabaya gets within range of his bird just in time for his equipment to go on the fritz. In the frigid winters of northern Japan, he has to warm his tape recorder with a cigarette lighter to keep it functioning.

Those who do not share Kabaya's singular obsession might imagine that boredom is his biggest enemy, as he crouches for hours on mountain precipices, sits in trees or camps deep in the woods, usually at sunset or sunrise. To ensure the integrity of his recordings and observe whatever his charges do while "performing," he passes the time without talking, moving or reading. "If the birds aren't singing, I'll just take a nap and wake up when they do," he says contentedly. "Since you can't talk, you should take it easy." He insists there is never a dull moment.

Once in a while, Kabaya hits pay dirt. "Sometimes a bird will land right on the microphone, and I tell myself, '*Yatta!*'" (roughly: "Eureka!").

Kabaya's fluency in bird chatter occasionally takes him far from the recording studio. Trying to invent a way of keeping rice paddies bird-free, he placed loudspeakers among the stalks and played ea-

gle calls. But the birds wised up fast, and the speaker "scarecrows" ultimately proved useless.

Police investigating phone calls from a kidnapper enlisted Kabaya's fine ear. He identified birds singing in the background (a brown-eared bulbul and a woodpecker) and told the police the probable location of the caller. Unfortunately, the criminals got away.

What began as a creative outlet for a bird-watching fanatic has become something of a broadcast crusade. Japanese universities do not offer courses on ornithology, and the government provides only sparse support for conservation efforts. The mission of educating the public falls to individuals like Kabaya. "Japanese always want to turn everything into amusement parks and golf courses," he says, scathingly. "My goal is to get people to care about birds and preserving nature."

Part III

HOME PLANET EARTH

What else is happening out there? The rest of the world awaits you—a global backyard that has been mapped, routed, poked, and prodded by those who have come before you (and by some who have since, regrettably, become no more)

5. *Everywhere Else But Here: Explorers At Large*

The story goes that even upon his deathbed, Marco Polo refused to admit to friends that his book, **The Description of the World,** *was full of fantastic lies. He stuck to his story, and was ultimately proven right. Now, we'll go look for the lesson, and you just enjoy the article.*

Marco Polo in the Court of Kublai Khan

reproduction from Calliope

Marco Polo: Describing the World

by Karen E. Hong

from Calliope

"Since God first created man, no Christian, Pagan, Tartar, Indian, or person of any other race has explored every part of the world as thoroughly as Marco Polo, nor seen so many of its marvels." With these words, Marco Polo prepared to tell the world of his adventures. His book, *The Description of the World,* now known simply as *The Travels of Marco Polo,* was indeed just that—observations of a world larger and stranger than Europeans had ever thought existed.

After being captured in 1298 during a war between Genoa and his native Venice, Polo often entertained his fellow prisoners with tales of his adventures. Although many in his audience did not believe him, he always drew a crowd eager to hear his story. Now, persuaded by his cellmate Rusticello, a romance writer from Pisa, Polo began to dictate his book. As he spoke, the world of the past three years, the world of Venice and its war, fell away, and he was once again in that exotic world of his youth.

Marco was fifteen years old in 1269 when his father and uncle, Nicolo and Maffeo, returned from their first trip to the Orient. The brothers had been traveling as jewel merchants when they were directed to the court of Kublai Khan. Years later, they returned to Venice aided by the Khan's gold tablets. These tablets ensured their safety by instructing the Khan's subjects to assist the brothers along their way.

The Polos had promised Kublai Khan that they would return with holy oil from Jerusalem after asking the pope for missionaries, but their journey back to Cathay, later known as China, was delayed by the pope's death. After months of waiting for a new pope to be elected, the brothers finally decided to leave Venice.

Taking seventeen-year-old Marco with them, they journeyed first to Acre, just north of Jerusalem, and then to Jerusalem itself for the holy oil. While there, they learned that the church legate they had met at Acre had been elected pope. They immediately returned to Acre to inform him of the Khan's request. Only two missionaries volunteered to accompany the Polos, and even they turned back rather than face the desert sands and mountain winds.

The three Polos continued eastward past Mount Ararat, where Noah's Ark was said to have rested after the flood; through Armenia, where a fountain discharged oil that could be burned in lamps; over the Pamir Mountains, called the roof of the world; and along the edge of the Desert of Lop, now called the Gobi Desert, with its mysterious spirit voices of shifting sand.

The Polos were forty days away from Shang-tu, Kublai Khan's summer capital, when they were met by escorts sent by the Khan. So efficient was the Khan's system of post houses, horses, and couriers that a message could be transported two hundred fifty miles in a single day. In this way, the Khan was able to follow the Polos' return journey to his court.

After three and a half years, the Polos arrived at the summer palace of Kublai Khan. The merchants Nicolo and Maffeo presented Marco to the Khan, who found him to be an accurate observer. In addition, Marco soon became proficient in four languages – Persian, Mongolian, Chinese, and Hindustani. His ability with languages, together with his powers of observation, made him a valuable asset to the great Khan.

For the next seventeen years, Marco was attached to the royal court. When he was not traveling throughout the empire on the Khan's behalf, he wintered at Cambaluc, now Beijing, and summered at Shang-tu.

Although Kublai Khan was of Mongol descent, he had adopted many Chinese ways. Entertaining in the most lavish Chinese manner, he had banquets for thousands of guests, serving forty meat and fish dishes, twenty kinds of vegetables, forty varieties of fruit, and vast amounts of milk and rice wine.

Traveling through the huge empire as the Khan's agent, Marco found a strange but wonderful world. Common people used public baths daily. Tree-shaded paved roads, parks, and bridges simplified travel. Paper money, unknown in Europe, was commonly used and accepted in all but the most remote areas. Coal, not generally used in England until four hundred years later, served as fuel.

In remote regions, Marco saw people who covered their teeth with gold, men who tattooed their entire bodies, and loaves of salt being used as money. He even saw a crocodile, which he described as "a great snake having a very large head, and eyes larger than a big loaf; a mouth so big that it can swallow a man whole."

Because Marco was so valuable, Kublai Khan was reluctant to allow him to return to Venice. But when the sultan of Persia sent a request to the Khan for a princess to be his wife, the Khan needed someone responsible to accompany her on the long, dangerous trip west. Regretfully, he selected Marco and the two older Polos.

The Polos sailed in a convoy of fourteen ships down the coast of China to Siam (present-day Thailand), then on to Ceylon and India. As was his habit, Marco noted the spices of Java, the gems of Ceylon, and the riches of India (cotton fabric, animal hides, delicate embroidery, exquisite gems, and precious spices).

Wealthy with gold and jewels, the Polos arrived home in 1295. Legend has it that their relatives and friends doubted their tales and prosperity until they gave a banquet for the three travelers. Ripping open the seams of their traveling clothes, the Polos spilled an abundance of diamonds, rubies, emeralds, and pearls onto the table.

Doubtful, too, were the readers of *The Description of the World*. Viewed as too fantastic to be true, the book was widely read in many languages as an imaginative tale rather than the factual account it was. Tradition holds that friends urged the dying Marco to retract the lies he had written in his book, but he insisted, "I never told the half of what I saw."

Gradually people recognized the validity of Marco Polo's descriptions. Mapmakers began incorporating his findings into their work. Prince Pedro, older brother of Prince Henry the Navigator, was presented with a copy of Polo's book when he visited Venice in about 1426. Christopher Columbus studied Polo's book, making notes in the margins and carrying it along on his historic voyage in 1492.

Marco Polo extended Europe's knowledge of other people, history, zoology, botany, and economics. Because his book helped make geography a science, Polo is sometimes called the "Father of Geography."

The explorer Thor Heyerdahl, author of Kon-Tiki, "inspired" the people of Easter Island to re-enact part of an intriguing puzzle that surrounds these enigmatic stone figures. Read all about it.

The Mystery Statues of Easter Island

by Daniel Pouesi, illustrations by Tim Foley
from Cricket

Easter Island is a little island in Polynesia surrounded by one million empty square miles of Pacific Ocean. The closest inhabited land is tiny Pitcairn Island, which is about fourteen hundred miles away.

People have lived on Easter Island for hundreds of years. Long ago, the islanders farmed, using simple planting sticks and hoes. They made arrowheads and adzes out of obsidian. But these long-ago people also made huge and magnificent stone

statues that have mystified scientists and everyone else for two centuries. Why did they do it? And how did they move the statues from the rock craters where they were carved to areas several miles away?

Of the six hundred statues on the island, more than 150 are unfinished. They remain near and around the rim of the volcanic crater Rano Raraku. The tools used to carve them from the rock were found in the crater. It is as if the workers were called away suddenly and never came back.

The statues have long earlobes, stomachs that stick out, jutting chins, and high foreheads. Their deep-set eyes make them seem old and wise. The largest, with its topknot, stands as high as a seven-story building and weighs close to fifty tons. Imagine moving it, and you can understand why so many people were baffled.

Some people thought the ancient islanders might have had help from outer space. Others thought the islanders had magical powers. None of the explanations made sense until archaeologists began to study the statues, the island, and the people living on the island today.

Archaeologists study extinct cultures by examining abandoned house foundations, stone tools, and food remains and making guesses from these clues about what life in the past may have been like. They try to piece the jigsaw puzzle of past traditions together. Fact-finding for them is tough and tedious business. If they're lucky, they might find living descendants who know something about their people's roots and their ancestors, and how they did things in the past. Unfortunately, on Easter Island, very few of the natives knew about their past.

A terrible disaster occurred on Easter Island long before people arrived to study the island. In 1862, slavers transported a thousand natives bound hand and foot to Peru, South America. They were to work on plantations there. Of the hundred that were finally sent back, only fifteen reached the island. The survivors, however, brought smallpox with them and, as a result, more of their people died. In 1877, only 110 natives remained on the island.

In 1955, Thor Heyerdahl, a Norwegian expert on the history of people in the South Seas, arrived with a team of archaeologists. Heyerdahl and the members of the expedition discovered things about the ancient people of Easter Island that no one had known before. But the experts still couldn't figure out how the statues had been raised.

One day Thor Heyerdahl offered the mayor of Easter Island, a man descended from one of the island's oldest families, one hundred dollars if he would place a statue back on its altar. The mayor accepted the challenge.

The mayor organized men to gather stones and use poles. The poles were pushed under the statue's buried face. Men leaned on them to raise the face enough so that the mayor could shove stones under it. After nine days of work, the statue lay on a pile of stones so high that the men working the poles had to hang from them by ropes. On the eighteenth day, the statue was slid onto its altar. The archeologists saw that the topknot could be rolled up the pile of stones to rest on the statue's head.

Thor Heyerdahl was happy to pay the mayor his one hundred dollars. And the mayor showed Heyerdahl that the statues were probably moved on sleds made of forked trees and pulled by many people. He had learned these things from his father and grandfather. Why had he never told this to any of the other scientists who visited the island? "No one ever asked me," he said.

Later, William Mulloy, a member of Heyerdahl's team of archeologists, stayed on the island to raise more of the statues. From his experiments, he estimated that it would take "30 men one year to carve a stone statue, 90 men two months to move it, and 90 men three months to erect it."

The statues cannot talk. But they do tell us something about the ancient people of Easter Island. To have carved, transported, and erected the statues, these people must have worked hard and cooperated with each other. The statues show us that not only can we learn *about* ancient people—we can also learn *from* them.

Modern-day explorer Will Steger talked with Louise Tolle Huffman about his early interest in adventure for Cobblestone.

Follow Your Dreams

by Louise Tolle Huffman

from Cobblestone

Sail Away artwork by Dick Daniels
from Sesame Street

When Will Steger was nine years old, he traded his hockey skates for a stack of *National Geographic* magazines. From that day, he was hooked on the outdoors. At the age of fifteen, he and his brother took a "Huckleberry Finn" boat trip from Minnesota, where he grew up, down the Mississippi River to New Orleans. Later his interests turned to cold and snow, and he began raising and training sled dogs. He has traveled thousands of miles on the Arctic ice by sledge. Steger is one of a few men who have been to both the North and South poles.

In 1986, Will Steger organized an expedition team with his co-leader, Paul Schurke. The team was made up of seven men and one woman. Their goal was to reach the North Pole by dog sled in a re-creation of Robert Peary's expedition. It would be the first dog sled trek since Peary's to reach the Pole without outside help. To ensure success, the team spent more than a year planning and training. During the trek, two men had to be flown to safety when one broke his ribs and the other suffered frostbite. On May 1, 1986, six of the original eight members triumphantly stood at the top of the world. Steger talks about the expedition:

When you were young, was there any one person or event that made you want to become an explorer?

When I was in fourth grade, Huck Finn made me want to travel down the Mississippi. That was my first trip. The IGY [International Geophysical Year] back in 1958, when I was fourteen, brought about a fascination for Antarctica. It was the first time they began exploring Antarctica internationally.

What were your qualifications for making the North Pole expedition?

I had twenty years of experience traveling in the north, of which fifteen were dog sled years. Also, I have the ability to raise money and run a business. I had run my own school for ten years prior to that. [Will organized a winter school where he taught his students how to run a dog sled team and survive outdoors without camping in tents. His "classroom" was the Minnesota and Canadian wilderness.] Exploring is a great big organizational and managerial feat. People don't realize you need those skills to be an explorer.

There were many dangers and hardships on your trek — the extreme cold, frostbite, and falling into open leads. Two of your team members were injured and had to be flown out. Your favorite dog, Zap, suffered a badly split front paw, and another dog, Critter, died. Why did you do it?

We did it because we wanted to go to the North Pole. It was pretty simple. For myself, I also was interested in the Peary controversy. I felt the best way to understand it was to travel in a similar means. Too many people who had never experienced the polar sea or driven a dog sled were making sweeping statements. I felt I could do something more decisive by going on the trip. That was part of the reason, but I'd say the real motivation was the adventure of doing it.

On the expedition, you crossed an open lead by ferrying over on an ice block, just as Peary did on his expedition. Were other parts of your journey similar to Peary's?

Most of it. Once you're on the ice, it all has a common denominator — men, dogs, and struggle. The ice has not changed. We had some advantages in our clothing, but it was still men and dogs, and in this case we had one woman on the team.

Peary claimed to have traveled twenty-five to forty miles per day at the end of his journey. You felt your team was less rested than his, yet you traveled thirty-five miles on two days as you neared the Pole. Do you think Peary made it?

I think he came real close. I've always said I thought he got within twenty, maybe ten, miles. Now the Navigation Foundation has uncovered other evidence through shadows in old photographs that indicate he made it or at least was very close.

Another team member, Ann Bancroft, was the first woman to reach the North Pole. Do you have any special advice for girls?

Don't limit your thinking. It's not just a man's world. Anybody can do this. Your thinking will be your biggest barrier. If you think you can't do something because you are a girl, you won't be able to do it. My advice to girls is the same as to boys — follow your dreams.

You used dogs to travel by sledge. Can you tell us about Sam?

Sam was a wild dog we found during a training expedition for the North Pole. We were along the north coast of Alaska. A little speck appeared on the trail way back on the pack ice. The speck got bigger and bigger until we could tell it was a dog. We thought it might be a wolf. He followed us, but he was shy and wouldn't allow us to get close. After three days, he walked up, and I harnessed him. I put him in the lead dog position, and he led to the North Pole and later to the South Pole.

What would you like to say to young people?

If you want to be an explorer or whatever, just go out and do it. It takes time to become a doctor or an explorer. You've got to put a lot of effort into it, but it's the effort that makes dreams come true.

Young people definitely need to be aware of the planet and take responsibility for it, maybe even more than adults. They may need to set aside some personal goals for the good of the earth. They should educate themselves to become aware of how we are all connected to this world.

Since going to the North Pole, you have completed another history-making trek — thirty-seven hundred miles across Antarctica. You have also written a book on the environment titled Saving the Earth. *What do you plan to do now?*

Unofficially, I will probably be going on an expedition to the Northwest Passage by dog sled and kayak, and I also might cross the Arctic Ocean. Some of the same effort I have put into organizing and launching expeditions will now be put into education. I want to help bring about an awareness of the environment.

SAIL AWAY

A triangle is a shape that has three sides.
Point to the sails shaped like triangles.
Can you find any other triangles?
What other shapes do you see in the picture?

Illustration by Dick Daniels

If you want to know more about Will Steger, beyond this excerpt, check out "Follow Your Dreams," in this section, or his article "North to the Pole," which appeared in National Geographic, *September 1986.*

Six Men, Six Nations, One Quest & Six Across Antarctica: Into the Teeth of the Ice

by Will Steger
from National Geographic

Six Men, Six Nations, One Quest

The pride of six nations is reflected in the faces of the members of the International Trans-Antarctica Expedition. Two of those members, Will Steger and Jean-Louis Etienne, discovered on a chance encounter in the Arctic in 1986 that they shared a common dream—to make the first unmechanized traverse of Antarctica. But beyond mere adventure lay an overriding concern for the environment and world peace. The expedition they envisioned must serve as an example of international cooperation, focusing the world's attention on this largely unexplored land and its critical environmental questions.

Such an undertaking would be daunt-ingly expensive; 11 million dollars was eventually raised. But the biggest investment, they agreed, would be in human terms. The right team had to be assembled, each man a valuable contributor to the expedition.

WILL STEGER of the United States, a former science teacher, led an expedition without resupply to the North Pole in 1986.

JEAN-LOUIS ETIENNE, co-leader, is a sports medicine specialist from France. In 1986 he made the first solo ski expedition to the North Pole.

VICTOR BOYARSKY is a Soviet veteran of six Arctic and Antarctic projects. His task: to oversee various meteorological experiments.

QIN DAHE, a glaciologist and geologist, spent two years in Antarctica as manager of China's Great Wall research station.

GEOFF SOMERS logged three years in

Antarctica as a member of the British Antarctic Survey. Geoff is a dog handler and navigator.

KEIZO FUNATSU from Japan is, at 32, the youngest member of the team. He has four years' experience working with sled dogs.

For seven months, under the most grueling conditions, these six men worked together in an atmosphere of harmony and cooperation. Sunset provides harmony of another sort above camp on the Antarctic Peninsula. Nighttime receded into 24-hour daylight in early November but returned in February.

Six Across Antarctica: Into the Teeth of the Ice

Tears of frustration and despair blinded me more than the stinging wind or snow. For 24 hours a storm had pinned us in our camp only 16 miles from our goal—the far edge of Antarctica. We had come too far, endured too much suffering, to lose a man now, I thought bitterly. We had to find him.

We clung to a long rope as we searched; the end was tied to a sled to keep us from straying, as he had, into the raging whiteout. "Keizo!" I yelled into the blizzard. "Keizo! . . . Keizo!"

Faintly I heard the others shouting his name as they too groped in a tethered arc around the tents and sleds. Our Japanese teammate, Keizo Funatsu—gentle, compassionate Keizo—had crawled out of his tent at 4:30 the afternoon before to check on his dogs. By six we knew he was lost. We searched into the night, calling and listening, flashlight beams futile against the swirling snow.

Now in the first faint wash of daylight we were searching again.

It was unthinkable that one of us could be gone after what we had come through together for nearly seven months: Trudging, antlike, across 3,700 miles of brutal terrain, from sea level to lonely elevations above 11,000 feet . . . battered for weeks by continuous storms . . . exhausted and frostbitten in temperatures that approached 60 below, winds that howled at 90 miles an hour.

We had challenged a foreign place, a place not meant for warm-blooded animals. Antarctica's terrible interior tries to turn men into its own image—frozen. Yet this endurance test had forged a deep and permanent bond among us: six dissimilar men from six nations, attempting to complete the first crossing of the continent by dogsled.

I envisioned the worst—carrying Keizo these last few miles wrapped in the flag of his homeland—and my stomach knotted in anguish. "Keizo!" I bellowed, over and over again.

I couldn't believe it when I glimpsed him—a wraith emerging from the driving curtain of snow. "I am alive," he said. In seconds we were clutching each other. Both of us were crying.

Keizo is a skilled survivor. Once lost, he scraped a shallow trench with pliers, the only tool he had, and curled up in it like a sled dog, allowing the blizzard to bury him.

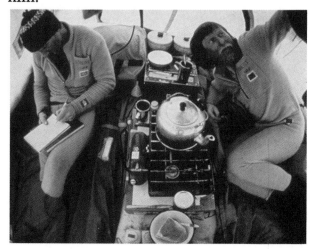

And there, with Zen-like calm, he waited for 13 hours, until he heard our calls.

It was then — but only then — that I was certain our expedition was a success. . . .

I was first fascinated by Antarctica as a boy, reading about Fuchs and Hillary in *National Geographic*. Poring over pictures of crevasses and mountains and scientific camps, I wondered how men dealt with this wild environment, how they survived. I knew then that Antarctica was a place I had to see.

I dreamed of it for 30 years. The reality was triggered by a one-in-a-million meeting in the middle of the frozen Arctic Ocean, when the path of my 1986 dogsled trek to the North Pole crossed that of Frenchman Jean-Louis Etienne, who was skiing solo to the Pole. We sat that night in a tent and drank tea and found that we shared the same dream. . . .

We wanted to prove that six men from six different nations, who had grown up with starkly different cultural backgrounds, could work together toward a common goal under some of the cruelest conditions on the planet.

We hoped our expedition would help focus the world's attention, and similar cooperation, on the icy continent. The next few years will be crucial to Antarctica's future. Increasingly it is beset by man-made pollutants; tourists are clamoring to visit. Most important, the international treaty that governs Antarctica comes up for review in 1991, leaving open to discussion such vital issues as scientific research, mining, military presence, and territorial claims. As the world's greatest remaining pure wilderness, Antarctica's harsh yet surprisingly delicate environment must be preserved.

Asked why six men, one each from the United States, France, the Soviet Union, the People's Republic of China, Japan, and Great Britain, would attempt such a challenge, Jean-Louis spoke for us all when we announced Trans-Antarctica: "You dream about exploration or you do not . . . but if you do, then the attraction is very strong, all of your life.". . .

Trans-Antarctica officially got under

way at sunrise on July 27, 1989: six men, three sleds, 40 dogs. The dogs lurched off so eagerly they overran and scattered the television crew filming our departure from Seal Nunataks. The temperature was a balmy 28°F, and the going was easy. But within ten miles we encountered the first of many blockades to come—a deep crevasse, wider than the length of three dogsleds; we were forced to detour around it.

We spent the first week establishing a traveling rhythm for the next seven months. Keizo, Geoff, and I were each responsible for a dog team; Victor skied ahead of the sleds, acting as a scout; Jean-Louis would maintain radio contact; Dahe did daily scientific studies. . . .

Each day began with Victor bursting from his tent clad only in Gore-Tex booties to take a "snow shower," after which he would visit the other tents to announce the day's weather.

"Mild today," he would shout through the tent wall. "Winds only 20 miles an hour. You'll need a face mask." Soon none of us would budge from the comfort of our sleeping bags until Victor issued his report.

After a quick breakfast of tea and oatmeal we would dig the sleds out from under the drifted snow, harness the dogs, and travel until 1 p.m. Spread out along the trail, we had little opportunity for conversation; we welcomed the chance to gather at lunch, even if the winds were too strong to talk. On those rare occasions when the sun shone during a lunch break, Antarctica seemed almost peaceful. "There's no place I would rather be," Keizo announced on one such placid day. . . .

The low point for me came the morning in mid-October when I crawled out to feed the dogs and found my old friend Tim dead. The perfect sled dog—part wolf, with thick, black coat—he had been the star of our North Pole team. Now five years old, he was weakened by the wet snow matting and freezing in his fur. I had tried keeping him in the tent at night and carrying him on my sled. But he lost his strength and his spirit, and he froze to death. . . .

Day 161, January 3, 1990: "Essentially our days have little pain or suffering to them now. It's a lot easier getting up in the morning, time passes a lot quicker. Day after day of blue sky, very calm at night. . . . Occupying your mind is now the real challenge."

We had been warned by both French and Soviet scientists that there would be very deep snow throughout the area of inaccessibility. The scientists had assured us that we would not be able to cross it by dog team. To our surprise it turned out that surfaces had been hard packed by the wind, making for relatively easy sledding. . . .

Nevertheless, a lot could still go wrong. Reaching our destination, the Soviet base at Mirnyy, was by no means a sure thing. More storms would be a certainty as we descended closer to sea level. Ferocious katabatic winds lay ahead. And in our race to beat winter, we would be approaching the coldest spot on the continent. . . .

We arrived at Vostok January 18, the first to cross the area of inaccessibility on foot. We were greeted by fireworks and the 40 Soviets who work there. Many of them knew Victor, who had been based here in the 1970s and '80s. They welcomed us Soviet style, with bread dipped in salt, Russian champagne, a sauna, and a shower.

Vostok is close to the coldest spot in the world, where an incredible minus 128.6°F was recorded in 1983. The morning we arrived, it was 48 below and dropping fast. I knew it would only get colder until we neared the coast, 850 miles away. Indeed, on February 6 we recorded our coldest day—54 below—and on the 15th, the worst windchill, minus 125. Windstorms like those on the peninsula swept us again, though thankfully they were now at our backs. . . .

Two days out of Mirnyy the storms came back with a vengeance. As always in such conditions, we staked skis and poles every few yards between the tents. It was here that Keizo, looking after his dogs in the blizzard, lost his way between ski markers and had to bury himself to survive.

His own journal tells the story best:

"Once I was in my snow ditch, blowing snow covered me in five, ten seconds. . . . I could breathe through a cavity close to my body, but the snow was blowing inside my clothes, and I was getting wet. I knew my teammates would be looking for me. I believed I would be found; it was just a matter of time. I had to believe that. . . .

"Very few people have that kind of experience, lost in the blizzard. I said to myself, 'Settle down, try and enjoy this.' In my snow ditch I truly felt Antarctica. With the snow and quiet covering me, I felt like I was in my mother's womb. I could hear my heart beat—boom, boom, boom—like a small baby's. My life seemed very small compared to nature, to Antarctica."

Finding Keizo alive was the greatest relief I have ever known.

The storms calmed the next day, and on March 3, 1990—after 220 days and 3,741 miles—we arrived at the other side of the continent. . . .

It wasn't until we stepped off the Soviet ship that carried us from Mirnyy to Perth, Australia, that we became aware of all the changes that had occurred while we were away. We stepped off into a new world: The Berlin Wall had tumbled, San Francisco had been rocked, Nelson Mandela was free, Eastern Europe was tasting liberty. . . .

Perhaps our expedition—as a small example of multinational effort focused on the last great frontier—would be accepted as a contribution toward the world's new awakening.

Newbery Medal-winning author Paul Fleischman (son of Newbery Medal-winning author Sid Fleischman) writes of the intense curiosity and drive to discover new species of flora and fauna that propelled two naturalists cross-country. Then read about the author, in his own words, in "Meet Your Author."

Journey into a Strange Land

by Paul Fleischman
from Cricket

On the morning of 13 March 1834, a coach clattered out of Philadelphia, bound for Pittsburgh. Inside it sat John Kirk Townsend and Thomas Nuttall. Winter was just giving way to spring, and the two men were in high spirits. They were heading west toward lands of undiscovered plants, strange birds, and new beasts. They did not plan to end their journey at Pittsburgh, but to proceed down the Ohio River, to cross the Mississippi, the Great Plains, the Rockies—to cross the entire continent—and to be the first trained naturalists to do so.

In Pittsburgh, Townsend and Nuttall booked passage down the Ohio River on the steamboat *Boston.* The hills of Pennsylvania, Townsend's home state, gradually disappeared behind him. He was twenty-four, well educated, a doctor whose real love was the study of birds. This would be his first trip west of the Appalachian Mountains.

Nuttall, however, had journeyed down the Ohio River several times before. Twice Townsend's age, he was North America's most-traveled plant collector. In the course of his explorations, from the Great Lakes and the upper Missouri to the Arkansas River and the swamps of Florida, he'd encountered quicksand, hostile Indian tribes, river pirates, had nearly starved to death, had become lost on the prairie, and had suffered through malaria.

In spite of all these hardships, Nuttall accepted at once when his friend Nathaniel Wyeth invited him to join his expedition to the Oregon Country west of the Rockies. Here was a chance to see plants no botanist had ever seen before! He'd met Townsend not long before, had been impressed with him, and invited him along.

On 24 March 1834, the *Boston* docked at St. Louis. The naturalists bought clothes for the journey ahead: leather pants, bulky overcoats, and hats that seemed stiff enough to repel bullets. The pair then walked to Independence, Missouri, and joined Wyeth's brigade there. On 28 April, all 70 men and 250 horses started west for Fort Vancouver, two thousand miles away on the Columbia River.

Lewis and Clark had been the first to travel overland to the Columbia thirty years earlier. West of the Louisiana Purchase, the Oregon Country was claimed by both the United States and Great Britain. Those going west with Wyeth had a variety of motives for traveling so far. Wyeth and his contingent of men hoped to take some of the trade in beaver pelts from the British Hudson's Bay Company, enriching themselves and bolstering America's claim to the region. A party of Methodist missionaries had joined them in hopes of converting the Flathead Indians. For Townsend and Nuttall the lure was neither money nor territory nor souls, but plants and animals waiting to be discovered.

Following the Kansas River, the expedition met white wolves and vast herds of antelope. It also met the Great Plains' violent weather. A daylong downpour drenched the men and their bedding. A hailstorm caused the horses to panic and flee. The men no longer bubbled with laughter and song. One morning one of the cooks was discovered to have left. A few days later three more men deserted.

On 18 May, the party reached the banks of the Platte, the river that would lead them west into the Rocky Mountains. It led them at once into Pawnee country — the brigade had to ride nearly all of one night to avoid a war party of 1,500 men.

Spring was giving way to a scorching summer. One day the expedition was attacked by swarms of gnats, causing all the men's faces to puff up from bites. Gale-force winds drove sand into their eyes. The naturalists, however, were not discouraged. Townsend discovered the lark bunting, which would become the state bird of Colorado.

Nuttall was exhilarated by the acres of bright prairie flowers. "Mr. N. was here in his glory," wrote Townsend. "He rode on ahead of the company and cleared the passages with a trembling hand, looking anxiously back at the approaching party as though he feared it would come ere he had finished and tread his lovely prizes underfoot."

Gradually the expedition climbed into the Rockies. They sighted the snow-covered peaks of the Wind River Range. Nearer at hand, Nuttall discovered a new whippoorwill, still known as Nuttall's poor-will. On 14 June, they traversed South Pass at 7,526 feet. The naturalists were now west of the Continental Divide. "The botanist . . . fails to recognize one solitary acquaintance of his former scenes," Nuttall wrote. "He is emphatically in a strange land. A new creation, even of forest trees, is spread around him."

After a two-week rest at the annual rendezvous of Rocky Mountain trappers, the brigade pushed west once again. They crawled through desolate, lava-covered hills. Mineral springs bubbled up beside them. After stopping again to build a trading post, they continued on into a land without water, shade, or game. The horses' tongues hung from their mouths as they labored to haul the party's gear up rock-strewn passes and down sheer mountainsides. The men, baking in the heat, sucked on pebbles to try to keep their mouths moist.

"We have no flour nor vegetables of any kind, and our meat may be aptly compared to dry chips," wrote Townsend. Dodging the Blackfoot Indians, the brigade lost its way among the mazelike Blue Mountains. The men could barely see ahead of themselves — vast wildfires were raging around them, filling the sky with smoke and blackening the grass that should have fed the party's horses. The men ran out of food entirely. Returning to camp after a meager dinner of rosebuds, Townsend discovered the owl he'd shot that morning and had intended to skin and stuff was being eaten by two men — one of them a ravenous Nuttall!

On 3 September, the expedition reached Fort Walla Walla and glimpsed the Columbia River at last. Their saddlebags stuffed with hundreds of pressed plants and stuffed birds new to science, the naturalists followed the river, then boarded canoes to take them the rest of the way to Fort Vancouver, only to be halted by a ferocious gale. The canoes were tossed violently about in the waves and rapidly took on water. Bailing for their lives, the men managed to reach shore, but not before Nuttall's huge plant collection was soaked. Townsend observed him hour after hour, sitting in front of an enormous fire "drying the papers, and rearranging the whole collection, specimen by specimen, while the great drops of perspiration roll unheeded from his brow."

The men proceeded, by canoe and on foot, drenched by a steady rain. At eleven o'clock on the morning of 16 September, the Wyeth expedition reached its destination, Fort Vancouver. By stage, steamboat, horse, canoe, and on foot, through rain, hail, sandstorms, and heat, Townsend and Nuttall had journeyed more than three thousand miles. Why? "None but a naturalist," Townsend wrote in his journal, "can appreciate a naturalist's feeling—his delight amounting to ecstasy—when a specimen such as he has never before seen meets his eye."

Meet Your Author: Paul Fleischman

from Cricket

I grew up in Santa Monica, California. My father, Sid Fleischman, was and still is a writer of children's books. I had no idea what *I* wanted to be. I didn't know that garbage cans, my shortwave radio, and our printing press would lead me to be a writer as well.

My sisters and I often rode up and down alleys, picking through people's trash. My favorite find was a World War II gas mask. This might seem to have nothing to do with writing. But when I'm looking for an idea for a book now, I often go to used-book stores and look through books

people have "thrown out"—old, dusty books that sometimes give me an idea for a book of my own. I never know what I'll find, just as I didn't in the alleys. When I do research for my books set in the past, I often read old diaries and letters—not unlike looking through the letters we used to find in garbage cans.

I got a shortwave radio when I was about ten, and grew up listening not only to the Los Angeles Dodgers, but Radio Havana and Radio Tokyo and stations from all over the world. I didn't speak Spanish or Japanese. When you listen to a language you don't understand, you hear just the music of the words, not their meaning. Words, I discovered, are made of beautiful sounds.

LARK BUNTING

NUTTALL'S DOGWOOD

RIVER CRAB APPLE

NUTTALL'S POOR-WILL

One day my parents came home with a hand printing press. I had my own printing business while I was in junior high school, printing cards and stationery for my parents' friends. The shapes of letters and the look of words on a page, I discovered, are beautiful as well.

Writing books today, I still find the sounds and shapes of words captivating, and the search for new ideas exciting. I think I'll take a walk down the alley.

Paul Fleischman

Elsewhere: Other Explorers and Discoverers

by D. P. Brown

from Cobblestone

Pytheas was a Greek navigator and astronomer who lived about 2,400 years ago. He explored England and made one of the first maps of the island. He also traveled to a place he called Thule—which may have been present-day Iceland or Norway—to witness the midnight sun. Ancient scholars doubted Pytheas's Arctic observations, as they believed that the earth was uninhabitable that far north.

In 1271, Marco Polo embarked on one of history's greatest adventures. He ac-

companied his father and uncle on a trading expedition from Italy to China. After 3 years, they reached the palace of Kublai Khan, China's ruler. Polo joined the court of the great ruler and for 17 years traveled Asia as his special envoy. Polo returned home after a 25-year absence. His family

and friends did not believe the stories he and his father and uncle told. When his autobiography was published, people thought that it was a fanciful story rather than a true account of his experiences.

In 1673, the French explorers Jacques Marquette and Louis Joliet were the first Europeans to see the Mississippi River. They canoed from present-day Wisconsin to Arkansas and then back to Michigan, a difficult journey of nearly 3,000 miles. Soon afterward another Frenchman, Sieur de La Salle, reached the Mississippi's mouth on the Gulf of Mexico. He claimed the land for the French king, naming it Louisiana in his honor.

Captain James Cook was one of the most famous English explorers. From 1768 to about 1778, he made 3 voyages across broad expanses of the Pacific. He discovered Australia's eastern shore, New

Zealand, Hawaii, and many other lands. He explored in the Arctic Ocean. He also charted the waters around Antarctica. Cook did much to advance the sciences of geography and navigation.

THE SPANIARD CORONADO EXPLORED ARIZONA, NEW MEXICO, TEXAS, AND KANSAS MORE THAN 60 YEARS BEFORE THE ENGLISH ESTABLISHED THEIR COLONY AT JAMESTOWN.

Incidents in the Life of My Uncle Arly

by Edward Lear, artwork by Mary Flock

from Cricket

I

O my aged Uncle Arly!
Sitting on a heap of Barley
   Thro' the silent hours of night,
Close beside a leafy thicket:
On his nose there was a Cricket,
In his hat a Railway-Ticket
   (But his shoes were far too tight).

II

Long ago, in youth, he squander'd
All his goods away, and wander'd
   To the Tiniskoop-hills afar.
There on golden sunsets blazing,
Every evening found him gazing,
Singing, "Orb! you're quite amazing!
   How I wonder what you are!

III

Like the ancient Medes and Persians,
Always by his own exertions
   He subsisted on those hills;
Whiles, by teaching children spelling,
Or at times by merely yelling,
Or at intervals by selling
   "Propter's Nicodemus Pills."

IV

Later, in his morning rambles
He perceived the moving brambles
　　Something square and white disclose;
'Twas a First-class Railway-Ticket;
But, on stooping down to pick it
Off the ground—a pea-green Cricket
　　Settled on my uncle's Nose.

V

Never—never more—oh! never,
Did that Cricket leave him ever,
　　Dawn or evening, day or night;
Clinging as a constant treasure,
Chirping with a cheerious measure,
Wholly to my uncle's pleasure
　　(Though his shoes were far too tight).

VI

So for three and forty winters,
Till his shoes were worn to splinters,
　　All those hills he wander'd o'er,
Sometimes silent; sometimes yelling;
Till he came to Borley-Melling,
Near his old ancestral dwelling
　　(But his shoes were far too tight).

VII

On a little heap of Barley
Died my aged Uncle Arly,
　　And they buried him one night;
Close beside the leafy thicket;
There—his hat and Railway-Ticket;
There—his ever-faithful Cricket
　　(But his shoes were far too tight).

6. When Outdoors and Indoors Are One

This is the serious part. When the great outdoors and its inhabitants, like the bald eagle and the tiger, are threatened, science can lend a helping hand within the controlled environment of the lab. This, in part, is what we understand by the word ecology. *It can also mean treating the outdoors as you do your own home.*

Test Tube Tigers Born in Omaha Zoo

from National Wildlife

Three tiger cubs, the first big cats ever conceived by in vitro fertilization, were born recently at Omaha's Henry Doorly Zoo. The tigers, born to a surrogate mother, were delivered by Cesarean section.

Although only one cub survives at this writing, the births represent a technological breakthrough that may have important implications for dwindling wild tiger populations, says the zoo's director, Lee Simmons.

By implanting laboratory-conceived embryos into wild females, Simmons says, scientists could introduce genetic material from animals thousands of miles away into isolated wild populations weakened by inbreeding.

The technique also could simplify captive breeding, because shipping embryos would be much less troublesome and costly than exchanging live animals among zoos, Simmons says.

World renowned entomologist E. O. Wilson invested a lifetime career in studying these little creatures' societies. There is more than enough wonder and fascination here to make you serious about and interested in the way you lead your own life — you may be inspired to think of one or more career ideas of your own.

Dr. Ant

by Don Lessem
accompanied by "New Ant Species Found in D.C. Office"
from International Wildlife

On a rainy morning, Harvard professor Edward O. Wilson, entomologist extraordinaire, is "rooting around like a hog," as he puts it, in the rain-forest soils of Costa Rica.

Wilson at work is a sight straight from a Gary Larson cartoon — a gaunt figure in thick glasses, swaddled in heavy work clothes and cap despite the tropical heat. In a Larson cartoon, some huge forest creature would be staring over the oblivious scientist's shoulder. In life, a three-toed sloth smiles from a nearby tree.

The sloth is well beyond the range of Wilson's nearsighted gaze. The scientist focuses on ants and their world, about which he is the world's foremost authority. "Come have a drool over this," he calls to his biologist companions from the Organization of Tropical Studies research station, motioning toward tiny ants he's whacked from the riot of branches.

For 50 years, Ed Wilson, now 61, has been "drooling" over ants like these — in this case a species previously unknown to

science. He has probed colonies of ants from Costa Rica to the Amazon, New Guinea to Jerusalem. In the process, the insects have led him along a bitterly controversial pathway of cutting-edge theory with sweeping ramifications.

The little world of ants that so fascinates Wilson is enormous, in numbers, variety and antiquity. Ants have worked the earth since the days of the dinosaurs — Wilson himself has identified ants preserved in amber nearly 100 million years old. Today about 8,800 known species and, Wilson suspects, at least as many yet to be discovered, build their colonies in every climate except polar cold. They turn over soil, pollinate plants and dispose of more than nine in ten small animal corpses.

Ants cover Planet Earth in almost unimaginable numbers — a million billion by Wilson's own "conservative" estimate — and in patches of almost unimaginable density. But it is in the tropics that ants achieve spectacular diversity. Concentrating on a single tree in the Peruvian

Amazon, Wilson once identified 43 species—roughly the number found in the whole of Great Britain.

The worldwide triumph of ants owes principally to their sophisticated societies. On the trail in Costa Rica, Wilson points out a great example—a clearing sprinkled with large mounds and many holes. This is the home of *Atta*, the leaf-cutting ant. In such homes, Wilson has been a frequent, if unwelcome, guest.

Galleries as wide as a fist plumb 20 feet down through an *Atta* nest complex, a labyrinth made of 40 tons of soil. "What they've done in a few years is comparable to building the Great Wall of China," says Wilson. "They" are 3 million workers, some as small as a grain of sand, with soldier sisters 100 times as large. The mid-sized *Atta* are the marathon runners, scurrying beyond the nest to bring back bits of leaves. By one of Wilson's favorite calculations, these ants' routine task is equivalent to a human running a mile in 3 minutes 45 seconds while wearing a 500-pound backpack.

Deep in the nest, ant siblings of the leaf-carriers, some microscopic, culture fungus on the leaves. The fungus processes plant cellulose that no ant, and few other animals, can digest. The ants harvest protein from the growth buds of the thriving fungus, a beneficial relationship for both parties.

The intricate behavior of these and other ants became a platform for Wilson's broader studies, which cast him as the principal advocate of the emerging and controversial discipline of sociobiology in the 1970s. Sociobiology is the study of the biological basis of behavior. Among animals, say the sociobiologists, the urge to protect one's shared genes in children and siblings influences all manner of actions, from establishing a territory to dividing labor.

Sociobiology theory fits the highly regulated and limited ant world. An ant colony is a huge family, made up of fertile queens and their many offspring. If, for example, some ants acted "altruistically," fighting to defend their colony at the cost of their own lives, they were still enhancing the survival chances of their genes—represented in their siblings.

But Wilson's huge, landmark book *Sociobiology: The New Synthesis,* published in 1975, applied sociobiology to higher animals as well. His efforts to suggest a role for genes in shaping some human behavior has met harsh criticism. Wilson cautioned that environmental influences were much more significant than biological ones, but suggested that genes might affect such common roles as females as cooks, and men as warriors. This approach struck many readers as fraught with possibilities for sexist and racist interpretations.

Among Wilson's sternest critics has been fellow Harvard biologist Stephen Jay Gould, who termed human sociobiology "dangerous nonsense." Irate demonstrators often heckled Wilson and once interrupted a lecture to douse him with water.

For the shy, gentle and unassuming Wilson, the ruckus over sociobiology was both surprising and troubling. "The lack of civility in the discourse" upset him, as he readily admits more than a decade later. But he did not back away from the controversy. He wrote three more books inquiring into the role of sociobiology in human behavior, including the Pulitzer Prize-winning *On Human Nature.*

The debate is far from resolved, but civility has returned. "Ed is one of the brightest men I know," says Gould, "and a good colleague, even if I disagree thoroughly with a lot of what he says."

"Sociobiology's become reputable to the point of dullness," Wilson says, chuckling. "It may be called evolutionary psychology or biosocial anthropology, but it's taught everywhere, including China and the U.S.S.R."

Sociobiology isn't Wilson's only contribution to grand evolutionary theory. In the 1960s, Wilson co-authored the theory of island biogeography. He and the late Princeton University biologist Robert MacArthur theorized that the number of species in any habitat is in equilibrium. If animals are added, others go extinct. If the habitat is reduced in size or suddenly isolated, the number of species will fall. According to Wilson's and MacArthur's theory, it is possible to predict precisely the number of species of trees, birds or ants in a habitat by specifying its size and degree of isolation.

This idea has profoundly influenced the planning of biological reserves. As Wilson explains, "We realized we need to preserve large areas, far larger than we used to believe, to protect species—and provide corridors of wilderness linking one reserve to another, so species won't be isolated."

The minute world of ants brought Ed Wilson to these great issues of conservation and evolution. If not born to study ants, Wilson was made into an entomologist early in life. As a frail boy growing up on the rural border of Florida and Alabama, "Snake" Wilson collected nearly all the 40 species of snakes known to the region. He was an avid fisherman as well. But at seven he lost most of the sight in one eye when he yanked up a catch and was scraped in the eye by the fin of a fish.

Ever since, Wilson's monocular vision hasn't been much good for spotting snakes, but his "good eye" is exceptionally adept at close-up viewing. Even without a magnifying glass, he can count the tiny hairs on an ant's body.

He has plenty of opportunities to do so

during 12-hour work days in his Harvard laboratory, surrounded by plastic tubs holding exotic ant colonies. When he leaves his office, it is often for his packed biology lectures to Harvard undergraduates. There, strands of black hair flopping in his face, chalk marks accumulating on his rumpled jacket as he paces beside the blackboard, Wilson is the image of the sweetly absent-minded professor. He is fond of ranging away from expected textbook material, for instance, drawing the pointed ears of Star Trek's Mr. Spock to illustrate mutations.

Aside from an obvious fondness for science fiction, Wilson is a man of only one notable quirk—an inexplicable fear of spiders. He has no known vices, few hobbies and little scientific interest outside of biology and conservation. Wilson's suburban home life with his wife of 30 years, Irene, is quiet. Their only child, Catherine, is a veterinary nurse. Only in recent years has Wilson stopped jogging five brisk miles each morning near his home, giving in to an aching back.

His single-minded diligence seems positively antlike. But, as he enjoys pointing out, ants are far less busy than he. "Like most cold-blooded animals, ants spend most of their time doing nothing."

He, on the other hand, is "trying to climb Mount Everest in my old age." That's how he refers to his current and unprecedented effort to describe thoroughly and draw every one of the more than 600 New World species of ants in the largest genus of ants on Earth, the *Pheidole*. He's been at it two years now, and anticipates he'll need three years more.

For the past three years, Wilson also labored, with Harvard colleague Bert Hölldobler, toward the publication last March of the first major overview of ant life since 1910. Theirs is a hefty work, titled simply *The Ants*—more than 700 oversized pages, including more than 1,000 illustrations and weighing more than 5 pounds.

Such voluminous research has not produced any practical applications, at least none that Wilson can think of. "I never worried about pest control," he says.

Controlling ant predators of crops or pests in the home is a daunting challenge. Despite a vulnerability to cold (they do not thrive in temperatures below 68 degrees F), ants are remarkably hardy. Some can survive flooding. One species can live up to 14 days submerged in water.

Against their natural enemies, ants deploy highly successful defenses. The inch-long and solitary *Bolla* ant of the American tropics possesses a sting so powerful it can temporarily disable a man. Withstanding several stings from *Bolla* placed upon their bodies is the manhood rite for adolescent Orinoco Indians. Borneo ants have pincers so sharp they can cut through leather. And perhaps most bizarre are soldier ants that compress themselves so violently when threatened that they blow up, spraying their foes with noxious chemicals.

Browsing in the ant world in Costa Rica, Wilson whacks at a snarl of branches, then squats to peer at the bark he has chipped away. He picks up one huge dark ant firmly from above. *"Bolla,"* he says. "I know how to handle them."

Wilson's big find for this morning is a small and unexceptional-looking black ant he uncovers beneath some bark. "It's a dacetine ant," he explains, "but the species is new." Deftly manipulating his tweezers, he drops several into a vial.

In the midday heat, while his companions enjoy a siesta in the dormitories, Wilson sets to work figuring out what prey the newfound ant prefers. (It chooses tiny insects called springtails). In mid-afternoon, Wilson is back in the jungle looking for more ants. And, after dinner, while his scientist companions extend conversations Wilson had taken an active part in, he excuses himself to patrol the outskirts of the screened and lighted dining hall, collecting yet more insects.

Catching the reporter's eye, he says, "You haven't asked me the question I'm most asked—'Dr. Wilson, what can I do about the ants in my kitchen?' My answer is always, 'Watch where you step.'"

New Ant Species Found in D.C. Office

Some biologists spend an entire career in the field hoping to discover a new species. But World Wildlife Fund president Kathryn Fuller found one right under her nose on the desk in her Washington office.

One day Fuller asked a distinguished visitor, noted ant expert and WWF board member Edward O. Wilson, to have a look at the tiny ants that had invaded her telephone. He took some specimens back to his lab at Harvard and after careful study concluded that they represented a completely new species.

The ants, which Wilson plans to name *Pheidole fullerae* ("Fuller's thrifty ones"), apparently hitchhiked from Central America via a potted palm that now resides in Fuller's office.

You live in an era in which grown-ups are admitting they haven't always done everything that's best for the earth. You're probably already helping out, and know that things are more complex than simple "either/or" issues.

Humans and Endangered Animals: Making Room for Both

from Current Science

More and more Americans are going green—that is, helping to preserve the environment. They're recycling garbage. They're demanding tougher antipollution laws. They're providing sanctuaries for endangered wildlife.

But like Kermit the Frog, they're also finding that "It's not easy being green." Environmental concerns often collide with other priorities, calling for difficult, painful decisions.

What would you do, for example, if helping an endangered animal meant that ranchers would lose some of their cows because the animal preys on livestock? Or worse, if protecting the animal meant closing off an entire forest, putting hundreds of lumberjacks out of work?

What follows are three real-life stories about conflicts that have arisen over attempts to save endangered or threatened species in the U.S. These are cases where

emotions have run high, where questions have outnumbered answers, where solutions are still being sought. Perhaps you have some solutions of your own. Read on.

Case No. 1: Owls vs. Jobs

Consider the conflict that has been raging for years in the Pacific Northwest (Washington, Oregon, and northern California). Conservationists there are at loggerheads with lumber companies that harvest the region's majestic ancient forests.

At issue is the survival of a bird, the northern spotted owl, that makes its home in the Pacific Northwest. The spotted owl needs large territories of old-growth forest to survive, and conservationists say that any more cutting down of the old trees could push the owl toward extinction. Lumbermen say that if they have to curtail their logging activities, many lumberjacks and millworkers will lose their jobs.

The timber industry employs 100,000 people in the Pacific Northwest. If the spotted owl is protected by fencing off the old forests, as many as 30,000 people could lose their jobs, say logging industry officials.

For many people in the Pacific Northwest, working in the woods is more than just a way to make money. It's a way of life. "We came out here in the 1850's," says Milton Herbert, the owner of Herbert Lumber in Riddle, Ore. "We spend our lives trying to understand trees, to live with the environment, not against it. I hunt and fish. This is my home."

Fighting over one species of animal may seem almost silly when so many livelihoods are at stake. But conservationists note that the northern spotted owl is really a symbol of a much larger concern: the survival of the ancient forests themselves and the dozens of other species that live in them.

Timber companies prefer harvesting the old cedar, Douglas fir, and redwood in the ancient forests because of the superior grain and strength of the wood in these trees. But the logging industry has already chopped down 90 percent of the old forests. In only a short time, the rest could be gone.

Lumber companies defend their case by pointing to the large replanting projects they've financed. In these projects, single species of trees that produce good lumber are planted. But conservationists say that the projects are an example of too little, too late. Forests take hundreds of years to mature, while reforestation programs have existed for only about 20 years. Besides, the newly planted single-species forests don't have anything like the diversity of the old forests.

Conservationists also say that Americans must practice what they preach. For several years now, the U.S. has been demanding an end to the destruction of the world's tropical rain forests. But can the people of Africa and South America be expected to save their forests when we can't save our own?

Case No. 2: Wolf Knocking on Yellowstone's Door

Sometimes saving one endangered species means sacrificing not just livelihoods, but the lives of other animals. This could happen if gray wolf packs are reintroduced to several areas in the northern Rocky Mountains, including Yellowstone National Park. Biologists are hoping to reverse the damage done during the taming of the American West, when the gray wolf was hunted nearly to extinction in the continental U.S. The gray wolf is now listed as an endangered species and lives only in Alaska, Canada, and northern Minnesota.

Biologist Renee Askins says that the demise of the gray wolf upset the balance of nature in places such as Yellowstone. Wolves were an important part of the park's *ecosystem* — the community of animals and plants in the park and their relationship to each other and to the physical environment.

Ms. Askins says that in Yellowstone and elsewhere, the gray wolf was the major predator of elk. It kept their numbers down by feeding mainly on the weaker members of the herds. "The elk and the wolf evolved together. There is a delicate balance between the two," says Ms. Askins.

Now that the wolf is gone, elk herds have grown by 80 percent and are now too large to be sustained by the park's limited resources. In winter, visitors to Yellowstone are struck by the pitiful sight of large numbers of elk, rooting through the deep snow, looking for any bit of vegetation they can find. Reintroducing the gray wolf could eliminate the weakest of these animals, resulting in smaller but stronger herds.

Though the restoration plan sounds sensible, ranchers and hunters don't like it. Ranchers worry that the wild canines will stray from the park and prey on their livestock (cattle and sheep), making it harder to earn a living. They estimate that the wolves could kill 1,000 head of cattle a year. Hunters also fear that straying wolves will compete for big game.

A recent 586-page government report on the restoration plan conceded that game wardens may have to enforce lower quotas on big game during hunting season. But the report also concluded that the wolves would not kill a significant number of livestock. Meanwhile, a U.S. conservation group, Defenders of Wildlife, has created a fund that would compensate ranchers for the loss of any livestock from wolf kills.

Some ranchers remain unimpressed. Teddy Thompson, a rancher in southern Montana, replies: "A compensation system will never work in country this rugged. You can lose livestock and not find the carcasses for months, and by then there isn't enough left to prove whether it was a wolf or something else that killed them."

Case No. 3: Sea Lions' Share of Fish

Sometimes an effort to help one species can backfire, putting the survival of an entire group of another species in danger. Take the case of the California sea lions who just won't stay put in their native state. Instead, they keep turning up 1,000 miles (1,600 kilometers) to the north, in Washington State's Puget Sound.

The problem with the sea lions is that they like to eat steelhead trout, a fish that is prized by sport fishermen and by two na-tive Indian tribes, whose treaties give them special rights to catch the fish. Sea lions pose a real threat to one particular *run* (population) of steelhead trout that uses a certain canal in the city of Seattle to reach its spawning ground in Lake Washington. The sea lions have discovered how easy it is to catch the fish if they station themselves at the entrance to the canal.

Joe Scordino, a deputy chief with the National Marine Fishery Service in Seattle, says that the sea lions gobble up so many fish that the run is getting smaller every year. "At this rate," says the biologist, "the run will become so small that it won't take much of an environmental catastrophe to eliminate it entirely."

Government scientists have tried everything to scare off the sea lions. They've detonated firecrackers under water. They've played tape recordings of killer whales, the enemies of the sea lions. They've fired plastic arrows at them, but "they got used to being bonked on the head," says Martin Fox, a biologist.

Finally, last March, the scientists captured a group of six sea lions and trucked them back to California. But not even that worked; by May, three of the animals were back. "We were surprised they came back so fast," says Mr. Scordino. "I guess they like the food up here better."

Some fishermen want the sea lions killed, but that is forbidden by the Marine Mammal Protection Act. Since the act was passed in 1972, the California sea lion population has increased by about 6 percent a year. In 1975, there were 27,000 California sea lions; today there are 177,000. As the population has grown, the sea lions have ventured farther and farther north.

Wildlife officials don't know what to do. How can they respect the Marine Mammal Protection Act, protect the steelhead trout, and keep fishermen happy, all at the same time?

Just because you think of something as trash doesn't mean it should be thrown out. Read on for some of the innovations taking place in the garbage world.

Whatta Buncha Junk!

from Ranger Rick

Thinking about trash got you down in the dumps? Here are some wacky, wild, and weird things that are happening with all kinds of junk.

Bottle Blowing

Have you ever made music by blowing over the top of a bottle? Justin Kramer has. In fact, he made a whole organ by recycling bottles—88 bottles in all. He also made a smaller bottle organ out of a six-pack. How does the music sound? Windy!

Garbage Museum

Sometimes museums collect what looks like old junk. But the folks in Lyndhurst, New Jersey, went a lot further. Their museum is crammed with *real trash!*

Folks in New Jersey wanted to teach people about what happens to the millions and millions of things we throw away each day. So they made the museum look like the inside of a landfill. The walls are plastered with cans and cartons, boxes and bottles, old teddy bears and broken toy trucks, inflatable boats, refrigerators— even a kitchen sink.

The museum also displays neat things people have made with recycled materials. And it asks people to buy things they can use again instead of things they'll just throw away.

What do you call a wastebasket filled with clocks?
A waste of time.

Plastic Playgrounds

A company in Chicago, Illinois, has found out how to turn used plastic into "lumber." They make plastic "wood" out of millions of used plastic milk jugs. The plastic is good for building outdoor stuff like playground equipment, docks, and fences. The plastic doesn't rot, splinter, or burn easily. And termites (insects that eat wood) don't like it.

This company is one of many that are finding ways to turn a tough problem—used plastic—into a tough solution.

What do you call little piles of trash?
Dump-lings.

How to Re-Tire

In the United States, more than 200 *million* tires are thrown out every year. That's nearly one tire for each person in the country. Most of these tires go into dumps or end up in rivers and streams.

But a company in Minnesota has found a way to grind up the tires and use them again. The ground-up tires are mixed with other materials to make a new kind of rubber. Then it can be used to make everything from shoes to new tires!

Mom, It's Recycled

Here's a way to convince your folks that the cereal you like is good for the environment. Open the box. If the cardboard inside is gray or tan, it's been made from recycled paper.

A Wreck! No, a Reef!

Scientists have found a new use for old ships. The ships are sunk in the ocean near a coastline in carefully picked places. The sunken ships soon become wildlife homes! Sponges and mussels grow on them, little fish hide in them, and big fish try to find and eat the little fish.

Dr. Garbage

William Rathje works as a professor at the University of Arizona. Get this—he teaches trash.

Dr. Rathje and his team of students dig through trash that's buried in landfills. (A landfill is a dump where each layer of trash is covered by a layer of dirt.) Then they bring back samples to the lab and pick through them. Why?

People who plan landfills need to know all they can about what happens to the stuff that gets dumped there. Then they can better decide how to handle all of our trash.

Landfill planners used to think that things rotted pretty fast inside a landfill. But Dr. Rathje and his students found out that most things we throw away stay around for a long time. They've even found 20-year-old newspapers that still look fresh! And they discovered that plastic — even the kind that's supposed to break down — doesn't rot at all.

Space Junk

When scientists look deep into the night sky these days, they see more than faraway planets and twinkling stars. They see trash! More than 7000 big pieces of trash are orbiting around the earth — everything from dead satellites to rocket parts.

Scientists know where the big pieces are, and they can make sure that spacecraft stay away from them. But there are thousands and thousands of tiny pieces of trash in space too — some as small as chips of paint from old spacecraft.

Scientists worry about the trash because of how fast it's zipping around the earth. A tiny chip may be going five miles (8 km) per second! It's getting dangerous for astronauts to step outside their spacecraft. They could get whacked by space trash!

Block of Bottles

Folks in Omaha, Nebraska, figured out a neat way to solve the problem of leftover bottles and jars. First, the city government asked people to save their glass containers. The city collected a total of 300,000. Then the people who make roads crushed the bottles. They mixed the ground glass with *asphalt,* the blacktop used to pave roads. Know what they called it? *Glassphalt!*

The city used the glassphalt to cover a street that's one block long and six lanes

wide. Other cities—such as New York—are using glassphalt to pave some of their streets too.

When the light shines on the glass mixed in the blacktop, it sparkles like diamonds. Now *that's* a bright idea!

Trash on Stage

Would you enjoy listening to a couple of puppets doing a rap on recycling? Lots of school kids in New Jersey get to do just that. Stage shows about garbage are being put on in many parts of the country. You might get to watch garbage collectors dancing ballet on stage. Or maybe you'll meet Mr. Recycle—he dresses up like a big aluminum can. And some school kids put on their *own* shows about trash and recycling. All these shows help to get the message out—garbage is everybody's problem.

What do you call three feet of trash?
A junk yard!

Beach Trash

People sometimes throw trash into the ocean without thinking. And a lot of it then washes up on beaches. A photographer found a whole bunch of this junk and lined it up in front of a nesting albatross. He wanted to take a photo that would warn people to be more careful.

Ocean animals such as the albatross may mistake pieces of junk for food. They

swallow the junk or feed it to their young. That's really bad news! Why? The trash can stick in their throat or their stomach and make them sick. Sometimes it can kill them.

So the next time you're at the beach or out in the water, help the wildlife—pick up the trash. And don't litter!

We don't know what to make of this. Is it good or bad? Or just ugly?

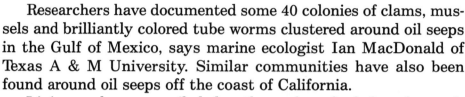

Sea Creatures Thrive on Oceans' Oil Seeps

from National Wildlife

Life thrives in some of the strangest places, including where oil and methane gas seep through the sea floor, scientists have discovered.

Researchers have documented some 40 colonies of clams, mussels and brilliantly colored tube worms clustered around oil seeps in the Gulf of Mexico, says marine ecologist Ian MacDonald of Texas A & M University. Similar communities have also been found around oil seeps off the coast of California.

Living as deep as a mile below the surface, far below the reach of any visible light, these oil-loving creatures include many species previously unknown to science. They survive in such a hostile environment by feeding on bacteria able to convert hydrocarbons to energy.

There really are book worms. And the way they take in the text may give you a chuckle.

Book Worms

by Elizabeth A. Foley

from Dolphin Log

Worms may not seem like the hardest workers on Earth, but in Dortmund, West Germany, they're doing a great job—recycling the town's old telephone books. Peter Ludwig, the worms' owner, keeps three million hungry earthworms in a big garden where he feeds them the town's old telephone books. By munching the books, the worms get food to eat and convert what would be a mountain of waste paper into fertilizer, which is then used by gardeners.

Scarlett O'Hara was always trying to make her waist look a little thinner. But this is a different symbol of the South, for a much different era.

Symbol of the South Grows Thin in Louisiana

from National Geographic

To the chagrin of Southerners with poetry in their hearts, Spanish moss, the ghostly gray plant that beards tree limbs and dances in the languid breeze, is in serious retreat. In parts of southern Louisiana it is gone with the wind.

Not a moss but an epiphyte, these air plants often secure their seeds in live oaks' craggy bark. Ken Whitam, a plant pathologist at Louisiana State University in Baton Rouge, suspects that Spanish moss has declined because of the effects of air pollution from chemical and oil refineries, as well as the debilitating attack of the fungus *Fusarium.*

During the 1970s the fungus plagued other southeastern states, where the moss seems to be recovering. The disease is now most active in Louisiana. In desperation, some homeowners there procure healthy moss specimens from distant sources and tie strands in their own barren trees, hoping that new generations will take hold.

So—what does *happen when you give cows chocolate to eat?*

How Sweet It Is

from National Geographic World

For some cows in Pennsylvania feeding time has become a sweet experience. A chocolate factory there gives nearby farmers scrap chocolate and damaged or misshapen candies. The farmers add about four pounds of the scraps to the daily feed of each cow.

The new diet doesn't make the cows give chocolate milk, but it does help them produce more and better milk. Here's why:

A pound of chocolate provides twice as much energy as a pound of corn. As the cow's energy level rises so does its milk output. The milk is richer, too. High in butterfat, it's the cream of the crop.

Minnesota's Lynn Rogers is known nationally for his photography. But while he has been checking out the locals, they've been checking out him.

Now Say Cheese! Eye to Eye with Wildlife

from National Geographic World

Picture this: You're looking through the lens of a camera and you see . . . something looking right back at you! That's what happened to photographer Lynn Rogers.

He set out to shoot pictures of birds in the Minnesota woods. A hungry red squirrel gave him another idea. Rogers put some sunflower seeds on the tip of his camera lens. The squirrel approached to get the seeds. The two saw eye to eye—then, click! Rogers snapped a close-up of the curious creature.

Although some good shots happen by chance, wildlife photographers work hard to make most pictures. They may climb a giant prickly cactus to look for a nesting owl, camp out in snow to photograph arctic wolves, or row to a distant island to find sea lions.

Patience is all-important, says photographer Jim Balog. He once spent several weeks in a Canadian national park, waiting for the right moment to make pictures of bighorn sheep. "I lived with those sheep, dreamed about them, even began to smell like them!" he recalls. His persistence paid off. When one ram challenged another in a two-hour battle, Balog was there to capture it on film.

Many wildlife photographers become experts in animal behavior. They learn how to read an animal's signals. "I've been studying black bears for 23 years," says Lynn Rogers. "I've discovered that they are curious but usually timid. A black bear that appears to be threatening is often only frightened."

When you think of endangered species, you probably think of lions and tigers and bears. But researchers are also plowing new ground in the fight to save ancient breeds of farm animals.

In Search of the Barnyard Ark

by Lisa Drew
from National Wildlife

Not far from where the Pilgrims came ashore to settle the New World, a dozen students take turns driving a team of Dutch Belted oxen. With spoken commands and a whiplike goad, they direct the yoked pair around a field. The overall effect on this sunny spring day is one of charm. The animals start, turn and stop in tandem, compliantly breaking in one handler after another. Their coloring, black interrupted by white bands encircling their middles, is echoed in the robes of one of the participants, a Benedictine nun. A student nervously yells, "Whoa!" near the beasts' sensitive ears, and the teacher says, "You don't have to be loud. I always say an ox's favorite command is 'Whoa.'"

Charm is important here. In another century, these animals might have been prized as hardy sources of meat and milk as well as brute strength. But the year is 1990, the place is Plimoth Plantation living history museum and the occasion is an American Minor Breeds Conservancy (AMBC) conference. These students,

mostly hobbyists, small farmers and historians, know that almost half the breeds of livestock in this country are near the brink of extinction—and that almost no one else is doing anything about saving them.

The modern farm has little use for animals like Dutch Belted cattle, as capable of pulling a plow as giving milk. Instead, it has developed single-purpose super breeds, like Holstein cattle for milk and Leghorn chickens for eggs. Though the older breeds hold genetic riches that one day may be priceless—for use in low-input farming, adaptation to climate change, even conservation and maintenance of wildlife habitat—they are endangered animals without an act of Congress to protect them. Many have survived only because they happen to have enchanted their keepers.

"We spend the least amount of money for our food—for probably the highest quality of food—anywhere in the world," says AMBC executive director Don Bixby. "How can you complain about that? But there are expenses that haven't been put on the ledger sheet, and genetic conservation is one of them."

Livestock conservation is not this haphazard everywhere in the world. It is most organized in Great Britain, which has a model nonprofit program called the Rare Breeds Survival Trust, and in the Eastern Bloc countries, which sponsor state-run programs. Some countries—most notably Hungary and Brazil—boast government farms for rare livestock. And the United Nations Food and Agriculture Organization has solicited livestock surveys from around the world, starting in developing countries. The United States now accounts for the biggest gap in the data.

The U.S. Department of Agriculture has been doing genetic research on some common and rare breeds of livestock for more than 30 years, and this winter it will release a national plan for animal gene conservation, including its first census. But as for actually saving breeds at risk, "We're just talking about getting all this pulled together," says Roger Gerrits of the USDA Agricultural Research Service. Eventually, the agency may store frozen semen and embryos of rare breeds. "After all is said and done," he adds, "a lot more has been said than has been done."

The closest thing in the United States to a livestock Noah's ark is the American Minor Breeds Conservancy, based in Pittsboro, North Carolina. Over the past decade, the nonprofit organization has helped give a sense of mission to owners of rare breeds, growing from 150 members to 3,000. "I'm raising American heritage farm animals," says AMBC member Margaret Marsh of Princeton, Massachusetts, whose 2 acres of pasture hold rare breeds of cattle, pigs and sheep between colonial stone walls. "What we're doing now may help farmers 50 years from now."

The AMBC has started some limited semen banking for certain breeds, but it has no funds for actually keeping animals; that is up to individuals and luck. And only since the organization conducted a 1985 census on a shoestring budget have members had any idea what breeds survive in this country and where they are.

During the weekend conference at Plimoth Plantation, 150 AMBC members ponder such issues as the future of draft animals and the importance of feral livestock, animals that have reverted to the wild and been toughened by the rigors of natural selection. Between meetings, participants show each other photographs of their animals, pulling snapshots from wallets and hauling out whole scrapbooks. In a very real sense, this is when they do some of their most important work: Survival for many dwindling breeds often means finding unrelated mates to forestall inbreeding.

Losing the old livestock could be a tragedy on a huge scale. The animals in the photographs—four-horned sheep, shaggy-haired cattle, draft horses, reddish pigs—are largely irreplaceable. Some are the closest living links to the wild animals from which domestic animals were first tamed thousands of years ago.

Some breeds are traceable to their wild roots: The ox ancestor of most of the world's cattle went extinct in the 1600s. Others are mysteries: Scientists can only guess at the ancestry of domestic horses. One theory holds that domesticity actually saved horses as forests and human hunters encroached on the grass-eaters at the end of the Ice Age. Only one truly wild horse still lives, the Przewalski's, which roamed Asia 60 million years ago. Ironically, the 1,000 surviving Przewalski's exist only in semi-captivity, while once-tame feral horses (like mustangs on our plains) run wild in parts of the world.

Many of the old breeds are a form of living history. The Crusaders used Percheron draft horses on the way to the Holy Land; they later became our most popular draft horses. In 1985 there were about 1,500 registered here, up from 85 in 1954. The sunburn-resistant Tamworth pig, one of the oldest surviving pigs, is similar to the domestic swine of medieval times, which in turn descended from ancient wild boars. About 2,000 were registered in this country in 1985. The gentle Guinea hog, once a common homestead pig in the South—and now almost extinct—came to this continent with the slave trade. Almost all livestock on this continent originated with animals that accompanied Spanish and European settlers or slave traders. Some of our minor breeds still exist in Europe, but generally are rare there too.

There is far more at stake than cultural history or a few unique traits. Until the farm technology of the past few decades, livestock survival had a great deal to do with natural selection—despite selection by breeders for productivity or more frivolous traits (like the markings of Dutch Belted cattle). Older breeds tend to forage well for their own food, resist disease and mother their young without help. They also were once key links on farms with many interlocking parts, consuming byproducts like whey and cider pulp, fertilizing fields, even controlling pests.

Over thousands of years, some farm animals have become integral parts of ecosystems. Some are named for the regions where they evolved, such as British sheep called Cotswold, Dorset or Oxford. Their counterparts among wild animals are subspecies, populations exquisitely adapted to specific habitats.

After an important Indian waterfowl reserve banned grazing in 1982, bird populations plummeted; the Bombay Natural History Society later blamed in part the withdrawal of water buffalo that had controlled aquatic grasses. Wildlife trusts in Britain advertise land available for grazing by rare breeds to help maintain habitat. In the United States, farmers have experimented with using Scotch Highland cattle in place of herbicides to control unwanted plants like poison oak and blackberry bushes. The cattle are also known for their lean meat; their long coats serve in place of fat to warm them.

The habitat of animals on the modern farm, in contrast, is often a sort of McDonald's environment, the same place no matter where it happens to be on the map. Animals adapt to antibiotics, assisted birthing, heated barns and high-energy foods rather than to weather or local plants. "You can go anywhere in the world now, and an intensive poultry farm will look identical in Iowa, Cotswold Hills and Addis Ababa," says Elizabeth Henson of Britain's Rare Breeds Survival Trust. "There are the same cages, same heating, same formula food and exactly the same birds. That is totally different to what it would have been like even 50 or 60 years ago, when every village in the world would have had slightly different birds."

Such farms generate enormous amounts of food; the worry is about what is being lost in the process. "Today's animals work extremely well for today's environments," says geneticist Phillip Sponenberg of Virginia-Maryland Regional College of Veterinary Medicine. But, he says, if we create a population of uniform animals, "We may not be able to redirect it."

One example may be the commercial turkey, one of the poultry industry's great success stories, which has such a large breast that it can't reach the opposite sex to mate. "There are very few turkeys, except maybe in somebody's farmyard, that can mate naturally," says George Farnsworth, chief geneticist of Nicholas Turkey Breeding Farms in California. Although turkeys are a marvel of modern breeding, with huge breasts of lean white meat and white feathers that leave the skin unmarred by color, their inability to mate is part of a general trend that concerns AMBC. "They're being modified out of any form of adequate biological fitness," says poultry geneticist Roy Crawford, "to meet a commercial demand for right now."

That notion is absurd to people like Farnsworth, who calculates intricate genetic formulas to increase the birds' vigor, size and efficiency. The company keeps more than two dozen strains as genetic libraries (and corporate secrets) to draw on in the future. But even among those breeds, only one or two can mate naturally. And, says Farnsworth, "If some strains don't seem to have any potential in a real way, we get rid of them."

That mentality, certainly common for a corporate world of what Farnsworth calls "cutthroat competition," is precisely what worries livestock conservationists. Says Henson of the Rare Breeds Survival Trust,

"We owe it to the next generation to hand them the same package of genes that was handed to us. It is very arrogant to say that people 100 years from now will want the same turkeys we eat and will want to continue to do artificial insemination."

If so, whose arrogance is it? If the case for keeping rare breeds is compelling, then can we blame someone for their status? "That is hard to do," says AMBC's Bixby. "Our society, and the short view of the profit motive, are to blame. Genetic conservation is one of those things we didn't know we needed to worry about."

Raising rare breeds is, all agree, no way to get rich. But who is to say that farmers of the future won't once again value abilities beyond food and fiber production? "These breeds evolved in an era of sustainability," says Bixby. "If we are to reachieve that sustainability, they will have a commercial niche." On the largely self-sufficient farm of the Abbey Regina Laudis, a Benedictine order in Bethlehem, Connecticut, Sister Telchilde Hinckley purchases no commercial feed for the Tamworth pigs. Instead, she gives them kitchen scraps, skim milk and whey from the dairy and bakery waste. "In very se-

© MAYRANNE MOTT

vere winters," she has found, "Tamworths have outwintered Yorkshires by a mile."

Last year, Rodale Research Center in Pennsylvania tried controlling an orchard's weevil pest with commercial chickens. "They were pretty pathetic," says Orchard Project Manager Sarah Wolfgang. "The first few weeks they were here, we had to literally pen them out of the shelter during the day."

The problem was no surprise to AMBC when Rodale contacted the organization for help. "The commercial chickens didn't understand the issue," says Bixby. This year, Wolfgang tried Dominique chickens — known as intelligent and self-sufficient. Though it is too early to tell whether the animals will control the pests, "These chickens are certainly better adapted," says Wolfgang. "They're excellent foragers, and they range across three connected plots instead of huddling in a group. They seem quite content in the environment."

That connection with the environment is key in developing countries, where well-meaning aid agencies are bringing in productive livestock to replace local breeds — without enough attention, say critics, to whether regions can support the coddled environments the animals need to survive. "The indigenous breeds," says poultry geneticist Crawford, "are falling like ten pins." There are no figures to support such charges, but there is plenty of anecdotal evidence. Just one example: In Africa's Chad Valley, commercial cattle largely replaced small local stock in the early 1970s. Then the region's usual seven-year drought hit, and, "Surprise, surprise," says Henson, "the imported stock died." Farmers rebuilt their herds with a few remaining local cattle.

The productivity of our commercial breeds is largely dependent on high-energy feed grain. "That doesn't make sense to some Ethiopian who really knows hunger," says Ronald Blakely of the Sedgwick County Zoo and Botanical Garden in Wichita, Kansas (home to a large rare livestock collection). "He says, 'Give me the grain; I can eat that. Why do we need to run it through a cow so I can get some milk?' That's one benefit of an animal that forages. A human being cannot eat grass, but he can eat it in the form of milk if an animal converts it."

Livestock conservationists worry that we may not have much time left in this country to save our equivalents of Chad Valley cattle, as many of our rare breeds are in the hands of aging farmers. "It doesn't take a lot of thought to realize those herds are going to be gone if we don't do something about it," says geneticist Sponenberg. One of those farmers is 69-year-old James F. Holt of Rochelle, Georgia, whose herd of Pineywoods cattle (also known as Florida Cracker cattle) has been in his family for 200 years. Fewer than 500 of the animals, descended from Spanish cattle brought here in the 1500s, survive in the whole country.

The cattle "practically feed themselves," says Holt, and calve regularly until the age of 25. Sponenberg calls them "indestructible." The last time Holt needed a veterinarian was five years ago, and that was for a crossbred animal. Other cattle may seem more productive, he says, "but here's the catch: In those Pineywoods cattle, you can feed five for the expense of feeding three of the others."

Holt's simple economics aside, herds like his could easily fall victim to the market — or worse. "There are dreadful consequences to a rare breed when even one key herd is forced to liquidate due to financial distress," says Canadian pig farmer Douglas Law of Moffat, Ontario. In the United States, Dutch Belted cattle suffered a blow in the 1986 dairy buy-out program. To relieve the glutted dairy market, the federal government offered cash for cows. Many older farmers retired, including a Florida farmer who sold about 1,000 Dutch Belts for slaughter. By 1987, fewer than 1,000 purebred Dutch Belts survived in this country.

In an even sadder chapter of U.S. history, the federal government almost killed off the Navajo Churro sheep, a particularly hardy breed with distinctive two-textured wool (wool that helped make Navajo textiles famous). The sheep became an integral part of Navajo culture after the Indians acquired them from Spanish settlers early in the 17th century. After the U.S. Army declared war on the Navajo nation in 1863, fighting decimated livestock populations. Then, between 1930 and 1950, the federal Navajo Livestock Reduction Program—an effort to reduce overgrazing on limited reservation land—indiscriminately slaughtered both good and poor Churro stock. Probably fewer than 1000 still exist, up from about 500 in 1985.

The only farm animal the U.S. government has actually saved is the Texas Longhorn. In 1927, 20 found a home on a wildlife sanctuary after Congress cited the animal's historical significance. Today, the demand for leaner beef has again made Longhorn genes commercially viable.

Although a one-time save by the government, the Longhorn case has much in common with other efforts to rescue breeds in trouble—efforts called "fire brigade stuff" by Elizabeth Henson. "In a way we're in the same position in livestock conservation as the World Wildlife Fund was when it first looked at individual species," she says. "It's hard to step back far enough to see the whole picture."

No one yet has a grand plan to ensure the animals' survival here. Bixby wants government support for semen and embryo storage, and use of rare breeds to control public grasslands. Michael Fox of the Humane Society of the United States would like to see tax credits for landowners who keep rare breeds. Henson envisions "some kind of program where you have live populations breeding naturally." She adds, "We have to do it as a conservation exercise. I don't think we can really expect the hard-nosed industrialists to do it." (Then there are the cases where a dollar sign has been just what was needed. Clydesdale horses, for example, could well have died out here if Anheuser-Busch hadn't made them a corporate symbol.)

Says AMBC's Bixby, "Conservation is sometimes practiced not because of any idea that one species or breed is more important than another, but just because it's threatened. The point is, we need to save genetic diversity."

Even fainting goats, which fall over with rigidly contracted muscles when startled? (The condition must set predators to licking their chops.) Yes, says Bixby, though even he agrees that the animal's peculiar condition "has no agricultural value." The goats are still sources of meat and milk, and they do have a place in medical research, as people can also be affected by the hereditary condition, called myotonia. Bixby insists that they are also valuable just because they are "different in a measurable, discernible way, and they may have some other characteristics we don't know about that will be valuable."

Philosophizing aside, for the time being the key to the goats' survival is simply that they charm us. And that, whimsical as it seems, continues to be critical not only for fainting goats but for the survival of this country's whole barnyard ark.

If you come across such words in the classroom as "science" and "Darwinism" and then you or someone else throws in another word for good measure like "ecology," you may end up with a question like this:

Should Scientists Unearth Indian Bones?

from Current Science

To dig or not to dig, that is the question. In recent months, this question has surfaced more and more often in debates between scientists and various groups of Native Americans. For years, scientists have been digging up the remains of ancient peoples to learn more about how humans lived many hundreds – and even thousands – of years ago. After the scientists made detailed studies of the remains, the bones often became part of scientific collections in museums and universities.

In recent years, however, many Indian groups have protested the digging up of their ancestors' bones. The groups say that scientists have no right to disturb the graves and that the bones now in museums should be returned to the tribes for proper burial. Only after the bones have been reburied, say some Native Americans, will the souls of their ancestors rest in peace.

Most anthropologists, or scientists who study the ancient records of early humans, are upset by the demands. The scientists say that studying ancient human remains is important to science and medicine. Analysis of bones and other grave artifacts help researchers learn about the health and habits of these ancient peoples who left no written history.

Responding to the concerns of the Indian groups, many states have recently passed laws against disturbing Indian burial sites. A few months ago Congress passed a law that would require museums and other institutions receiving federal funds to return the remains of ancient humans to a tribe who can prove a link of kinship to the remains.

Although many remains may leave museum collections because of this law, many skeletons, especially the very old ones, will stay because they have no link with living tribal groups.

Not all anthropologists and Indian groups are on opposite sides of the debate. Some are working together to ensure that both scientific and tribal goals are achieved. For example, before scientists at the University of Nebraska return the remains of 93 Omaha Indians to the Omaha tribe, the Indian group has given Dr. Karl J. Reinhard permission to make a new study of the bones. An Omaha tribe member, Dennis W. Hastings, will cooperate with Dr. Reinhard and go with him on field trips to Omaha cemeteries and other Indian sites.

Mr. Hastings, an anthropologist himself, says that "more might be lost than gained for the tribe if the bones were reburied before they were adequately studied. It is very much in our interest to learn as much as possible about our past, especially now that the days are past when oral histories preserved our traditions."

Other anthropologists strongly agree.

7. Regarding Dinosaurs

For those of you who happen to be dinosaur fans—and that may mean all of us who are not ourselves extinct. Presenting . . .

Dinosaurs Were Babies Too!

by Petra de Groot

from Ranger Rick

illustrations by Robert Byrd from Cricket

Ask Jack Horner about dinosaur eggs and his eyes light up. "They're like great gifts!" he says. "The shell is like the wrapping paper, and the baby inside is the surprise."

Jack is a paleontologist (PALE-ee-on-TAHL-uh-jist)—a scientist who studies the remains of animals that lived long ago. And he has lots of "presents" to unwrap.

Jack was the first person to find dinosaur nests and eggs in North America. First, he found fossil egg shells scattered on a hill in eastern Montana. When he dug into the hill, he found the nests. Finally, he found a few unbroken eggs nearby.

As Jack looked at one of the eggs, he wondered: Could an *embryo,* or unhatched dinosaur, be inside? How could he find out without breaking the shell—and maybe the dinosaur's bones?

Then he had a great idea. He decided to use a medical machine called a CAT scanner. Doctors use a CAT scanner to see inside a person's body. It shows more details

than the simple X-rays you may have had taken.

Sure enough, the CAT scan showed an unhatched dinosaur curled up in the egg. It was the first dinosaur embryo ever found. And it was the embryo of a new kind of dinosaur called *Orodromeus* (OAR-uh-DROH-me-us), which means "mountain runner."

Jack had already discovered the bones of this new dinosaur near the eggs and nests. They were bones of an adult *Orodromeus.* And now he had eggs and an embryo to study.

Ready to Run

Jack used the CAT scan of the egg to guide him as he "unwrapped" this incredible find. He carefully chipped away the shell until he got to the "gift"—the em-

bryo's bones. What kind of clues were hiding inside those tiny, 80-million-year-old fossils?

When Jack studied the bones under a microscope, he saw something exciting. The unhatched dinosaur had well-formed bones. They were as well formed as the bones of baby chickens. And since chicks can run around as soon as they hatch, maybe these dinosaurs could have too.

As Jack searched for more eggs, he found another clue about the mountain runners. Their nests were in big groups, or *colonies.* Jack knew that many birds protect their nests by nesting in colonies. Maybe mountain runners nested in colonies for the same reason. This was a brand new idea about dinosaurs!

Family Help

Jack soon discovered other kinds of dinosaur nests. This time he didn't find any unbroken eggs. But he did find bones of young dinosaurs piled inside the nests. And he also found bones of adult dinosaurs that were scattered nearby. When Jack studied one of the dinosaurs' skulls, he knew he'd discovered another new dinosaur. This one was a kind of duckbill.

It was neat to find another new dinosaur, but Jack was puzzled. The young dinosaurs had been several months old when they died. Why hadn't they left the nest after hatching, as mountain runners had?

Once again, Jack thought about birds. Some of them, such as songbirds, have to stay in their nests until they get stronger. Maybe these baby dinosaurs were like baby songbirds: They *couldn't* have left their nests.

To find out if his hunch was right, Jack studied the bones of the dinosaur nestlings. Sure enough, their bones weren't as well formed as those of the mountain runner. Their parents needed to feed and pro-

tect the nestlings for many months while they became stronger.

This was big news! No one had thought that dinosaurs took care of their young. But these duckbills lived in a kind of family. So Jack named this dinosaur *Maiasaura* (MY-uh-SAWR-uh), which means "good mother lizard."

More Gifts to Open

Jack keeps searching for dinosaur eggs, and he finds more each year. He's excited about unwrapping these new "presents"—there might be more new dinosaurs inside. But cracking 80-million-year-old eggs isn't easy.

Jack is patient, though. He explains, "We don't exactly know what we have. But who knows? Maybe each egg is hiding another clue about how dinosaurs lived!"

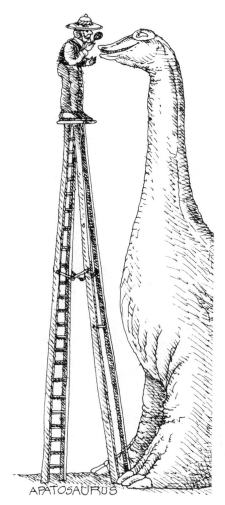

APATOSAURUS

Children's book author/illustrator Hudson Talbott has written other books since his debut with We're Back! A Dinosaur's Story, *but this one remains his most popular. You'll see why.*

We're Back! A Dinosaur's Story

by Hudson Talbott

from Cricket

HI, MY NAME IS REX.

One day as I was beginning a little afternoon snack, I noticed a small but tasty-looking creature approaching me.

"Hi there, sir," he began. "My name is Vorb, and I'm with Mega-Mind, Inc. We're test-marketing a new ultra-megavitamin on your planet. It's called . . . Brain Grain, IQ Enhancer! In regular or mint flavor . . ."

I would have caught him if he hadn't been showering me with Brain Grain. Little did I know that my life would never be the same.

164

Where am I??? A weird feeling jolted me. I began to utter strange but somehow meaningful sounds!

"As I was saying," Vorb panted, "we're testing a new Mega-Mind product, and for the lucky volunteers there's an extra-special bonus prize!"

I wondered what he meant. Then he added, "*And* free snacks." I said yes.

The other folks on board were surprisingly friendly considering my years of terrorizing them. I was amazed at how easily they accepted the new "me." It wasn't long before we became a new "us."

Together we studied geography, math, penmanship, reading, and all sorts of things.

Then one day Vorb came in and announced . . .

"You've passed! Thanks to you all, our research has been a success. And now for your *prize!* It's a trip to the twentieth century! There you'll meet *our* favorite contact person, Dr. Miriam Bleeb of the Museum of Natural History! What an adventure awaits you! Just *getting* to the museum should be the thrill of a lifetime!"

"Thrill of a lifetime?" I asked.

But before there was time for Vorb to reply, we were suddenly plunging downward in the dark toward water.

We all sat in silence as we *putt-putted* toward our destiny, wondering what sort of welcome we would receive.

"Excuse us, sir," we asked of the first little creature we saw. "Could you tell us how to get to the Museum of Natural History?"

"You're looking for the start of the parade? Just keep heading uptown. Traffic's light 'cause it's a holiday. Great costumes!" he said.

Costumes? Parade? Well, we didn't want to seem like out-of-towners, so we nodded, thanked him, and marched on.

We walked and walked until someone waved at us and shouted, "Quick! Get in line behind the Wichita Falls Marching Band! They're about to start!"

Perhaps this is some kind of welcoming ceremony, we thought. The crowd loved us! But they did call out curious questions such as ''Where are the motors?'' and ''How many guys are in there?''

We simply smiled and waved and acted as if we knew what they were talking about.

Suddenly I caught sight of what I thought was a familiar face.

''Say, isn't that old Worgul?'' I exclaimed. ''That Allosaurus who used to hang out by the tar pool! Maybe he can tell us where to get a bite around here.''

That was my first mistake . . . PANIC STRUCK!

THE DAILY POS

LATE EDITI

Somehow we found our way to the museum. And not a moment too soon.

"May we come in?" I said as Dr. Bleeb opened the door.

"Sure, but hurry!" replied Dr. Bleeb. "I have a plan, but we'll have to act quickly. I can't hold them off for long.

"Now listen carefully. I want you to act like dinosaurs. That shouldn't be too hard," she said, kneeling down and baring her teeth. "Like this. And when I say freeze, hold perfectly still!"

As she got up from her demonstration, we timidly tried to imitate her pose. She hurried toward the door, then turned and yelled, "FREEZE!"

The door creaked open, and the stomp of combat boots echoed throughout the halls. We didn't move a muscle.

"So you see, officer," I heard Dr. Bleeb say, "the only beasts we have are these models in our diorama. The creatures you speak of have been extinct for a hundred million years. I don't know who you saw run in here. Perhaps it was a publicity stunt for some movie or the *Enquirer*.

"They probably went out this way. Come back and see us again when you have more time. Yes, I'm sure you like dinosaurs—you were only doing your job. I must go now. Good-bye and good luck."

"Dr. Bleeb, " I said. "Thank you for saving us. But is it too late to get out of this bonus prize?"

"Not having a good time?" she replied. "Aren't you just a *little* curious about this new world? There's so much to learn from each other if you could stay a while and work with us here at the museum. But you don't have to decide right now. Why don't you sleep on it. We've got your beds all made."

After we were settled in, Dr. Bleeb opened a book.

"Once upon a time," she read, "in the early Paleozoic era, there was a little trilobite who wanted more than anything to walk on land. . . ."

"Go for it," I muttered. We've come this far, why not?

A TRILOBITE WAS AN ANCIENT SEA ANIMAL WITHOUT A BACKBONE. SAY IT: TRY-LUH-BITE.

Part IV

THE COMPANY OF OTHERS

It may be true that he who travels alone travels fastest, but most of us prefer to have other wayfarers nearby. Ramble through these paths, and remember: Haven't you ever needed a little help from your friends? And, have you ever had a really good laugh all by yourself?

8. Friends

Whatever else it is about, this epic tale is first a story about true friendship, perhaps the earliest ever recorded, between Gilgamesh and Enkidu.

Gilgamesh: The Quest for Immortality
&
The Story of Gilgamesh

by Susan Gundlach

from Calliope

Gilgamesh: The Quest for Immortality

Powerful and arrogant, the young king, Gilgamesh of Uruk, was two-thirds god and one-third man. He was destined to have many great adventures during his life. When the elders of Uruk complained that Gilgamesh was not a wise and loving ruler, the gods listened and responded. They created a wild man of the steppe, Enkidu, as a "second image of Gilgamesh," a man equal to the mighty king. Enkidu would be sent to Uruk to fight Gilgamesh and teach him humility.

When the day came for Enkidu and Gilgamesh to do battle, the two heroes wrestled so strenuously that they broke the doorpost of the marketplace and shook the wall. But then a wonderful change took place. Although Gilgamesh won the fight, he recognized that Enkidu was indeed his equal and praised his opponent: "Enkidu has no match. . . . In the wilderness he was born; no one stands against him." Enkidu also realized his special relationship with Gilgamesh. The two men embraced, and Enkidu called Gilgamesh "friend." Thus was formed a friendship that changed the life and ways of Gilgamesh forever.

So that Gilgamesh could make a name for himself, the two heroes took on spectacular challenges. They killed Humbaba, fearsome monster guardian of the Cedar Forest. They also killed the Bull of Heaven, but their actions angered the Great Goddess Ishtar, who caused Enkidu to get sick and die. Gilgamesh mourned for six days and seven nights. He then held a lavish funeral for Enkidu and vowed to discover the secret of immortality.

To fulfill this promise, Gilgamesh set off to find Utnapishtim, the only man who had survived the Great Flood and had been given life everlasting. Gilgamesh discarded his royal garments and clothed himself in lion skins. After weeks of travel, he came to Mount Mashu, the "mountain of the rising sun." He told the scorpion-men guarding the gate about his plan to talk with Utnapishtim. They answered, "Never has a mortal man done that, Gilgamesh." Gilgamesh did not give up. He entered the mountain tunnel and walked in darkness until light appeared "at the end of eleven double-hours." Soon after, he reached the sea. There he met the boatman Urshanabi, who ferried him across the waters of death.

On the opposite shore, Gilgamesh at last faced Utnapishtim. When Gilgamesh explained his quest for immortality, Utnapishtim responded with discouraging words: "Do we build a house forever? Do we seal a contract for all time? . . . From the beginning there is no permanence." Utnapishtim did, however, agree to tell Gilgamesh the secret of how he had escaped death and achieved everlasting life.

Utnapishtim told how Enlil, ruler of the gods, decreed that a terrible flood be made to destroy all human beings. But Ea, ruler of the earth and god of wisdom, loved humans and instructed Utnapishtim to build an ark and load it with the seed of every living thing. Utnapishtim did so. When the waters came, even the gods were horrified at the destruction they saw. The goddess Ishtar wailed and spoke against Enlil, who then granted everlasting life to the only survivors, Utnapishtim and his wife.

After relating this story, Utnapishtim further discouraged Gilgamesh by asking, "Who will assemble the gods for you, so that you may discover the life you seek?" Even though he knew that Gilgamesh would not find what he was seeking, Utnapishtim proposed a challenge to test Gilgamesh's suitability for immortality. He asked Gilgamesh not to sleep for six days and seven nights.

Gilgamesh failed this test by falling asleep right away. When he awakened seven days later, he was filled with despair. Utnapishtim ordered Urshanabi to take Gilgamesh to the washing place to purify himself. The tattered skins Gilgamesh had been wearing were cast into the sea, and he put on a fresh garment, "the robe of life . . .

The people of ancient Mesopotamia built shrines, known as ziggurats, to honor their gods.

an elder's robe," that would remain forever new. Thus did Gilgamesh prepare to return to his city a wiser man.

When Gilgamesh and Urshanabi arrived back at Uruk, Gilgamesh was ready to resume his role as king. He had not achieved immortality, but he had gained wisdom. He recorded his story on stone tablets, which he placed on the walls of the city. He knew that he would die one day, but his name would live on through his good deeds and the tables he left behind.

All quotes are from *Gilgamesh: Translated From the Sin-leqi-unninni* version by John Gardner and John Maier. Published by Alfred A. Knopf, Inc., New York, 1984.

The Story of Gilgamesh

This epic is the story of the Sumerian king Gilgamesh, ruler of Uruk, who lived in southern Mesopotamia sometime between 2700 and 2500 B.C. At the beginning of the tale, we learn that Gilgamesh has angered the townspeople and the council of elders by his insensitive treatment of his subjects. The gods hear these complaints and answer by sending an equally strong man, Enkidu, to fight Gilgamesh and put him in his place. Although the two men fight as planned, they later become close friends and embark on daring adventures together.

When Enkidu dies, Gilgamesh forsakes his kingdom and sets off on a quest to discover the secret of immortality. He seeks help from Utnapishtim, survivor of the Great Flood. Utnapishtim says that Gilgamesh cannot achieve eternal life and sends him back to Uruk.

As Gilgamesh is leaving, however, Utnapishtim tells him about a magical plant that can bestow immortality on those who eat it. Gilgamesh succeeds in plucking the plant from the bottomless sea, but a serpent steals it from him. Gilgamesh finally accepts the fact that everlasting life is only for the gods. Only then is he ready to return to Uruk. He also realizes that he must take pleasure in what he has.

At the end of the tale, the ghost of Enkidu escapes from the netherworld. He tells Gilgamesh about the fate, mostly sad, of those who inhabit the world of the dead.

Gilgamesh can be read on two different levels. On the surface, it is the story of a hero's quest for adventure. But on a deeper level, it is the tale of his search for wisdom.

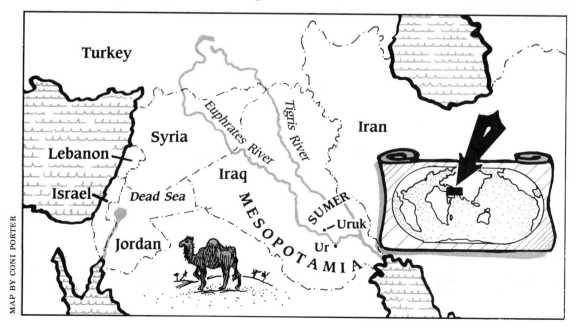

MAP BY CONI PORTER

We're not saying that the Babylonians dressed like the picnickers in Ronda Krum's illustration. But gatherings, from ancient feasts to your own Thanksgiving, are always a time for bringing together family and friends.

Some Tasty Recipes for a Babylonian Feast

from National Geographic

illustration by Ronda Krum
from Wee Wisdom

A stew of kid spiced with garlic and onion and prepared using fat, soured milk, and blood probably won't be part of your Christmas dinner. But 3,750 years ago it may have been haute cuisine to inhabitants of Babylonia.

Recipes for this and more than two dozen other dishes—such as stews of pigeon, mutton, and spleen—are recorded on three clay tablets in the Yale Babylonian Collection in New Haven, Connecticut. Dating from about the time of Hammurapi and fully deciphered only in the past decade, the tablets are believed to be the world's oldest cookbooks. They originated in what is now Iraq. The largest of the tablets measures 6.5 by 9 inches. All are somewhat damaged.

They contain a "very elegant handwriting without visible errors in all respects answering to the highest standards of cu-

neiform writing," says William W. Hallo, curator of the Yale collection. Although the collections catalog has listed the tablets since 1933, there is no record of where or when they were discovered.

Neither Professor Hallo nor Jean Bottéro, a French scholar who is publishing a full translation of the wedgeshaped script, knows exactly why the tables were inscribed or for whom. Most ancient Babylonians ate subsistence foods, but these assorted recipes, which call for a variety of rich ingredients, almost certainly were prepared for the elite, perhaps royalty.

A good friend is hard to find. Enough said.

Ants Answer Caterpillar's "Cry" for Help

from Current Science

How does a butterfly caterpillar protect itself from attack? It sounds an alarm by sending out calls for help. The sounds attract ants, who rush to the side of the lumbering insect. The aggressive ants then protect the caterpillar from its enemies.

According to Dr. Philip DeVries, an entomologist at the University of Texas, the sounds are produced by tiny organs known as vibratory papillae (puh-PIL-ee). The papillae produce sounds that vibrate the stem, leaf, or other surface that the caterpillar is on. The vibrations are easily detected by the ants. When Dr. DeVries placed a tiny microphone on a surface occupied by the caterpillar, sound vibrations were recorded up to 2 inches (5 centimeters) from the caterpillar.

The protection of the ants is very important to the butterfly larva. Studies have shown that if insect predators such as wasps find caterpillars unprotected by ants, the caterpillars have no chance of survival, says Dr. DeVries.

While the caterpillar benefits from the ants' protection, ants also benefit from this relationship because they feed on sugars and other nutrients produced by the caterpillar. Such a beneficial relationship between two different organisms is called *symbiosis*.

Bug Buddies

by Elizabeth A. Foley

from Dolphin Log

illustration by Mary Kurnick Maass from Wee Wisdom

What would you do if you were in trouble? Call a friend for help? Some scientists say plants might do the same thing. When a leaf-munching caterpillar threatens to consume them, some plants release chemicals that attract certain female wasps, which then sting the caterpillar. The sting immobilizes the caterpillar while the wasp lays her eggs in its body. When the hungry larvae hatch, they eat the caterpillar.

Not all scientists believe that plants can use their body chemicals to call their waspy friends for help. But caterpillars beware — better safe than sorry!

U*S* Kids *has a monthly advice column called* Kids Helping Kids, *where people your age write in with their problems. From these pictures, you can see that Laura Cornell, who illustrates the column, knows a thing or two about friendships and about dealing with others.*

Broken Friendships, Crying, Cheating, & Pets

illustrations by Laura Cornell
from U*S* Kids

182

The art that appears with this story is by a Danish artist, and seemed too inviting to bypass. Claire Blatchford has written an intriguing holiday story with a lesson about jumping to conclusions.

Weird, Wonderful Mrs. Becker

by Claire Blatchford

illustrations by Svend Otto S. from Cricket

"**M**rs. Becker is weird," Cat said at suppertime one evening soon after Thanksgiving.

"Caitlin, please don't talk that way about our new neighbor. We hardly know her," Cat's mother replied.

"But she *is* weird," Cat insisted. "Her front door was wide open when we got off the bus today, and she was carrying rocks into her house."

"*Big* rocks," Lisy added.

"They were covered with mud," Cat continued. "Who in the world would want a lot of dirty rocks in their house?"

"Maybe she has an aquarium," Cat's father suggested.

Cat shook her head. "They were way too big for that. They were as big as the rocks in Mr. Turnbull's stone wall."

Mr. Yates raised his eyebrows. "How old do you think Mrs. Becker is?" he asked Mrs. Yates.

"About Gammy's age."

"She got us mixed up again, too," Cat added.

Cat was eleven, and Lisy, although she was only half an inch shorter than her sister, was eight. When people confused the two or, worse yet, asked if they were twins, Cat got cross. Very cross. It wasn't fair that she had such a tall younger sister.

"I'll make cookies for her sometime soon," Cat's mother decided.

"Cookies?" echoed Lisy. She loved making cookies. Even more, she loved eating raw cookie dough.

The next afternoon when Cat and Lisy got off the bus, there was Mrs. Becker in a blue parka in front of her house. This time she was shoveling earth from her garden into three bushel baskets.

"Hi," she said, pausing to wave at them. The bun of white hair on top of her head looked as though it was about to unravel.

"Hi," said Cat.

"Did you have a good day?"

"O.K.," answered Cat. She really had had a good day, but she wasn't sure how friendly to be with this strange lady who dug in her garden in December.

"Looking forward to Christmas?"

Both girls nodded.

"Me, too. It's my very favorite time of year."

"I have to do my homework now," Cat said. She nudged Lisy with her elbow, and they started up the driveway to their house.

"She's watching us," Lisy whispered while Cat fumbled for the key in her pocket and then unlocked the door.

Once inside, Cat dumped her schoolbag on the kitchen table.

"What's she doing?" Cat wondered.

Together they went into the living room and peered out from behind the curtains. Mrs. Becker had resumed her digging. When the baskets were full she carried them, one by one, up the front steps and into her house.

At suppertime that night, Cat announced, "Mrs. Becker is *really* weird."

"Caitlin . . ."

"She took a lot of earth into her house," Cat said quickly.

"*Black* earth," Lisy added.

Mr. Yates raised his eyebrows again. "She seems nice enough," he said, "but that is an odd thing to do."

"Are you still going to make cookies for her?" Lisy asked.

Mrs. Yates nodded. But there was no time for baking that evening, nor the next, nor the one after that. Mrs. Yates was too busy wrapping packages to send to relatives. Then there were the Christmas cards to write and address. Secretly Cat hoped her mother would forget all about cookies for Mrs. Becker.

On the afternoon of the nineteenth, everyone was predicting the season's first snowfall, and on the morning of the twentieth, Mr. Yates woke the girls with the good news: "No school!"

"Yippee!" Cat yelled, jumping out of bed.

The snow was coming down so thick and fast she could barely see their own garage. Mr. Yates left early to catch the train, but Mrs. Yates stayed home.

After breakfast the girls bundled up, went out, and waded around the backyard, heads bent, snowflakes stuck to their eyelashes. Lisy got cold and went in, but Cat continued to brave the storm. She crouched under the forsythia bush and pretended she was in an abandoned wolf's den.

Sugary smells greeted her as she came in for lunch.

"Don't take your snow pants off yet," her mother said. "I want you to take these cookies to Mrs. Becker."

"Me?"

"It'll only take a few minutes."

"What about Lisy? Isn't she coming?"

"Her snow pants are soaked."

"Mine are, too."

"Caitlin . . ."

Cat stuck her tongue out at Lisy, who was licking the mixing bowl. Cat took the bag with the cookies and stomped back outside. If she fell into one of the holes in Mrs. Becker's yard and froze to death, they'd be sorry!

She made it to Mrs. Becker's front door without any mishaps and rang the bell.

A second later the door flew open, and there was Mrs. Becker in a red sweater with a spray of holly sticking out of the bun on top of her head.

"Here-are-cookies-from-my-mother," Cat said in one breath.

"Thank you," Mrs. Becker said, taking the bag. "I'm baking, too. Let's have a swap."

Before Cat knew what had happened, she was inside the house, and the door was shut.

"My mother expects me home for lunch."

"I'll be quick."

Mrs. Becker hurried into her kitchen.

Cat looked around. There was a cuckoo clock on the wall in front of her. She peered

into the living room, and her mouth fell open.

"*Wow!*"

The entire floor in that room was covered with moss and grass—*real* moss and grass! There wasn't a chair or a table or a TV in sight. Instead there were potted plants of all sizes and shapes half-buried in the grass. Rocks (the big rocks Cat had seen Mrs. Becker carrying into her house) lined a path leading to a Christmas tree in the center of the room. Candles and straw birds adorned the tree. A gold star shone from its top.

"Come," Mrs. Becker said.

Cat jumped. She hadn't heard her return.

"Those are paper-whites, here are tulips," Mrs. Becker said, pointing at some buds as they went down the path. "I'm hoping they'll bloom on Christmas Eve."

"Is it . . . is it always like this in here?" Cat asked.

Mrs. Becker laughed. "No, this is my Advent garden."

Cat looked puzzled.

"The rest of the year I have furniture, but the four weeks before Christmas I change everything. We did it as children. My father would tell my sister and me a fairy tale as we made the garden. It's about a poor family that lived deep in a forest. One Christmas Eve when they had nothing to eat, the ice and snow suddenly melted away. The light grew warmer, and the flowers opened. They found all kinds of nuts and berries to eat while the birds sang, 'It's Christmas!' "

Cat didn't say anything. She felt she'd slipped into another world. She stood there smelling the earth and grass while the snow outside swirled up against the windows and the wind whistled.

"I know you wondered what I was doing the day you came home and I was carrying the rocks into the house," Mrs. Becker said. "I decided I wouldn't tell you then; I'd invite you and your sister over for a surprise on Christmas Eve."

Cat turned to her. "Can we still come?"

"Yes."

"Mum and Dad, too?"

"Of course! But try to keep it a secret till then."

"Lisy can't keep secrets," said Cat, "but I can."

"I know you can," Mrs. Becker said with a smile. "You're older." Then she leaned over, broke a little spray of holly off a plant, and gave it to Cat.

Farewell to a True Friend

by Jay D. Hair
from National Wildlife

The familiar and lovable Kermit the Frog reports to us from Mount Rushmore. In the background, well-known presidential visages wheeze and cough.

"Air pollution is bad for all of us," Kermit tells us. "We all care about clean air."

With that and many similar messages, Kermit uses his unequaled ability to reach countless young people to instill a message of environmental concern.

When Kermit's creator and alter ego Jim Henson died on May 16, all people—young and young at heart—lost a true friend. Those who work directly on environmental issues also lost a creative talent who gave freely of his abilities to promote protection of our natural resources.

Since 1984, Jim Henson, his Muppeteers, writers and crew worked with the National Wildlife Federation to help teach the public about environmental issues. Over the years, Kermit and Company made several appearances in National Wildlife Federation public service announcements for television broadcast.

Each announcement reached millions of people a year nationwide.

Jim's extraordinary talent for making the Muppets universally appealing meant conservation messages could be conveyed to a wide audience. Children everywhere were charmed by Kermit's mild-mannered humor, but part of Jim's magic was that when the Muppets spoke, grown-ups listened, too.

The Federation honored Henson with a Special Achievement Award given at this year's annual meeting in March in Denver. Jim was there with his sidekick Kermit to accept the award.

When asked why he took the time from his hectic production schedule to make free public service announcements on the environment, Jim's considered response was characteristically lowkey: "The whole thing is just getting the awareness of people. In the last year or so, we've certainly seen a major change in overall awareness. I think it's the only way we'll ever see any major changes."

The same degree of care and professionalism that characterized all Jim's work was evident in his creation of public service spots for television audiences.

In one of the most memorable announcements he did in cooperation with the Federation, Miss Piggy instructs her household companions to do their environmental share, such as check on insulation and recycle their trash.

"What can we do to save energy?" Kermit asks, with his usual naiveté.

"Turn out the lights," responds the irrepressible Miss Piggy, as she flings herself at Kermit for an obviously opportune embrace in the dark.

Thank you, Jim. We'll miss you.

Jay D. Hair
President
National Wildlife Federation

Cathy Newman goes in search of the honorable Charles Dodgson, his young friend Alice Liddell, and the Cheshire Cat in this piece, excerpted from a much longer, truly frabjous article in National Geographic.

The Wonderland of Lewis Carroll

by Cathy Newman
from National Geographic

At the edge of an English meadow a rabbit expert flipped through my copy of *Alice's Adventures in Wonderland* and stopped at the picture of the large, white rabbit studying his watch.

"*Oryctolagus cuniculus,*" John Sandford, chairman of the British Rabbit Council, pronounced. "An albino. Pink eyes, you know. Absolutely domestic. Can't survive in the wild."

Pointing to a hedgerow, he showed me a rabbit hole, guarded by bramble and nettle.

"Unlike the one Alice fell into, burrows never go straight down," he said. "They run parallel to the surface."

He snapped off a twig from an overhanging tree and dropped it into the hole. It went straight down.

"Strange," he said, and stooped for a closer look.

Charles Lutwidge Dodgson, the shy Oxford don who wrote *Alice* under the pen name Lewis Carroll, would have been delighted. He reveled in the unexpected. In *Alice* and its sequel, *Through the Looking-Glass,* he celebrated manic absurdity. In his tales, logic spins like a carousel ("If you'll tell me what language 'fiddle-de-dee' is, I'll tell you the French for it!"). Puns teeter on the brink of outrageous (a tree can bark; it says "boughwough"). Words dance with joy ("O frabjous day!").

Even his pen name was a play on words. He transposed Charles Lutwidge, transformed it to Ludovic Carolus, and emerged as Lewis Carroll. . . .

I went to England hoping to gain a deeper understanding of the enigmatic Dodgson—and determined also to find a Cheshire cat.

"There are 75,000 cats in Cheshire; what did you have in mind?" Ken Oultram of the Daresbury Lewis Carroll Society inquired.

I didn't mean just any cat. I meant the cat who, in *Alice,* makes one of literature's most amazing exits. He dissolves, tail first: Nothing remains but his luminous grin. My request didn't surprise Oultram, my guide to Dodgson's birthplace.

Daresbury is in Cheshire, a green county abutting industrial Merseyside and Manchester's urban sprawl. Dodgson was born here on January 27, 1832, eldest [stuttering] son in a family of 13. His father was the vicar of Daresbury. . . .

"But what about that Cheshire cat . . .," I prodded.

"We don't know for sure where he got the idea, but to 'grin like a Cheshire cat' was a common expression in his day." Possibly it originated from a popular Cheshire product of the time: cheeses molded in the shape of a cat.

"Of course, if you want the real animal," Oultram said, "you might check the Cheshire Area Cat Championship . . . except that it's held in Wales!" He grinned, eyes blue as a Siamese. . . .

Dodgson was 14 when he arrived [at Rugby School], an awkward age exacerbated by his shy, sensitive nature. . . .

The school librarian showed me Dodgson's old dorm building, School House. "In those days," she said, "the butler would lock the boys in at night. He'd slam the heavy door shut and say, 'Goodnight, gentlemen.' " . . .

After Rugby's ordeal came Oxford, the great old university 55 miles from London. To envision the school as it appeared to Dodgson as a first-year undergraduate in 1851, walk through the lush expanse of Christ Church meadow to the footpath that edges the Thames. Look back. From there Oxford is all spires and towers, and parade columns of plane trees set against a limpid blue sky. . . .

There is a room in Christ Church that breathes the very presence of Charles Lutwidge Dodgson, a room of leather books, cool and dark, except in late morning, when the sun edges in and turns everything to gold.

It is not where he slept or studied but rather the library office, where as sublibrarian he glanced through a window and saw the young daughters of Dean Henry Liddell playing in the garden. They were Edith, Lorina, and Alice—a three-year-old with bangs and thoughtful eyes.

He cultivated the children. "The three little girls were in the garden most of the time, and we became excellent friends," he wrote in his diary on April 25, 1856. "I mark this day with a white stone." A white stone, adopted after a Roman custom, signified a special day. . . .

Children were a tonic, he said. "They are three-fourths of my life. I cannot understand how anyone could be bored by little children." And with them, he didn't stutter.

And how could any child be bored by Mr. Dodgson? Once when a child walked by, sopping wet from having fallen into the sea, he tore off a bit of blotting paper to ask: "May I offer you this to blot yourself up?". . .

He died of pneumonia at 65, in the house in Guildford, Surrey, where his unmarried sisters lived. The doctor, descending the staircase to break the news, gently said: "How wonderfully young your brother looks!"

9. The Other Sex: What Boys Have that Girls Don't; What Girls Do that Boys Won't

You may know—from your own experiences or those of older brothers and sisters—that the course of romance ne'er did run smooth. And that seems to go for non-humans, as well.

Will You Be Mine?

by Kay Ingalls, drawings by Pidgeon
from Ranger Rick

Whether it's Valentine's Day or not, attracting a mate isn't always easy!

A male *balloon fly* may try to win over a female with a gift. First he catches a small insect. Next he uses silk from his body to spin a glistening balloon around the dead insect. And then, while the female eats her "present," the male mates with her!

Mating can be tough for male spiders—females might want to *eat* them instead of mate with them! So a male has to tell the female what he wants. To do this, he may use his legs to vibrate a female's web. That tells her he wants to be a mate, not a meal.

The male *fiddler crab* really has his work cut out for him. He has to wave his big, heavy claw in the air to try to attract a female. He'll keep on waving all day long if he has to. It's as if he were saying, "Hey, look over here. Aren't I cute?"

When a male *blue bird of paradise* wants to attract a mate, he fans out his feathers and hangs upside-down from a tree branch. That's his way of showing females he wants to "hang around" with them!

Male *humpback whales* sing songs that may be heard under water more than 100 miles (160 km) away! Scientists think one reason the males sing may be to attract a mate. Whale songs don't sound like songs you'd hear on the radio. But they may be music to a female humpback's ears!

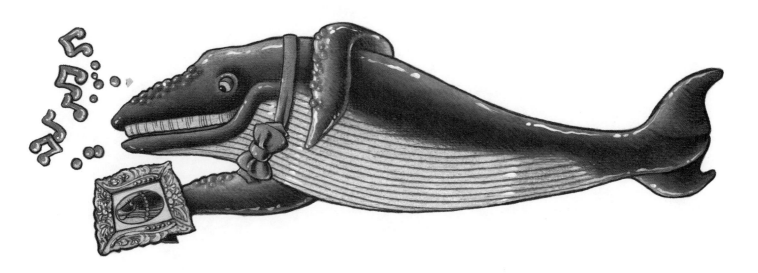

ILLUSTRATIONS BY PIDGEON

Romance Spells Trouble for Some Animals

from Current Science

When a male frog's thoughts turn to romance in Panama, he warbles his feelings with a song. If a nearby female frog likes the song, she will be attracted to the frog.

There's one problem for this budding romance. If a fringe-lipped bat cruising in the area hears the male's song, the flying mammal will zoom down and capture the frog, wiping out any further thoughts of love.

Biologists are finding that sounds and other romantic ploys used by some animals to attract the opposite sex unexpectedly turn out to be dinner bell sounds for some predators. For example, the "juggerump" of the American bullfrog, which is commonly heard during the frog's mating season, attracts not only females but also snapping turtles. Fortunately, for the bullfrog's future, enough bullfrogs survive to ensure future generations of the chunky amphibian.

A similar problem arises for some male fireflies when they advertise for females by twinkling their lights while flying on a warm summer night. If a female firefly perched on a leaf likes the winking lights, she will blink back with her light. A male will descend and land next to her.

However, sometimes another firefly species that likes to eat other fireflies (a predator called *Photuris*) will wink back. A male firefly, thinking it's a female answering, will come close to investigate. *Photuris* will capture and eat the firefly.

The lack of communication between a wife and a husband leads to a near-tragic occurrence in this tale. But love conquers all.

The Little Bell

by Danaë Tsoukalá, translated by Edward Fenton
from Cricket

There are some lucky people who have a little bell in their hearts, a bell that constantly rings, joyously and festively. Those who have it cannot hear it. They only feel that their hearts are light, without knowing why, and all their days are like holidays.

There was once a woman who had such a bell in her heart. Whenever her husband came home, worn-out from his hard day of work, he would find her with a smile on her lips.

"Don't you ever feel troubled, wife?" he would ask. "Our house is only a hovel, our field is small, and though we work from morning till night, we will always be poor. How does it happen that you are so cheerful?"

"I don't know myself," she would answer, smiling at him.

Then harder times came, when even their goat took sick. The man was in despair, and his wife racked her brain trying to think of a way to help. Finally she remembered stories of a sorceress who lived in the forest and could perform wonders with her spells. So early one morning she set off to find her. She walked and walked,

but when she came to the witch's cave at last, she nearly took to her heels and ran back home. The sorceress was terrible to look at as she sat inside her cavern with serpents writhing all around her.

The woman's knees nearly gave way with fright, but she had decided to help her husband and she was going to do that at any cost.

"Madam," she said to the witch, "hard times are upon my husband and me, and it is said that you have the power to help."

"I will help you," the sorceress told her, "if in exchange you give me the little bell that is in your heart."

"I have a bell in my heart?" the woman asked in astonishment. "Is that really so?"

"Yes," the sorceress said. "It is only a little bell, but I will give you a world of riches for it."

"Then you may have it," said the woman. She would have given her life for her husband, so why shouldn't she give a little bell?

The sorceress placed her hand on the woman's breast, murmured a few magic words, and in that way took the little bell away from her.

When the woman returned home, she found her husband overjoyed. Fields, vineyards, herds of cattle, and flocks of chickens had come to them as though they had dropped from the sky.

But the woman couldn't share her husband's happiness. It was as though something had died inside her, and she grew more and more unhappy all the time. If only one of their many heifers fell sick, she was miserable. If the crops were not the most plentiful in the valley, her heart ached to bursting.

"What has changed my wife?" wondered the man. "I don't recognize her anymore!" And since he couldn't bear to hear her wailings, he stayed away from home.

This made the woman weep harder, until finally her husband scolded her. "What are you crying for?" he asked. "When we were poor, you were always cheerful. And now that everything is going well for us, you sit and weep!"

So she confessed to him what had happened when she visited the sorceress. "And since the day I gave away my little bell," she finished sadly, "I haven't felt any happiness."

At first the husband couldn't believe his wife's words, but he saw for himself that she had become a different person. He said to her, "Tomorrow morning you must go to your grandfather and tell him everything you have told me. He is wise and will know how to help you."

So the next day the woman set out for the mountain where her grandfather was grazing his goats. The old man listened carefully to her story.

"You made a bad bargain," he said finally. "What you gave away was beyond price, for that little bell's joyous ringing always made a holiday in your heart. But you still have time to put matters to rights. Within one year you can return whatever you were given in exchange for what you gave away, because the sorceress was dishonest. She did not tell you the bell's true worth, and without your wish she cannot keep it. Once a full year has passed, however, the little bell will belong to her, by right and by might. Therefore, visit her again soon and make your request. Take this little plant with you. If anything should stop you on your journey, nibble one of its leaves and you will find a way past all obstacles."

The woman thanked her grandfather, took the plant, and returned home. But when she told her husband how she could get back the little bell, he was beside himself. "The old man doesn't know what he's talking about," he said angrily. "We could give the old witch something, a yoke of oxen or a nice cow, but not everything we have! Whoever heard of such a thing?"

The woman's longing to get back what she had given away was so great, she agreed to take a pair of oxen to the sorceress and beg her to return the little bell.

She went to the forest with a heavy heart, knowing that what she was doing was not right, and she reached the cave just as the old witch was feeding her serpents.

"What do you want now?" asked the sorceress.

"I brought you a pair of oxen to trade for my little bell."

"What?" the sorceress asked. "Do you take me for a fool? We made a bargain, and I will return your bell only when you bring back all I gave you."

The witch spoke with certainty, sure that the woman's husband would never sacrifice his newfound wealth for a little bell.

And she was right. When the woman told her husband what the witch wanted, he would hear none of it. The days went by, the end of the year approached, and the woman's heart grew heavier. She and her husband quarreled often now.

One evening, the worst of all, the husband became so enraged during an argument, he raised his arm to strike his wife. After that, he left the house and went out to the fields. Usually the sight of his well-tended vineyards brought a warm feeling to his heart, but tonight he got no pleasure from his wealth. His mind raced back to the house, and he kept seeing the terrified expression in his wife's eyes when he had raised his hand to her. It was the first time he had ever done such a thing.

How did we arrive at such a state? he asked himself. And the time came to his mind when he and his wife had lived together as one. Then, in spite of all their poverty, a smile had been on her lips, and her happiness had lightened his own heart. Was it possible that all this had been because of a little bell?

The sun was rising when the man turned suddenly and went back into the house. At last he understood the value of the little bell.

"Come," he said to his surprised wife. "We will go to the sorceress and make the exchange, properly this time. What can we do with all our riches if we don't have joy?"

The woman wanted nothing else. But the last day of the year had arrived, and if they did not get back the little bell by sunset, it would be lost to them forever.

Hand in hand, they went to the forest. But they had not gone far when a dragon suddenly appeared, holding out a thick piece of rope and a slender needle.

"Unless you can thread this needle," the dragon told the woman, "you will go no farther."

The woman realized with a sinking heart that the sorceress had placed the dragon in their path to stop them. How could she possibly accomplish this task in time?

All at once she remembered the little plant her grandfather had given her. She took it from her bodice and nibbled one of the leaves. At once the rope became the finest of silk threads, and she easily threaded the needle with it. The dragon bellowed with rage and vanished.

The path was free again, and the couple rushed on. Soon they came upon a violent, rushing river. But this time the woman knew what she had to do. When she nibbled one of the plant's leaves, the river dwindled. She chewed on a second leaf, then a third, until finally the river was only a little rill that they could cross easily.

But now the leaves were all gone. Would they get to the witch's cave before it was too late? "We must leave the path to shorten our way," said the woman.

And so they ran through underbrush and bushes. Brambles caught at their clothes and stones cut their feet, but they reached the witch's cavern just as the sun was sinking out of sight. The wife cried, "Old woman, take the fields, take the vineyards and the herds, take everything—only give me back my little bell!"

"And what does your husband say?" asked the sorceress slyly.

The man stepped forward, still holding his wife's hand. "Give us back the little bell!" he said firmly.

The sorceress had to submit. And the moment the little bell was back in place, the woman found her smile again.

Hand in hand, she and her husband returned home. They found themselves in their old poverty, but they didn't care. The woman worked with a smile on her lips, and her husband, seeing that she was happy again, forgot his sufferings and his bitterness, and together they began a new life.

Give yourself a break when you're talking to members of the opposite gender. There may be scientific reasons for the difficulty you two have in reaching an understanding.

Time to Talk

from Current Health

Have you ever noticed that males and females show differences in the way they speak with people? Research done at the University of Michigan found that boys and girls as young as age 4 spoke differently to the adults who were talking with them. When the girls were asked a question, their answer was more complete. They used more words and gave more information than did the boys. The boys also interrupted women who were interviewing them more often than they did men. The researcher who led the study felt that the females worked harder to make conversation. She said that understanding how people do something as simple as talking with each other helps us to learn more about how men and women are treated differently.

If all your communication efforts fail (see "Time to Talk" in this section), hop in a homemade car and race. That will solve just about any dispute.

Soap Box Speedsters

from National Geographic World

Mark Mihal streaks across the finish line to win first place in the Kit Car Division of the 53rd All-American Soap Box Derby. Mark, 13, from Valparaiso, Indiana, shows off his winning car. Like all derby cars, it is homemade and has no motor.

Tops in the Masters Division, Sami Jones, 14, from Vancouver, Washington, sits up after opening her car's hinged flap. The masters competition is the fastest. In it drivers lie on their backs. What does it take to win? According to Sami, "It's the design of the car, your wheels, and luck—a lot of luck!"

The Soap Box Derby has been held in Akron, Ohio, since 1935. Gravity pulls the cars along a steep downhill course at speeds up to 30 miles an hour. In the 1990 derby Mark and Sami competed with more than 150 other racers from 9 to 16. They came from all parts of the United States and from Canada, Germany, Ireland, and the Philippines.

Finally, this word on X's. Before you leave your mark anywhere, be sure you haven't any vows you don't intend to keep.

Why Do X's Stand for Kisses?

from National Geographic World

If you sign valentines with X's, you'll be following a custom that started in the Middle Ages. At that time few people could read or write. When they had to sign an official paper, they made an X — a shape associated with Andrew, a Christian saint. Kissing the X on paper, like kissing the Bible, was a sign of good faith. It showed that the signer intended to keep the promises made on paper. Nowadays X's on valentines and letters simply stand for kisses, a kind of shorthand for "I love you."

10. Other Faces, Other Places

For more about Chinese-Americans, look to Cobblestone's *March 1991 issue. Below is only a glimpse of the lively communities integral to the American way of life.*

Chinatown

by Walton Duryea
from Cobblestone

"All day long, and often until late at night, the streets are crowded with Chinamen of all ages and sizes . . . with shaven crown and neatly braided cue [sic], sauntering lazily along, talking, visiting, trading, laughing, and scolding in the strangest and . . . most discordant jargon," an 1870s visitor to San Francisco's Chinatown wrote.

Another visitor, German photographer Arnold Genthe, completed the description of this colorful and exotic community in 1895: "The painted balconies were hung with windbells and flowered lanterns. Brocades and embroideries, bronzes and porcelains, carvings of jade and ivory, of coral and rose crystal, decorated shop windows. The wall-spaces between were bright with scarlet bulletins and gilt signs inscribed in the picturesque Chinese characters." He also noted the smells: "the scent of sandalwood and exotic herbs from the drugstores, the sickly sweetness of opium smoke, the fumes of incense and roast pork, and the pungent odors from the sausages and raw meat."

The San Francisco community they described was the United States' first Chinatown. By the late 1800s, many others had grown up in cities around the country. Wherever Chinese immigrants went to find work, they gathered together to live. Discrimination forced them together; they were not welcome in many residential areas, were not allowed to rent in some areas, and often could not buy property.

Chinatowns were places where Chinese immigrants could live freely with friends, find support and help when they needed it, speak their own language, eat familiar foods, and carry on the traditions they had brought from China.

Until 1943, Chinatowns were largely bachelor societies. Men lived in boarding houses and met at family and clan association headquarters for conversation, to receive news from home or to send letters back to their families, and to enjoy games of mahjong and fan-tan. The men worked in Chinese stores and restaurants; clothing, cigar, and shoe factories; laundries; banks; and import-export houses. They enjoyed performances at Chinese theaters, attended Chinese temples, and frequented gambling halls and opium parlors.

From 1882 to 1943, only merchants could bring their wives to this country, and many did as they prospered. For the most part, the women remained indoors. But children roamed the streets of Chinatown, safe in the protection of the close-knit community.

By 1900, Chinatowns had developed in many cities. In 1887, more than one thousand Chinese lived in New York City's Chinatown. Others had gathered in Seattle, Los Angeles, Sacramento, Phoenix, Philadelphia, Boston, Honolulu, and Washington, D.C.

In 1940, twenty-eight U.S. cities had Chinatowns. The number of Chinatowns dwindled over the next decade, as few new immigrants entered the country, and by 1955, only sixteen remained. Since the mid-1960s, however, new laws have allowed approximately twenty thousand Chinese to immigrate each year, and most have settled in areas with large Asian populations.

Today fewer than half of all Chinese Americans live in Chinatowns. But the communities still keep many of the old tra-

A 19th-century Chinese pharmacist weighs ingredients for a prescription. Drawers of herbs and medicines line the wall behind him.

ditions alive and provide a comfortable welcome to new immigrants. Chinese Americans who live nearby often go to Chinatown to celebrate traditional holidays.

Chinatowns today are communities with families, businesses, churches, and service organizations. Their rich traditional culture sets them apart in appearance and activity from the cities surrounding them.

But like those cities, they have problems of urban crowding, poverty, crime, drugs, unemployment, and juvenile delinquency. Pay is low in the restaurants and garment factories where many Chinese Americans work, and apartments are scarce. Some community organizations, such as Chinese for Affirmative Action, are trying to improve working conditions and wages and defend Chinese Americans' civil rights. Others work to preserve Chinese traditions and Chinese Americans' pride in their heritage. Like many other immigrant groups, Chinese Americans face the challenge of preserving their ethnic identity while they live within a different culture.

Shoes
&
Shoes from
Around the
World

from Scienceland

If you want to know a person, the old saying goes, walk a mile in her shoes. Here's just a few stylish ped-covers to choose from.

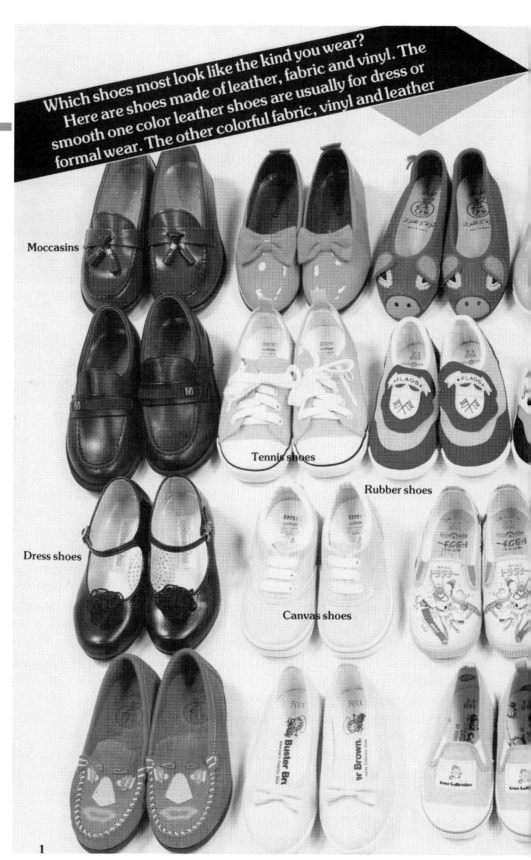

Which shoes most look like the kind you wear? Here are shoes made of leather, fabric and vinyl. The smooth one color leather shoes are usually for dress or formal wear. The other colorful fabric, vinyl and leather

Moccasins

Tennis shoes

Rubber shoes

Dress shoes

Canvas shoes

1

Rain boots (galoshes g ə losh′ iz)

Basketball shoes

Sneakers

Sandals

lip-ons

Which Is Which?

The name and shape of shoes change. What are called sneakers some people call canvas *kan′ ʋə s*, rubber, or tennis shoes. They all have rubber soles that make no sound. Perhaps that is the reason why they are also called sneakers.

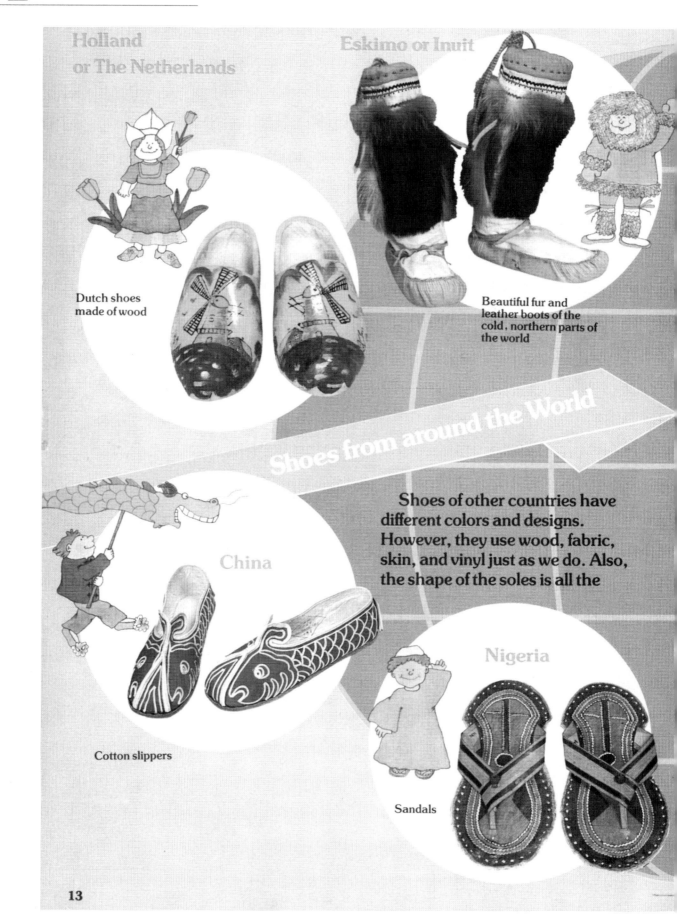

Holland or The Netherlands

Dutch shoes made of wood

Eskimo or Inuit

Beautiful fur and leather boots of the cold, northern parts of the world

Shoes from around the World

China

Cotton slippers

Shoes of other countries have different colors and designs. However, they use wood, fabric, skin, and vinyl just as we do. Also, the shape of the soles is all the

Nigeria

Sandals

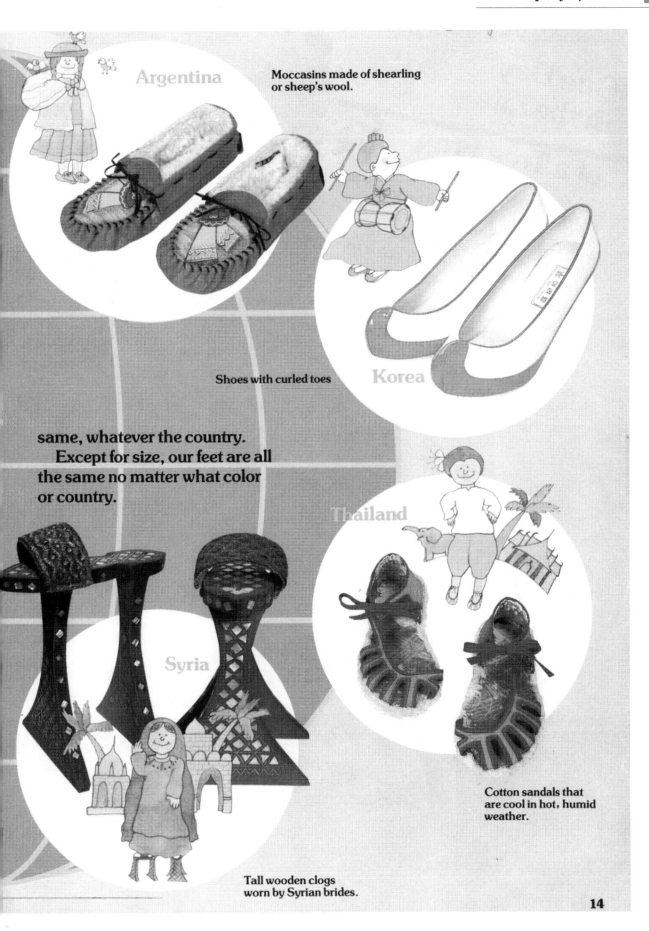

Argentina

Moccasins made of shearling or sheep's wool.

Shoes with curled toes

Korea

same, whatever the country.
Except for size, our feet are all
the same no matter what color
or country.

Thailand

Syria

Cotton sandals that
are cool in hot, humid
weather.

Tall wooden clogs
worn by Syrian brides.

14

Breads of the World

from Scienceland

If you want to make a friend, another saying goes, break bread together. Here's a few savory samples to chew on.

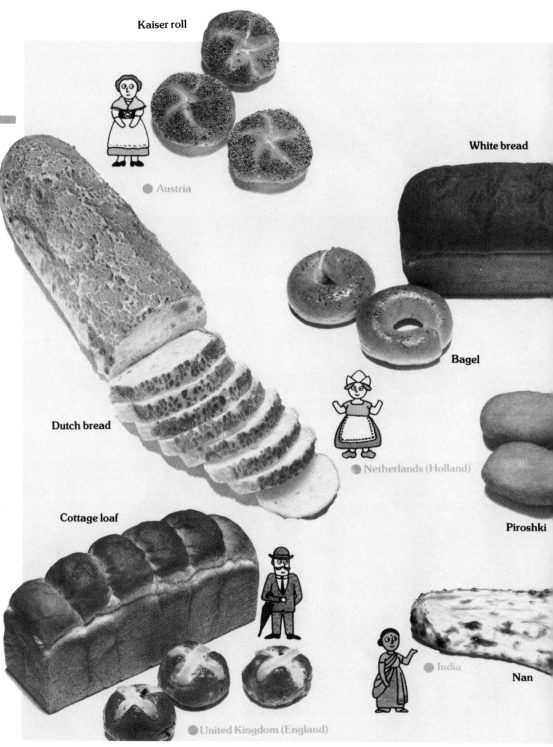

Kaiser roll

Austria

White bread

Bagel

Netherlands (Holland)

Dutch bread

Piroshki

Cottage loaf

India

Nan

United Kingdom (England)

208

Rye bread

United States

Pumpernickel

Germany

Mone zemel

Baguette

Brioche

Black bread

Croissant

Soviet Union
(Russia)

France

Milton Meltzer has won awards and acclaim for his nonfiction writing for young readers. Here he takes you to the origins of a famous wordsmith, in this look at the life of Langston Hughes.

Harlem Poet

by Milton Meltzer

from Cobblestone

accompanied by a poem by Langston Hughes
from Highlights for Children

The subway train rushed madly through the tunnel as Langston Hughes counted off the numbered signs to 135th Street, where he got off. The platform was jammed with black people on their way to work. Lugging his heavy bag up the stairs, he came out on the corner of Lenox Avenue. It was a September morning in 1921. Nineteen-year-old Hughes stood there feeling good. But being there felt a little crazy, too, as if he had finally come home, though he had never been to Harlem before.

With a week to go before beginning classes at Columbia University, he got a room at the YMCA. That afternoon, he crossed the street to visit the Harlem Branch Library, where the librarians made him feel right at home. That night, he went into the Lincoln Theatre to hear a blues singer.

He spent the next few days mapping Harlem with his feet. The great dark expanse of this island within an island fascinated him. In 1921, Harlem ran from 125th Street north to 145th and from Madison Avenue to Eighth Avenue.

Eighty thousand African Americans were packed into the long rows of tenements as the flood of southern blacks continued to roll north.

Hughes had begun to write poetry in high school in Cleveland. One of his teachers had introduced him to the work of American poets such as Carl Sandburg, Vachel Lindsay, and Robert Frost, all of whom were exploring new ways to create poetry. His teacher encouraged him to find his own lyric voice, and the school paper published some of his work.

Hughes found Columbia too big and too cold and the instructors too busy to bother with a black student who needed help. But he kept writing poems and sent several to *The Crisis,* a black magazine. It published one, which began, "I am a Negro/Black as the night is black/Black as the depths of my Africa." The readers liked the poem so much that *The Crisis* published more.

College did not seem right for Hughes, and he left after one year. After a year of working and writing poetry in New York, he found a job as steward on a freighter bound for Africa. He was twenty-one now and on his own. As the ship made stops at ports along the western shore of Africa, he saw that blacks lived under white laws made abroad for the black colonies, laws that were enforced by whip and gun.

His next job on a freighter brought him to France. He left the ship to discover the Paris every young poet dreamed about. He worked in night-clubs as a doorman, dishwasher, and cook. Alone in his tiny room, he continued to write poetry, fitting the rhythms of jazz into the rhythm of words, and sent his poems off to New York. A magazine bought three of them for $24.50—the first time he had ever been paid for writing. When he lost his job in Paris, he worked his way home on an American ship.

Back in Harlem, Hughes found himself among several black writers and artists and began friendships that would endure. But he was penniless and could not find work. In early 1925, he moved to Washington, D.C., taking jobs in a laundry, as a clerk, and then as a bellboy in a hotel. His big break came when the popular white poet Vachel Lindsay read Hughes's poems to a large audience, praising them highly. Overnight, newspapers across the country spread the story of this new poet.

It was the beginning of Hughes's fame but not his fortune. He won literary prizes, was published in many places, and found his way back to Harlem in 1925. There Carl Van Vechten, a widely known white writer who befriended many black artists, took Hughes's poems to a publisher, suggesting that they would make a good book. When Hughes's book *The Weary Blues* appeared in 1926, critics hailed it as powerful, warm, and lyrical.

Still, Hughes felt that his education was unfinished. He wanted to go back to college "in order to be of more use to my race and America," he said. The oldest black school in the country, Lincoln University in Pennsylvania, admitted him. But how could he afford to go without a dime in his pocket? Amy Spingarn, a white woman who admired his poetry, offered to pay his way through Lincoln.

He spent summers in New York, working and immersing himself in Harlem life. All his artist friends were trying to find their roots and new ways to shape black life into art. Hughes experimented with forms derived from black culture. He voiced the spirit of the blues, of spirituals, folk ballads, and gospel songs. With a deceptive simplicity, he suggested the variety and complexity of the black experience. His pioneering use of blues forms and jazz rhythms would be the major innovation in the poetry of the Harlem Renaissance.

The poems and stories written by Hughes during the Harlem Renaissance are a small but important part of his contribution to literature.

A second book of his poems came out in 1927. And soon after graduation from Lincoln, his novel *Not Without Laughter* appeared in 1930. Through its characters, he explored the challenges young blacks had to face in a racist society.

In 1929, the Great Depression hit the United States. Even with millions of people jobless and homeless, Hughes decided to try to make a living solely by writing. He made ends meet by traveling the country in an old car and giving readings of his poems at black schools, colleges, and churches. This was the first chance for cotton pickers and college students to see and hear an African American poet. They no more expected an African American to be a poet than to be president. Until his death in 1967, Hughes read to, talked with, and encouraged young African Americans. His work opened their eyes to a new universe.

Hughes's travels would take him across this country and around the world. He wrote articles, poems, and stories based on his wanderings. He founded a theater in Harlem and wrote plays for it. He wrote a movie script, his autobiography, and stories about Jesse B. Semple, a Harlem character he had met in a bar. So universal was their vision of human strengths and weaknesses that these books were translated into many languages.

Hughes often worked with composers, writing the story and lyrics for operas, musical folk comedies, and gospel shows. He wrote many books for young readers on black heroes, musicians, jazz, the West Indies, and Africa. He took part in many festivals of music, poetry, and the arts both at home and abroad.

Hughes's life sounds as though it was great fun, and in truth it was. But it was also a life of hardship and many disappointments. Throughout it, he suffered from the discrimination and segregation so common among African Americans and was hounded because of his political views. None of his writings earned him great financial reward, but he lived generously, devoted to helping anyone whom he could. He had a special gift for friendship as well as for the arts.

He died in 1967 at the age of sixty-five. It was a great loss for everyone who knew him and for the millions of people who loved his work.

Misery is when your
very best friend
calls you a name she really
didn't mean to call you at all.

Misery is when you call
your very best friend a name
you didn't mean to call her, either.

Langston Hughes

Many people in various countries listened when Nelson Mandela talked of all South Africans' inalienable right to be free. Thanks to the man and his simple appeal—for which he spent 28 years in prison—the outlook for South African children may be hopeful.

Nelson Mandela: Champion of Freedom
&
Further Exploring

by Carol Gelber

from Faces

When his first son was born in 1918, Henry Mandela, a chief of the Tembu people of South Africa, gave his child two names. One name, Nelson, was English. The other, Rolihlahla, was African. In Xhosa, the language of the Tembu, Rolihlahla means "stirring up trouble." It would prove to be a suitable name. Henry's son would one day lead black South Africans in their fight for justice and human rights.

Nelson Rolihlahla Mandela grew up on his family's farm in the grassy hills of the Transkei reserve, the home of the Tembu people. He spent his days herding his family's sheep and cattle or plowing their fields. In the evenings, Nelson loved to sit near the bonfire that burned outside his family's whitewashed huts. Here he could listen to the old people tell stories about a time when "our people lived peacefully under the democratic rule of their kings and their councilors and moved freely . . . up and down the country."

Those days were only a memory. Before Nelson was born, white Europeans had conquered the land. Now black Africans could not vote or choose where they lived. Men had to carry a pass. They were forbidden to enter a city unless their pass showed that they had a job there. Many men had to work far from their home and could see their wife and children only once a year.

Nelson's parents sent him to a local school run by white missionaries. Although some of the students made fun of his shabby clothes, he loved his studies and was a hard-working student. Then, when he was 12 years old, his father fell ill. Nelson was moved to the home of a relative, the paramount chief, where he lived with other boys from the Tembu royal family.

In his new home, Nelson could attend the traditional African courts in which the tribal elders served as judges. He was fascinated by the elders' skill in questioning witnesses. As he listened, he developed a love and respect for law.

At age 18, Nelson enrolled at Fort Hare College in South Africa. Tall, strong, handsome, and a natural leader, he was elected to the student council. When the college took away the powers of the council, Nelson joined a student boycott. He was suspended and sent home.

The paramount chief was not pleased. He wanted Nelson to give up the boycott. Nelson writes, "My guardian felt it was time for me to get married. He loved me very much and looked after me as diligently as my father had. But he was no democrat and did not think it worthwhile to consult me about a wife. He selected a girl, fat and dignified . . . and arrangements were made for the wedding."

Nelson ran away to Johannesburg, South Africa's largest city. For the first time, he saw how Africans lived in the shantytowns outside the cities. Thousands of people lived in shacks made of cardboard and packing crates without electricity or running water. Men worked long hours for so little pay that they could not feed their families.

Nelson's days in Johannesburg were long and tiring. He worked while he finished his college education by correspondence course. When he got his degree, he found a job in a white law firm. The lawyers were impressed with Nelson and sponsored his admission to law school. Every day he took the long train ride from the law office to the university. He had to return home before the curfew that applied only to black people.

In the black township where he lived, Nelson Mandela's friends were members of the African National Congress (ANC). This organization was founded in 1912 by four black lawyers to fight injustice and discrimination. The ANC wanted all the peoples of South Africa to unite in the battle for democracy. Some groups, such as the Zulu and the Xhosa peoples, had been rivals long before the arrival of the Europeans.

With Oliver Tambo, a friend from Fort Hare College, Mandela joined the ANC. Tambo and Mandela, both lawyers, opened an office in Johannesburg—the only black law firm in the city. Both men were dedicated to the fight for human rights, and they would soon be recognized as leaders of the ANC.

In 1948, the South African government set up a system of apartheid aimed at the complete separation of the races. The people of South Africa were classified into four categories: Europeans, Asians, Coloreds, and Bantus (Africans). Each group was to live in areas assigned by the government. Many families were separated—husbands from their wives and children from their parents. The mission schools, like the one Nelson Mandela had attended as a boy, were closed. Black children were told to attend Bantu schools, which would prepare them to be farmers or servants.

Mandela and Tambo organized an ANC campaign urging people to refuse to accept the segregation laws. They led boycotts, workers' strikes, and protest marches that made the whole world aware of the injustice of apartheid.

In 1955, the ANC and other groups drew up the Freedom Charter, which stated, "We the people of South Africa declare that South Africa belongs to all who live in it, black and white, and that no government can justly claim authority unless it is based on the will of all the people." Mandela was arrested.

For the next 35 years, Mandela and Tambo spent much of their time in exile or in prison. Mandela could see his wife, Winnie, only a few times each year. Their two daughters grew up without their father. In fact, Nelson Mandela was in prison for 28 years. He became the most famous prisoner in the world.

In the mid-1980s, South Africa's president said he would free Mandela if he would renounce the policies of the ANC. Mandela refused, saying, "Let him free all who have been imprisoned, banished or exiled for their opposition to apartheid. . . . What freedom am I being offered when I may be arrested on a pass offense? What freedom am I being offered to live my life as a family with my dear wife who remains in banishment? What freedom am I being offered when I must ask for permission to live in an urban area? What freedom am I being offered when I need a stamp in my pass to seek work?"

In 1990, Nelson Mandela was unconditionally released from prison. Since then he and Winnie have toured the world, speaking out for human rights. Rolihlahla still fights for justice and equality for black South Africans. And he has come to symbolize the struggle for democracy for all peoples.

Further Exploring: A Guide to Recommended Reading

• *Nelson Mandela: A Voice Set Free,* by Rebecca Stefoff.

Nelson Mandela spent 28 years of his life in jail because of his beliefs. For many South Africans and people around the world, he is a symbol of the fight against apartheid and the fight for freedom. This book, from the Great Lives Series, examines his life from birth to his release from prison in 1990. (Fawcett Columbine, New York, 1990.)

• *Somehow Tenderness Survives: Stories of Southern Africa,* edited by Hazel Rochman.

This collection of short stories for older readers written by people who have experienced South Africa depicts the fear, violence, and beauty of this complex part of the world. The collection includes the works of some famous South African authors such as Nadine Gordimer, Mark Mathabane, Dan Jacobson, and others. (Harper and Row, New York, 1990.)

• *Southern Africa,* by Peter Brooke-Ball and Sue Seddon, illustrated by Mei Lim and Ann Savage.

Photographs, illustrations, maps, and charts highlight this book on the history, geography, and climate of this troubling part of the world. The material is especially accessible to younger readers. (Silver Burdett Press, Englewood Cliffs, New Jersey, 1989.)

• *The Land and the People of South Africa,* by Jonathan Paton.

In this overview of South Africa—its people, geography, economics, and history—the author draws on a wide variety of material, including poetry and discussions of language. (J.B. Lippincott, New York, 1990.)

• *Cry, the Beloved Country,* by Alan Paton.

Published in 1948, this novel for older readers was one of the first books to explore the cultural diversity and tension in South Africa. The story revolves around two families, one black and one white, and the tragedy that brings them together. (Charles Scribner's Sons, New York, 1948.)

- *Journey to Jo'burg,* by Beverley Naidoo, illustrated by Eric Velasquez.

When their baby sister becomes very sick, 13-year-old Naledi and her 9-year-old brother know that they must find their mother, who lives and works as a maid in Johannesburg, and bring her home. Their journey to the city brings them face to face with the cruelty of apartheid. (Harper and Row, New York, 1988.)

- *Chain of Fire,* by Beverley Naidoo, illustrated by Eric Velasquez.

This book continues the story in *Journey to Jo'burg.* Nadeli, who is now 15 years old, and her friend Taolo attempt to fight the forced removal of the people of their village to a barren tract of land called Bophuthatswana. Although Naledi, Taolo, and their friends who join the protest suffer many setbacks, they find within themselves a steely determination to fight on. (J.B. Lippincott, New York, 1989.)

Boys' Life published a series of articles in celebration of the 200th anniversary of the Bill of Rights. Here, Robert W. Peterson outlines some of the significance behind one of our most basic freedoms.

Freedom of Religion

by Robert W. Peterson
from Boys' Life

"Congress shall make no law respecting an establishment of religion, or prohibiting the free exercise thereof; or abridging the freedom of speech, or of the press; or the right of the people peaceably to assemble, and to petition the government for a redress of grievances."

The First Amendment forbids:

- *Laws favoring any religion*

- *Laws that tell anyone how he must worship God*

In many countries one religion is favored over all others. Some countries have official religions that are given tax money and special privileges. In a few nations, people who don't follow the official religion are persecuted.

Not in the United States. Our government keeps hands off churches, synagogues, and mosques. It neither helps nor harms religion. And the government may not do anything to keep you from worshiping God in any way you please.

The reason is contained in the Bill of Rights. The First Amendment reads, in part: *"Congress shall make no law respecting an establishment of religion, or prohibiting the free exercise thereof."*

Simple, right? Not always. Suppose, for example, you were a member of Jehovah's Witnesses. They believe that people should not salute the U.S. flag because the Bible forbids worshiping a "graven image." If you were a Witness, could you be forced to salute the flag in school?

In 1943, the U.S. Supreme Courts said, no. Because the flag salute goes against their religious beliefs, Jehovah's Witnesses do not have to pledge allegiance to the flag in school.

The First Amendment also protects some school dropouts. Children of the Amish, a religious sect that rejects modern ways, can leave school after eighth grade.

The Amish, who don't own cars, telephones, or television sets, fear that their children might lose their religious faith if they get too much public education. Twenty years ago, the State of Wisconsin tried to make Amish children stay in school until they were 16.

"Stop!" the Supreme Court ordered in

1972. The Court held that the right of the Amish to follow their religious beliefs was more important than the state's interest in having well-educated citizens.

The court cases involving the Jehovah's Witnesses and Amish schoolchildren were about an American's right to religious liberty. Another type of case asks the question: Can government ever help to advance a religious body's interest? The Supreme Court has maintained that it cannot. But it *can* help people to practice their religion.

Thus the Court has ruled:

• Religion classes cannot be held in public schools. But pupils can be excused from school to attend religion classes in church.

• Tax money can be used to bus pupils to church schools because the main benefit is to the pupils, not the schools. For the same reason, church (or "parochial") school students can borrow books from public schools.

• Tax money cannot be used to pay parochial schoolteachers. Nor can public schoolteachers be paid with tax money to teach in parochial schools.

• Religious clubs can meet in public high schools if the schools welcome other clubs that are not related to the curriculum.

The Supreme Court has turned back several attempts to put prayer into the public schools. (You are free to pray silently all you want in school. But the school cannot have recitation of a prayer, or even a minute of "meditation or voluntary prayer.") Also forbidden are Bible readings and posting of the Ten Commandments in classrooms.

Many Americans favor group prayers in public schools. But all proposals to amend the Constitution to allow prayer in school have failed.

The men who wrote the Bill of Rights thought religion was too important for government to have anything to do with it.

11. Western Civ Rap: Public Places Large and Small

In the tradition of the Iliad and Jabberwocky, rap rhythms give facts (or fictions) a spirited gait, particularly when the stuff that makes for good storytelling is none other than the memorable drama of Western civilization.

The Western Civ Rap

by Nancy Porta Libert

from Plays, Inc.

photograph of Mycenae by Karen Mason
illustration of Orpheus by Bonnie MacKain from Cricket

Characters

RAPPERS:

JACK

GROUP I
GROUP II } *mixed voices*

BOYS, *with low voices*

GIRLS I, *with low voices*

GIRLS II, *with high voices*

TIME: *The present.*

SETTING: *A classroom. Blackboard or painted backdrop on back wall reads* WESTERN CIVILIZATION FINAL EXAM. *Student desks line back and sides of stage.*

AT RISE: *Rappers, carrying books, notebooks, and talking amongst themselves, enter right and left. They place books on desks, then gradually form semicircle, arranged by group. When JACK makes his way to the middle of semicircle, murmuring dies down. Note: Each group steps downstage or away from semicircle in turn, and steps back when finished. Rappers may mime* certain portions of story as the opportunity presents itself.

GROUP I (*Leaping downstage, center*):
Now this story of ours,
If you want to know,
Goes a way, way back
To where the rivers flow.

In the Middle East,
North Africa, too,
India, China,
and even Peru.

BOYS:
Well, a way back then,
So the story goes,
They had no language
and they had no clothes.

Even their food
Was the simple kind—
Seeds and berries,
Anything they could find.

JACK:
Then they learned about hunting,
And they learned about fire.
And the prospects of man
Rose higher and higher.

There was ice all over —
Just glaciers and snow.

But the earth warmed up
And the ice departed. (*To* CHORUS)
What's the next big step?
CHORUS (*Shouting*):
Farming started!
GROUP II:
Now the earliest people,
You'll know them by name,
Came from different places
Of equal fame.

Sumer and Egypt,
They left their traces —
Strong early folks
Of different races.
GIRLS I (*Confronting* JACK):
Now, hold on, Jack!
We happen to know
That the ancient Greeks
Were a part of this show.

They came from the north
Had a war to fight
With Macedonia,
They showed 'em their might.
GIRLS II:
It was mountainous country
With a lot of separation,
Took a long, long time
To make one nation.

Every city state
Had its own pursuits,
But Athens and Sparta
Had the strongest roots.
JACK:
They defeated the Persians,
Had a Golden Age,
Made democracy the rule,
And sports the rage.

They had poets like Homer
Who wrote with ease,
And some dudes named Plato
And Socrates.

Alexander the Great
Spread the Greek ways.
The Hellenistic Age —
Those were civilized days.
1ST GIRL (*Stepping forward*):
Whoa! there, Jack,
It wasn't all Greek —
There are many other groups
Of which we can speak!

© 1991 KAREN A. MASON

CHORUS (*All except* JACK *leaping forward and singing to the Ray Charles tune, "Hit the Road, Jack"*):
Tell me more, Jack,
And won't you go back some more, some more, some more, some more,
Tell me more, Jack, and won't you go back some more.
JACK (*In gravelly voice*):
What you say?!
CHORUS (*Repeating refrain*):
Tell me more, Jack. . . (*Etc. Meantime,* JACK *paces, deep in thought.*)
JACK:
Well, ten thousand years,
Maybe longer ago,

JACK (*Holding up hands defensively*):
O.K., O.K. . . now,
Give me some time.
I can give you the facts,
But they've got to rhyme! (*He paces as though pondering, then spins around to audience.*)
On seven low hills
Some Latin tribes
Set up their huts
By a riverside.
They fought their neighbors,
Hardly ever stayed home,
But they founded the great, great
City of Rome.

GROUP I:
Ah, the noble Romans
As an early nation,
Formed a strong republic
With representation.

There were consuls, a senate,
And a twelve-law credo —
And would you believe,
They invented the veto!

BOYS:
Soon the Romans fought others
And before they knew it,
They took on Carthage
And almost blew it.

But Hannibal was beaten
And in a short time,
They had Spain, and Greece,
And Palestine.

GIRLS I:
But the seeds of greed
Were in the grain,

And the Roman sense of duty
Was on the wane.

Some army generals
Had such great power
That the senators and consuls
Began to cower.

GROUP II:
So when Caesar declared
He would rule for life,
The only solution
Seemed to be the knife.
(*In stage whisper*)
Plots to kill him
Grew unabated.

CHORUS:
In a group attack,
He was assassinated!

GIRLS II:
Then the Roman Empire,
Rotten within,
Collapsed from folly,
Greed, and sin.

When German tribes
Took over their land,
Those ancient Romans
Made their last stand.

BOYS:
In the years that followed
Things were pretty dark.
There was great disorder
And it left its mark.

The Vikings and the Goths
And the Franks caused scandals.

They robbed, they pillaged
They were nothing but vandals!

GROUP I:
For the people of Europe
A new way of life
Was needed to save them
From war and strife.

So the king decided
To stand and deliver
His plan was to make him
A big land giver.

In return for land,
Men pledged to fight,
And with the tap of his sword
He dubbed each his knight.

JACK:
People lived in cities
Surrounded by walls
Where the king and his army
Protected them all.

A system of mutual aid
Had arisen
That got the name
Of Feudalism.

(CHORUS *sings "Tell Me More Jack" refrain;* JACK *chimes in with "What you say?";* and CHORUS *sings refrain again.* JACK *continues rapping.*)

By the year 1,000
They had it down pat,
Life on the manor —
That's where it was at.

Anything they needed
They made right there,
So trips into town
Were really quite rare.

GIRLS II:
This was the time
Of knighthood in flower,

When men were brave
And the gallant had power.

BOYS:
They marched to the east,
Fought eight crusades;
Showed skills in jousting,
Protected fair maids.

GROUP II:
But sooner or later
All things must cease,
And manor life declined
As travel increased.

With travel came trade
Which flourished and grew.
Smart people with skills
Could make money, too.

JACK:
So an age of business
Developed in stages,
As people with crafts
Were paid real wages.

They spent their time
Making products to sell,
The population grew
And merchants did well.

GIRLS I:
There you go again, Jack!
It wasn't so sunny!
Don't paint this picture
Of milk and honey.

There were lots of things
That weren't so hot.
If you're gonna make soup —
Put it all in the pot!

JACK (*Aside, to audience*):
I see these girls
Aren't easily led.
They're sharp, they're quick,
They're very well read.

I've got to get down
To the serious facts,
Or my scholarly image
Is bound to show cracks. (*He pauses
to consider his next move.*)
In 1215 in England
With clouds overhead,
King John taxed his nobles
Right into the red.

He was forced to sign a charter
That cut his power
At Runnymede the people
Had their finest hour.

GROUPS I AND II:
Soon a grand new age
Got a real good start,
With a lot of new thinking
In science and art.

2ND GIRL:
It was the Renaissance,
An age that glistened.

JACK:
When the poets spoke —
The people listened.

GIRLS I:
Now, the Renaissance
Had some really fine fellows:
Botticellis and da Vincis
And Donatellos.

Their sculpting and painting
Sent the people reeling.
Especially Michelangelo,
Who loved his ceiling.

JACK:
Great men of letters
Also rose,
They began to write verse
And classic prose.

Their works got read much more,
I guess —

CHORUS:
When Gutenberg invented
The printing press!

GIRLS II:
Near 1500
Some religious views
Were tossed around
'Til they made big news.

The German, Martin Luther,
Said the church must change —

BOYS:
It's the hierarchy
I'd like to rearrange!

GROUPS I AND II:
No immediate action
Came about,
So Luther, being
Quite devout,

Led the people
In a new congregation,
And founded
The Protestant Reformation.

GIRLS I:
It was during this time
That ideas were big,
But there was one Italian guy
No one could dig

ALL GIRLS:
It was clear he marched
To a different drummer,
Said the world was round —

3RD GIRL:
Now, what could be dumber?

CHORUS (*Gathering downstage*):
He said, "To reach the east,
You gotta sail West!"
He got three Spanish ships
To make the test.

He found a brand new world
When he crossed that ocean —

JACK:
He took America,
And set it in motion!

CHORUS:
An age of exploration
Changed the lives
Of future generations,
Their kids and wives.

And before you knew it,
The west was won,
And history had
A whole new play to run.

The modern age entered
In all its glory,

JACK:
But the truth is, friends,
That's a whole other story! (*All nod
and murmur in agreement as lights
dim to black. Curtain*)
                    THE END

Although the horses in the photograph that accompanies this article are cast in bronze, they are far from immobile. Allegedly, they have traveled from Greece, to Rome, to Constantinople — read below. And they have outlasted the empires which displayed them.

Muses' Corner

from Calliope

Every nation takes great pride in the art and architecture of its own citizens. Yet many countries also promote the artistic creations of foreigners. Throughout history, nations around the world have purchased, taken, or acquired as spoils of war works of art and architectural designs. These works often achieve a place of honor in their new home due to their historical value or the fame of their creator.

When Constantine the Great redesigned his city on the Bosporus, his aim was to make it the center of the civilized world. To provide a sense of grandeur and culture, he imported sculptures from Rome, Greece, and Egypt. Later emperors followed his example.

Many of these objects were displayed in the Hippodrome, where they were highly visible reminders of the fact that Constantinople was so powerful that it could acquire artifacts from anywhere in the world. Constantine imported the center column of the Hippodrome from the sacred temple of the sun god Apollo in Delphi, Greece. The Greeks had built this column, which branched out in the shape of three serpents, as a sign of thanks for their decisive victory over the Persians at Salamis in 480 B.C.

One of Constantine's successors undertook the task of transporting to Constantinople an Egyptian obelisk dating to 1515 B.C. This too was placed in the Hippodrome.

Perhaps the world's most widely traveled sculpture is four bronze horses created originally, it is believed, in Greece during the fourth century B.C. The horses were taken to Rome by the emperor Nero, but as the focus of the Roman world turned east, so too did the horses. This time they traveled to Constantinople to embellish the monuments in the Hippodrome. They remained there until the Crusaders invaded Constantinople in 1204 and took the horses back to Italy, to Venice. In 1797, Napoleon, the emperor of France, became the ruler of northern Italy. He so admired the horses that he had them transported to Paris, where they stayed until he abdicated in 1815. They were then returned to Venice, where they still stand guard above the entrance to St. Mark's Cathedral.

Not all works of art have changed loca-

Four bronze horses stand guard above the entrance to St. Mark's Cathedral in Venice, Italy.

tions because of war or emperors building new and grander cities. In 1878, the English paid for an Egyptian obelisk to be transported to London, and in 1880, New Yorkers imported another magnificent obelisk to adorn Central Park. When transporting such objects is not possible, replicas may be made. For example, an exact model of the Parthenon in Athens,

Greece, can be found in a park in Nashville, Tennessee. The great French chateaux inspired the construction of the Vanderbilt estate near Asheville, North Carolina. And the excavated Roman Villa dei Papyri at Herculaneum, Italy, was the model for the J. Paul Getty Museum in Malibu, California, built in 1954.

"You could not get a human to put together anything unless the child put together a set of bricks," said Jacob Bronowski, in The Ascent of Man. *There are some people who would tell you that entire civilizations were and are as fleeting as castles in the sand.*

Building Sand Castles

by Pam Grout

from Career World

Most people take money and shopping bags to the mall. Last time Lucinda Wierenga visited a mall, she took 150 tons of sand.

As a professional sand sculptor, Wierenga spent two weeks at Chicago's Lincolnwood Town Center, transforming the 150 tons of sand into a giant sculpture of Wrigley Field. It included the logos from all 26 major league baseball teams and Harry Carey's "Holy Cow."

Wierenga, known as Sandy Feet, travels the country building sand castles at malls. She also enters approximately 140 competitions across the country, hosts competitions in her home state of Texas, and writes articles and books on the proper way to build a sand castle. Her book, *Sand Castles Step by Step,* has already gone into a second printing.

Sandy Feet met her husband, the Amazing Walter, on the beach (where else?). In fact, their wedding last February was decorated with a 1-foot by 1½-foot sand castle.

Perhaps her crowning achievement is a 10,760-foot sand sculpture that's listed in the *Guinness Book of World Records* as the longest sand castle in the world. She built this two-mile castle in 1987 with the help of 2,000 college students who were vacationing at South Padre Island, Texas, over spring break.

According to Sandy Feet, who left teaching to build sand castles, the money isn't too bad. She and the Amazing Walter are paid $300 each Saturday during the summer to build a castle at the South Padre Island Holiday Inn. The artistic duo earned $20,000 for the two-week project in Chicago. Prize money at competitions often reaches into the thousands.

When she's not working on a commissioned sand castle, Wierenga makes miniature castles called "Sand Drops" that, with the help of Elmer's Glue, can last forever.

She sells them at art galleries in South Padre.

Unfortunately, her major masterpieces don't last too long. Either they're washed away by an ocean wave or swept away by a mall janitor.

"Sometimes it's hard to watch six hours of work destroyed in 10 seconds, but it's that temporary nature that gives a sand castle part of its appeal," she says. "Somebody likened a sand castle to a rose. You know it's eventually going to wither and die, but that doesn't stop you from buying one anyway."

This article is about the Mohawks' highwire work on skyscrapers. It's not for readers with feet of clay or fear of heights.

Walking High Steel

by Trudie Lamb Richmond
from Faces

The Haudenosaunee, "People of the Longhouse," are better known to most people as the Iroquois. At one time, the Iroquois network extended from the Atlantic seaboard to the Mississippi River and from Canada to the Carolinas. Today the Iroquois live on reservation lands on both sides of the U.S.–Canada border, with the majority of people concentrated in what is now upstate New York. The two largest Mohawk reservations are located on the St. Lawrence River. Kahnawake (pronounced Cog-na-wa-ga) is in Canada, just south of Montreal. Akwesasne, the only international reservation, straddles the St. Lawrence, with part in Canada and the rest in New York State.

Today the Mohawk are known for their prowess in high-steel work. In the East, when one thinks of bridge builders, one thinks of Mohawks. How did they gain this special aptitude or ability?

In the years following the American Revolution, life was not easy for the Iroquois, particularly the men, who were reluctant to abandon their traditional ways of life. The missionaries tried to get the Iroquois men to farm, but they refused. Growing food had always been the women's responsibility. The men wanted to hunt and fish in groups the way they always had. Many signed up with trading companies as canoeists, transporting goods up and down the St. Lawrence. It was an occupation they knew, were good at, and took pride in. But by the 1840s, the fur trade had declined, and the Mohawk felt they were declining as well.

In the spring of 1886, the Canadian Pacific Railroad began erecting a bridge across the St. Lawrence and needed to go through a portion of Kahnawake. To gain access to the reservation, the railroad agreed to provide jobs for the men loading and unloading supplies. As the men worked, they became fascinated by those who were building the bridge. The challenge and danger of the work intrigued them. After convincing the railroad company that they were capable, the first group of Mohawks began their apprenticeship as ironworkers. By 1900, Mohawks had exchanged their traditional headgear, the *gustoweh,* for the yellow hardhat of the

Hundreds of feet above the streets of New York City, ironworkers break for lunch during a skyscraper project in 1928.

construction workers. Walking high steel, they became the warriors of the twentieth century.

Following is an interview with Donald and David Richmond, two brothers from Akwesasne. Born and raised on the reservation, they became ironworkers in the 1950s. They take great pride in the fact that they once "walked the steel," fearlessly climbing and working high in the air.

Donald, why did you become an ironworker?

It sounded like it would be a great adventure. Looking back, I realize it was a great opportunity for Indian men. Working steel was challenging. It was a chance to prove yourself. In my day, you would get up so high and there would only be Indians working. No one else wanted to climb that high. It made you feel good.

What is the highest you had to climb?

I'd say 1,100 feet. That's about 100 stories.

What was the most frightening experience you ever had?

When I was on the Chesapeake Bay Bridge, another span of bridge was being floated into place. Suddenly it drifted free and slammed into the section I was working on. The impact was so great I thought the whole bridge would go. I just hung on and prayed.

Why do you think Indians became ironworkers?

We have the ability to perform well in spite of fear. To me, that's part of being Indian. Maybe ironwork was a natural transition for the traditional warrior. You were held in high esteem for what you did.

What was the longest job you worked on?

As foreman on the St. Lawrence Seaway. The Seaway brought a lot of changes to the reservation, both good and bad. It brought ocean-going ships to the middle of North America. It gave Indian people jobs and the opportunity to earn good money. But it was the beginning of our environmental problems. And, worst of all, we lost a lot of land to the Seaway.

David, when did you start working with iron?

I was 16 years old, and my first job was on the Seaway putting in the reinforcement rods. My brother didn't want me to become an ironworker, but I went up to Montreal, took the test, got my journeyman's book, and got in the union.

What was your most difficult job?

Working on the Verrazano Bridge in Brooklyn, New York. The wind was bad all the time. It made it difficult to work.

Why did you want to walk the steel?

Working on structural steel carried prestige. Ironworkers were role models for us kids on the reservation. You'd see the way these men walked on the iron. They were good. They seemed to be the ones who had the most guts, and everyone wanted to be like them. Ironwork gave Indians a sense of pride. I always worked with Indian crews, and the majority were Mohawk. It made you feel good because you were all like family. I guess we did feel like modern warriors way up there on the high steel.

L'Enfant, called Monsieur "Lanfang" by General George Washington, was the son of a painter employed by the French King Louis XVI. But no matter how large his father's canvases were, they couldn't match L'Enfant's vast plans, alluded to in the excerpt below, for the place we call our nation's capital.

L'Enfant's Washington

by Alice J. Hall

from National Geographic

Daybreak comes with thick mist and drizzle. President George Washington, tall and distinguished at 59 years, and 36-year-old Maj. Pierre Charles L'Enfant leave their lodgings in the port of Georgetown on the Potomac River and mount horses. The younger man, an architect-engineer, is also tall and courtly but has a beaked nose and a manner some consider arrogant. They ride east across swollen Rock Creek, past corn-stubble fields and timber, to inspect uneven Maryland countryside that will become the nation's capital. The land, an English visitor later observes, "waves in gentle curvatures, never rising into a hill, never sinking into a valley . . . surrounded by a complete amphitheater of hills."

On this historic Tuesday, March 29, 1791, Washington is attracted to a ridge with a view south to his beloved Potomac: Here will rise a house for the President. The mounted party rides another mile to Jenkins Hill; L'Enfant calls it "a pedestal waiting for a monument." That monument will be the U.S. Capitol.

Washington finds the weather so bad that he derives "no great satisfaction from the review." But for the visionary L'Enfant lengthy conversations with the President encourage him to plunge ahead on a "grand pland of the whol city."

That grand plan would be revised several times by L'Enfant, under Washington's watchful eye. But the only draft in the designer's hand to survive is a large pencil-drawn map, one of the great treasures of the Library of Congress. Age-worn and obscured by varnish, its lines are hard to read. So, for the map's 200th birthday, in August 1991, the National Geographic Society helped sponsor a clear reproduction. Thanks to computer digitization by experts at the U.S. Geological Survey, the original legibility has been restored. Now everyone can compare L'Enfant's ideas with the city as it exists today.

The reproduction of L'Enfant's plan is a cornerstone of a four-year joint program with the Library of Congress, funded in part by a $348,250 Society grant, to improve access to and preservation of the library's unique collection of 2,000 maps and atlases on the evolution of Washington, D.C. . . .

Map historian Richard Stephenson, who oversees the L'Enfant map at the Library of Congress, sums up: "What I find most amazing is that when our country was nearly broke and so small in population—four million, according to the 1790 census—our leaders had the vision to create a city plan that still works today."

If you had a dragon-prowed ship, you couldn't find safe harbor in Iceland, because its people were worried you'd scare off protective spirits. If you think that's a goofy rule, just remember: In 1930, Iceland celebrated 1000 years of parliament. They must have been doing something right.

Iceland: Where Law Was King

by Diana Childress
from Faces

When we think of Congress and the Supreme Court in Washington, impressive buildings and black-robed judges come to mind. But in Iceland 1,000 years ago, the earliest national parliament in modern Europe, the Althing, met outdoors on a plain set between steep lava cliffs and the Oxara River. Crowds gathered at Law Rock to hear the Lawspeaker recite the laws.

Iceland is a rugged, volcanic island about the size of Kentucky, with wide expanses of good grazing land and excellent fishing. In spite of its name and its nearness to the Arctic Circle, the coastal areas of Iceland have a mild climate because the Gulf Stream warms them.

Many of the first settlers of Iceland came from Norway in the ninth century to escape overpopulation and King Harald Fairhair, who imposed heavy taxes on them. Others came from Norse colonies in Britain. Eager to preserve their newfound freedom, they met to plan their future. They were familiar with the Scandinavian custom of meetings called *things* held to settle disputes. But they came from many regions, each with its own laws. To live peaceably together, they needed one law code for everyone.

A settler named Úlfljótr (OOLF-lee-oter) was sent to Norway to study law for three years. He returned with a constitution that introduced many new ideas. Among the most important was the national assembly, or Althing.

Held every summer, the Althing brought together much of the property-owning population. Every free man who owned an ox, a horse, and at least one cow (or something of equal value) for every family member and servant in his household had to attend the assembly or pay a special tax. The taxes collected from those staying home helped pay the traveling expenses of the rest.

Úlfljótr's code provided for 36 chieftains, selected from among the settlers. These men voted in the Law Council and named the judges in the Law Courts. A chieftain could leave his title to his son, or he could sell or give it to another free man. Every landowner was required to pay the *thing tax* to a chieftain of his choice and would thus become the chieftain's *thingman.*

Riding on horseback together, sometimes for days, chieftains and thingmen, along with their wives and children, would cross the rough landscape, past birch forests, barren heaths, rocky fields of lava, and thundering waterfalls, to reach the plain called Thingvellir. There they would live in tents and in cloth-roofed huts built of stone and turf.

For two weeks, this campground was the closest thing to a town in Iceland. It was the scene of communal worship, bartering and trade, sports competitions, and reunions with relatives from other settlements. But above all, it was a site for peacefully negotiating claims, arranging marriages, drafting new laws, and listening to the Lawspeaker explain the complex details of the law code that Úlfljótr originated.

The Lawspeaker was the only paid public servant in Iceland. He was elected by the chieftains and served a three-year term. Many Lawspeakers were reelected. They were held in such high regard that early Icelandic historians date events by naming the Lawspeaker who was in office at the time.

Like the speaker of the U.S. House of Representatives, the Lawspeaker presided over the national assembly. Unlike his modern counterpart, however, one of the Lawspeaker's duties was to memorize all the nation's laws and recite them at the Althing.

Whereas today everyone in Iceland learns to read, 1,000 years ago few people could do so. Nevertheless, it was important for all Icelanders to know the laws because law enforcement was in the hands of

the people. People had to know and assert their own rights. Those found guilty of breaking the law paid fines or were outlawed. Since there were no prisons, some outlaws had to leave the country for three years, while others were banished for life.

The laws are full of information about early Icelandic life and beliefs. One law forbade dragon-prowed ships from approaching Iceland because they might scare the island's protective spirits. That the Althing convened on Thor's day (the day we now call Thursday) probably reflects Icelandic respect for the god Thor.

Laws regulated the calendar, dividing the year into two seasons—summer, beginning on the second or third Thursday in April, and winter, beginning on the second or third Thursday in October. Laws also defined the hours of the day. For example, *eykt* was the time when the sun had passed two-thirds of the southwestern eighth of the sky. (The sun's not being visible was a legal defense for being late!)

By law, age was counted in the number of complete winters survived. A child born in early October would turn 1 the following April, while a child born in late October would have to wait 18 months for his first "birthday."

Úlfljótr's code separated judges from lawmakers. It called for courts to settle disputes and a Law Council to propose laws. It also provided for panels of neighbors who would listen to arguments and deliver their verdicts under oath, much as juries do in the United States today. The constitution was amended as needed to provide better means of settling disputes, and new laws passed by the Law Council were added to the Lawspeaker's recital.

The laws were finally written down beginning in A.D. 1117. They form the largest, most complete set of medieval laws we have from northern Europe.

This form of government survived for more than 300 years. Elsewhere in Europe, people were ruled by kings and lords who owned the land and controlled the peasants. A German historian writing in the 11th century remarked on the unusual Icelanders, who were "governed not by a king but only by laws."

The Icelanders themselves did not speak of their country as a nation but as "our laws." Yet in the end, these laws were unable to maintain internal peace. The constitution did not prevent power from accumulating in the hands of a few large landowners. Battered by feuds between these powerful families, the Icelandic Commonwealth voted in 1262–64 to accept Norwegian rule.

You may have read the d'Aulaires' many stories about the Greek gods. Here's the basic structure of the Olympian court.

On Mount Olympus

by Ingri and Edgar Parin d'Aulaire
from Cricket

In the gleaming hall of the palace, where light never failed, the Olympian gods sat on twelve golden thrones and reigned over heaven and earth. There were twelve great gods, for Zeus shared his powers, not only with his brothers and sisters, but with six of his children and the goddess of love as well.

Zeus himself sat on the highest throne, with a bucketful of thunderbolts beside him. On his right sat his youngest sister, Hera, whom he had chosen from all his wives as his queen. Beside her sat her son, Ares, god of war, and Hephaestus, god of fire, with Aphrodite, goddess of love, between them. Next was Zeus's son Hermes, the herald of the gods, and Zeus's sister Demeter, goddess of the harvest with her daughter, Persephone, on her lap. On the left of Zeus sat his brother Poseidon, the lord of the sea. Next to him sat the four children of Zeus: Athena, the twins Apollo and Artemis, and Dionysus, the youngest of the gods. Athena was the goddess of

wisdom, Apollo, the god of light and music, Artemis, goddess of the hunt, and Dionysus, the god of wine.

Hestia, the eldest sister of Zeus, was goddess of the hearth. She had no throne, but tended the sacred fire in the hall, and every hearth on earth was her altar. She was the gentlest of all the Olympians.

Hades, the eldest brother of Zeus, was the lord of the dead. He preferred to stay in his gloomy palace in the underworld and never went to Olympus.

The gods themselves could not die, for divine ichor flowed in their veins instead of blood. Most of the time they lived happily together, feasting on sweet-smelling ambrosia and nectar, but when their wills clashed, there were violent quarrels. Then Zeus would reach for a thunderbolt and the Olympians would tremble and fall to order, for Zeus alone was stronger than all the other gods together.

Ron McCutchan, art director of Cricket *magazine, offers up a sampling of medieval tale-telling and Arthurian lore.*

The World of King Arthur

by Ron McCutchan

from Cricket

Do you love tales of knights, castles, and the days of King Arthur? Here are some books that will help you discover what life was like in those long-ago times.

Who was King Arthur? Did he really have a Round Table? Learn about the Arthur legends and the sixth-century warrior who may have been the *real* King Arthur. (*Quest for a King:* Catherine M. Andronik; Atheneum)

The Once and Future King tells the story of Arthur's life. As you read, you'll feel as though you were sitting on the castle walls with the young Wart (Arthur) and his tutor, the wizard Merlyn. (*The Once and Future King:* T.H. White; Putnam)

To find out about a true medieval queen, you might begin with Eleanor of Aquitaine. This strong-willed queen tells her own story—with the help of several opinionated friends. (*A Proud Taste for Scarlet and Miniver:* E.L. Konigsburg, art by the author; Atheneum)

"An illumination is a picture, design, or decoration drawn on a manuscript page." *Illuminations* is a colorful alphabet book that shows daily life in medieval times, from the castles of the nobles to the cottages of the common folk, from Alchemist to Zither. (*Illuminations:* Jonathan Hunt, art by the author; Bradbury)

Harald loves to hear tales of the Great Stag living in the Baron's forest. But when the boy learns that the Baron and his hunters plan to kill the majestic animal, he knows he must do something to save the Great Stag. (*Harald and the Great Stag:* Donald Carrick, art by the author; Clarion)

12. Americanarama: Home-Grown Pieces

Using a fictional family, Cobblestone *offers an overview (a summary) of the origins of American folk art that may have you looking at household objects in a creative new way.*

American Folk Art
&
From Every Culture

from Cobblestone

American Folk Art

The autumn harvest was in, and the days were getting shorter. Sarah Ann looked forward to the cozy winter evenings when the family gathered around the crackling fire. The early darkness and cold that drove them indoors also gave them time to work on the many projects that they were too busy to do during the growing season.

Sarah Ann loved those evenings by the fire. It was peaceful to sit stitching. Per-

Silhouette of Tinker,
from Faces

242

Hunters carved decoys in the shapes of ducks and other game birds to lure wild birds to the places where the hunters waited.

haps she would finish her sampler by Christmas. She liked hearing Father's tales of the early days, when he and Mother had come to western Pennsylvania to settle the farm.

As Father talked, he would sit on a stool, carving new tool handles and wooden mixing bowls and spoons for Mother. Sometimes he had a harness to mend or would cut pieces of tin for a new lantern. Nine-year-old Jared liked to imitate Father. Just yesterday he had asked whether he was old enough to carve himself a wooden horse.

Mother would be busy mending old clothes and making new ones, something eleven-year-old Sarah Ann could help with this year. Last week Mother had said it was time for them to start a quilt for the new bed Father was making for Annabel, who was getting too big for the cradle.

Sometimes when Father finished a tool handle or kitchen utensil, he'd sit back and look over at three-year-old Annie. With that gleam in his eye that told Sarah Ann something fun was coming, he'd say, "Well now, I suppose I ought to be carving out something useful." And a couple of evenings later, there would be a dancing jointed doll that made all the children shriek with laughter as Father dangled it on his knee.

During the long winter, early American families, like this farm family, kept busy making things they needed and used in their daily lives. Many items they produced we now call folk art. They usually learned the skills they used to make quilts, dancing dolls, and so many other things from older family members, neighbors, or coworkers. For instance, Sarah Ann learned to quilt from her mother and would probably help teach her younger sister the skill.

Folk art is handmade, and no two pieces are identical. Many folk art objects are useful and were made to fill a need. Others are decorative, made as gifts, to decorate a home, or as a personal expression of creativity. Folk artists usually did not think of themselves as creating art but rather as making something they needed in a pleasing way.

Farm families were not the only early American folk artists. Sailors at sea whittled gifts for their loved ones from whalebone. Ship carvers created fancy figureheads to decorate the finished ships. Sign makers carved and painted images showing the activities or goods of various

Ink, watercolor, and careful work with scissors made this Pennsylvania German cutwork valentine.

businesses. Traveling painters produced family portraits, views of towns, and landscapes as decoration for people's homes. Stonecutters decorated buildings and gravestones.

By the late 1800s, many things that people needed were being made in factories. Less traditional folk art was made as manufactured items became easily available. Old quilts, thick pottery and wooden ware, and the wooden figures and signs that marked village shops were destroyed or put in attics and old barns and forgotten.

Folk art was "discovered" by the 1920s. Antique collectors and bargain hunters bought pieces that were sold when attics and barns were cleaned out, and people began to notice the artistic quality of many handmade tools, toys, and decorations. The first exhibit of American folk art was held in 1924.

At first, folk art pieces were called "early Americana" and thought of as antiques. But as collections grew and were studied, collectors realized that there was a unique group of objects that, through their creation and decoration, told us things about people's lives. These pieces of private lives are now preserved as art.

Folk art continues today, perhaps for different reasons than in the 1800s but in the same tradition. Although twentieth-century folk artists no longer need to make objects for daily use, they still use materials that are at hand – scraps of cloth, poster paint or house paint instead of artists' oil paint, pieces of wood taken from the forest, and even collected junk.

Today's folk artists are still mostly untrained in formal art. They create to express a feeling about something. In 1976, Howard Finster, a former preacher in Georgia, felt inspired and picked up a paintbrush and a can of tractor enamel. He began to paint ideas and messages from the Bible.

Simon Rodia came from Italy when he was twelve years old and worked as a tile setter and handyman. In 1921, when he was in his forties, he decided he wanted to "do something big." He began to build a tower with whatever materials he could find. For thirty-three years, Rodia cemented together scraps of chicken wire, pieces of glass, seashells, and other objects. His Watts Towers still stand in Los Angeles as a monument to American folk art.

From Every Culture

Much American folk art comes from the eastern states, inspired by European folk traditions brought here by immigrants. Germans came to Pennsylvania with a special way of painting and lettering. America's first tinsmiths used skills they had learned in England.

Long before the colonists arrived, however, Native Americans started the first American artistic traditions. Throughout the continent, they made beautiful pottery, baskets, woven goods, carvings, and paintings. The materials used and the style of the objects varied, but each group passed its traditions down from generation to generation. Some also learned arts from their neighbors. The Navajo, for instance, learned to make silver jewelry and woven goods from the Mexicans and Pueblo.

Folk art often is part of a group's religious beliefs. The Hopi used carved and painted kachina dolls (representing supernatural beings) to teach children about their religion. In the Southwest, the influence of Spanish missionaries led to the creation of religious paintings, carvings, and statues that decorated homes and churches.

Spanish settlers also brought folk art traditions to the Southwest. These are still seen in the region's distinctive weaving and furniture styles. And in the Southeast, African slaves introduced traditions from their homelands. Today their descendants practice these arts as they weave sweet-grass baskets and sew colorful quilts.

Most of the weather vanes we've seen have been roosters. In this article, you'll learn how these hand-crafted objects figured in some of the earliest advertising.

Sitting on Top of the World

by Joan Hiatt Harlow
from Cobblestone

Children in Colonial Boston loved to gather at the Province House when the clock struck noon. As the bell tolled, they watched the weather vane perched on top of the cupola. Shining in the sun, an Indian archer, with bow and arrow poised to shoot, turned in the breeze. According to legend, one day the Indian would shoot the sun out of the sky.

This four-and-a-half-foot copper weather vane, created in 1716 by Boston coppersmith Shem Drowne, was described in a story by Nathanial Hawthorne as "an Indian chief gilded all over . . . bedazzling the eyes of those who looked upward like an angel in the sun."

People have watched weather vanes for thousands of years. Ancient Greek sailors looked to a Tower of Winds, where a figure of the sea god Triton pointed out the wind's direction. Seafaring men in early America checked the rooftops in their ports. High above the homes, shops, and public buildings, ships, whales, mermaids, fish, and sea serpents swung in the wind to show them when it was a good time to sail.

Inland, American farmers also kept track of the wind, but their vanes were more likely to take the shape of a rooster, horse, or other farm animal. Farmers needed to know what the wind was bringing. They planted crops with the warm spring breezes and watched carefully for damaging storms and the return of winter winds. This verse from the 1851 edition of *The Old Farmer's Almanack* gives some helpful advice:

Wind from the east—bad for man and
'for beast;
Wind from the south is too hot for
them both;
Wind from the north is of very little
worth;
Wind from the west is the softest and
best.

246

*The Peaceable Kingdom. Reproduction by Edward Hicks
from* Cobblestone

The rooster was probably the first barnyard animal to be a weather vane. The earliest settlers brought weathercocks from Europe, where they had long been used. It is said that in the ninth century, a pope commanded that a rooster be placed on every church as a reminder of the time Jesus told Peter, "I tell thee, Peter, the cock shall not crow this day, before thou shalt three times deny thou knowest me."

In Colonial Pennsylvania, some weather vanes had a second job. Perched atop many barns, wooden and metal Indians guarded the farms. The area's first set-tlers used these sentinels to show that they had bought their land from the Indians. Without such a sign, a farm might have been attacked by Indians who thought the farmer had taken the land.

The first weather vanes were made by hand by the people who used them or by a local sign carver or metalworker. They cut, sawed, or carved the vane from materials at hand—an old piece of wood or an extra sheet of metal. Most vanes were simple, flat shapes cut in silhouette to stand against the sky above the letters N, S, E, and W, which marked the compass directions. A board was chiseled or sawed by hand, and a flat sheet of iron, zinc, or tin was cut with metal shears. Many vanes were painted bright colors to protect them from the weather.

More elegant vanes were made from copper, brass, or iron in three-dimensional shapes. These fancy designs were most likely to be seen in town, where weather vanes drew customers to shops—a pig for the butcher or an eagle at the inn—and sat atop public buildings and churches. Many of them were made by professional craftsmen, like Shem Drowne, who were metalworkers and woodcarvers.

While some vane makers took their design ideas from the world around them, others were inspired by current events or subjects of personal interest. During times of war, the American eagle and the Goddess of Liberty were patriotic weather vane designs. As the railroad crossed the country in the mid-1800s, it caught America's imagination, and soon locomotives were flying over rooftops, especially at railroad depots.

George Washington chose a symbol of peace for the weather vane on his home, Mount Vernon—a dove with an olive branch in its beak. Another president,

Thomas Jefferson, designed a special weather vane for his home, Monticello. He built an arrow of wood and metal, then connected it to a shaft that went through the roof to the ceiling of the room below. When the vane on the roof turned, the shaft turned another arrow on the ceiling, pointing out the wind's direction. Jefferson did not have to go outside to check the wind.

Perhaps the most famous weather vane is the copper grasshopper that still sits on Boston's Faneuil Hall. It watches the world with green glass eyes, and for many years, it carried a secret message. When discovered, the message told of the grasshopper's eventful life:

Shem Drowne Made it May 25, 1742

To my brethren and Fellow Grasshopper, Fell in ye year 1753 November 18, from ye Market by a great Earthquake . . . repaired by my old master above. Again like to have met with my Utter Ruin by Fire but hopping Timely from my Publick Scituation came off with broken bones, and much Bruised, Cured and again fixed by Old Master's son Thomas Drowne June 28th, 1780, and though I will promise to Discharge my Office, yet I shall vary as ye wind.

What could be more a part of any Americanarama than a sweet apple dessert? And surely the picture by children's book illustrator Tricia Tusa will make you smile while you bake.

Apple Appeal

by Caroline Bates, illustrations by Tricia Tusa

from Faces

If you had to pick an apple dessert with the most appeal, which would you select? Many people would choose apple pie, surely one of the most appealing of all American desserts. But there are other sweet apple endings to a meal, such as this sugar-crusted apple crisp with the added flavor of currants. Present it to a high court of judgment, such as your family, for a decision. I have a hunch you will win the case.

You need:
1 cup dried currants
2 tablespoons butter or
    margarine
6 large tart green apples
juice of 1 lemon
3 tablespoons white sugar
3/4 cup dark brown sugar

3/4 cup flour
1/2 cup quick-cooking oatmeal
1 teaspoon cinnamon
1/2 teaspoon ginger
1 stick (1/2 cup) butter or margarine,
    melted
vanilla ice cream

illustrated by Tricia Tusa

small and medium mixing bowls; measuring cups and spoons; small saucepans for boiling water and melting butter; sieve; 9-inch-square baking pan; apple peeler, corer, and slicer or knives for paring and slicing; lemon squeezer; wooden spoon; 6 dessert plates

1. Pour 1 cup boiling water over the currants in a small bowl. Let them soak for 10 minutes, then drain them thoroughly.

2. Preheat the oven to 375°F.

3. Grease the bottom and sides of the baking pan with the 2 tablespoons of butter. Peel and core the apples, slice them thinly right into the baking pan, and sprinkle them with the lemon juice and white sugar. Scatter the currants over the apples.

4. In a medium bowl, use a wooden spoon to mix together the dark brown sugar, flour, oatmeal, cinnamon, and ginger. Stir in the melted butter.

5. Pour the mixture over the apples and currants. Bake the crisp for 40 to 45 minutes, or until the apples are tender and the topping is brown and crunchy.

6. While the crisp is still warm, spoon it into the dessert plates and top each serving with a scoop of vanilla ice cream.

Richard Meryman wrote about one of the Wyeth boys in Andrew Wyeth, *published by Abrams. In this excerpt, you'll meet many of Andy's brothers and sisters, and their imperious, spirited father, N.C. Do read more about them in* National Geographic.

The Wyeth Family: American Visions

by Richard Meryman
from National Geographic

Newell Convers Wyeth, the great American artist and illustrator, can best be described as two men fighting in a sack. Torn apart all his life by the opposites in his nature, he was at once a questing intellectual, open to new ideas, and an untrammeled romantic with virtuoso imagination imbuing whatever it touched with meaning, personality, and excitement.

This blend in N.C., as he was known, produced some 3,000 works, including illustrations for 112 books. Generations of Americans, imagining Jim Hawkins in *Treasure Island* and David Balfour in *Kidnapped,* see in their minds N.C. Wyeth's images. . . .

Just as his creations were larger than life, N.C.'s romantic idealism was boundless. He considered the "spirit of family reverence" a lost art, and when his own family came, he set out to be the ultimate father. Until his death in 1945, he managed a hothouse of creativity to develop each child's talents to the utmost.

He succeeded to an extraordinary degree. Three generations of Wyeths have become one of America's most famous and remarkable families, a dynasty of applied fantasy. N.C.'s daughter Henriette Wyeth, the oldest at 83, has had a distinguished career as a portraitist, especially of young children. Carolyn Wyeth, 81, named for her mother, established herself as a painter of intense originality, her output prized for its brooding, abstract power. Nathaniel Wyeth, who died at 78 in 1990, adapted N.C.'s schooling in imagination to science and was named the first senior engineering fellow at the Du Pont Company, the highest technical position at the time. Holder of 25 patents, he invented the prototype of the plastic bottle used today for carbonated drinks. Ann Wyeth, 76, became a gifted composer. . . .

The youngest child, Andrew, now 74, has achieved the nearly impossible, broad popularity while assured of a major place in the history of American art. . . .

And N.C. Wyeth's legacy continues into the third generation. Twelve of his thirteen surviving grandchildren work in the arts. . . .

The romantic side of N.C. also embraced a near pantheistic relationship with nature. To ingrain into his children his own "sense of identification and unity with nature" and to develop their "fine power of observation," he took them on walks and picnics in the woods. They searched for mushrooms and birds' nests and found in the wet leaves of melting winter the first, starry spring beauties. . . .

Systematically stoking their imaginations, N.C. joined his children at play, helping them build dams in the brook below the house, making paddle wheels of wood with a jacknife. . . .

Everything within N.C. — his hyperbolic imagination, his Swiss tradition, his unbridled enthusiasm — climaxed at Christmas. Being the producer and stage manager and lead actor of Christmas, N.C. once wrote, "set me *crying* in pure and exultant joy."

On Christmas Eve empty stockings hung from the children's bedposts. Andrew says, "I remember waking up in a sweat and in the dark feeling for the stocking and the different shapes inside. One year there was this strange figure made out of wood with big feet and a marvelous head with a pointed hat. I clutched it to me in the dark, smelling the new paint on its face, feeling the nose and wondering what it was." . . .

On the roof the children heard Old Kriss. Heavy boots stamped, sleigh bells rang, a booming voice called to the reindeer by name. Soon the children heard Old Kriss on the stairs coming in full costume to shake hands with each child. One year Andrew, listening to Old Kriss's approach, held his breath till his eyes popped and, in a frenzy of fear and excitement, wet his bed. When they at last could rush into the big room, warmed by the logs in the fireplace, N.C. made them stop and savor the tree, decorated with real candles burning.

Under the tree was the raw material for the children's own intense fantasy lives. Ann yearly received at least one large, beautifully realistic doll bought by her mother, who often sewed period dresses and nightgowns. And Carolyn received toy animals. Nat built Andrew a castle on which N.C. painted the stones and climbing vines, reciting a story with each detail. Brushing a stain below one of the windows, N.C. said, "That's where one of the lazy guards had to go to the bathroom and just let it go out the window."

N.C. once wrote to his mother about the children, "As they weave the textures of their lives the background of memories will give them untold pleasures, and *perhaps* be the basis upon which they can build an important life work." Andrew Wyeth has said, "It was the most imaginative, rich childhood you could ever want. That is why I have so much inside of me that I want to paint."

Adults haven't been the only ones to create artful objects; girls, especially, worked on samplers that would be passed on to us as testaments to their craft and skill.

Stitches in Time

by Deb Felton
from Cobblestone

The girls sat with their backs straight, concentrating on their work. Each held a needle, a length of shiny silk, wool, or linen thread, and a piece of linen fabric stretched tightly in a wooden hoop. Carefully, they made tiny stitches, forming pictures on the fabric as they worked. The pictures showed huge birds on cone-shaped trees, angels floating among vines and flowers, and ships sailing off the shore of little New England villages.

The girls were in school, learning to stitch samplers as part of their preparation for being wives and mothers. In the 1700s and 1800s, none of them realized that their work might go down in history as examples of American folk art.

Samplers did not start out as artwork at all. In fact, the first samplers were used as tools to record different types of stitches. As girls learned a new stitch, they would practice it by adding another design, making the sampler long and narrow. These samplers were easily rolled up and stored until the seamstress needed to remember how to make a particular stitch.

During the 1700s, samplers began to change. They became shorter and broader, and they almost always included a border design, the name of the seamstress, and the date. Girls embroidered their age into the design, too. For example, twelve-year-old Phebe Bratton proudly stitched the names of her parents, the date she was born (March 13, 1783), and the name of the school where she learned to sew.

One of the first of those schools, or academies, opened in Boston in 1706. By the time of the Revolutionary War, needle-art academies were springing up all over New England. These boarding schools taught a few academic subjects, such as music, English, and French, but many of them began by teaching only needlework.

In 1799, both boys and girls attended Philadelphia's Westtown Boarding School, but the girls spent less time with math to allow time for sewing. "Two weeks in six are spent in the sewing school," said a flier distributed to parents, "from which the girls go to reading and writing classes as usual, but during the rest of the time they are busy with the needle." Apparently the embroidery practice paid off. Records from

Ten-year-old Elizabeth Richards sewed the alphabet with cross-stitch, worked the border in eyelet, and used real hair on her people.

the time show that some girls became so skilled that they could do the intricate work by moonlight.

Girls put the designs together in a variety of ways. Often the figures were out of proportion, such as squirrels climbing trees filled with enormous acorns. Although the sizes and shapes were not perfect, the scenes on the samplers show us what life was like at the time. They include bouquets and baskets of oversized flowers and family members wearing bonnets or carrying Revolutionary War muskets. In 1798, Elizabeth Helms, a thirteen-year-old from Philadelphia, finished a sampler that included a two-story house, a picket fence, weeping willow trees, sheep and shepherds, two dogs, and an enormous deer.

The girls often stitched scenes and verses from the Bible or other moral lessons. For example, in 1737 ten-year-old Jane Simons stitched this verse in her pattern sampler:

The Gracious God Did Give Me Time To Do th[i]s Work You See that Others Mayd L[e]arn The Same When I Shall Cease to Be.

Some of the verses were composed by the girls' parents or teacher, some were lengthy and hard to stitch, and many started out with something morbid, such as "When I am dead and laid in my grave." (Of course, this was a time when people died young and death was more of a daily threat.)

The samplers also gave girls a chance to learn the alphabet, but in a slightly altered version. In most samplers, there were only twenty-four letters in the alphabet, because the upper-case I and J were the same letter, as were the U and V. In the late 1700s, only four out of ten women in the Colonies could write their names, so stitching an alphabet, a signature, or a moral verse was an accomplishment.

By the mid-1800s, needlework had all but disappeared in the schools. But many early samplers have been saved, passed down through generations or packed away in attics. Because of the names, dates, and ages stitched into these early samplers, genealogists have been able to trace the family histories of several of the young embroiderers. And thanks to the girls' painstaking work, we are able to get a glimpse of lives led years ago, captured for us through two centuries of children's folk art.

There are still people who "quilt," but do they work from real patches, or do they purchase fabric for the project? In one family, the scraps of collected fabric from children's home-sewn clothing were piled high before the grandfather at last picked up his needle and thread and set to work.

Patchwork Art

by Mary Morton Cowan

from Cobblestone

In the early days of America, cloth was scarce. Many settlers had looms, but it was time consuming to make new cloth. So women who could not afford to send to England for new fabric saved every scrap of cloth and worn-out clothing. They sewed their small scraps together to make quilts. In cold climates, a layer of warm filling—everything from unspun wool to cornhusks and dry leaves—was stitched between the pieced top layer and a cloth backing.

At first, quilt pieces were odd shapes and sizes. As time went on, women cut and arranged pieces carefully, creating elaborate designs. Some patterns told stories and family histories. Others, such as Water Wheel, Pine Tree, and Weather Vane, symbolized their daily lives. The Log Cabin pattern was made from strips of fabric, or "logs," around a center square representing a chimney. Turkey Tracks portrayed turkeys' tracks in the snow, while Mohawk Trail symbolized sunny and shady spots along a forest trail. The Friendship Ring pattern was made from pieces supplied by friends. Many patterns were created to honor people or commemorate events.

There are hundreds of variations of patchwork quilt patterns, many of which have more than one name. Can you identify the traditional patterns in the quilt on the next page? In the smaller diagram, label the square that corresponds to the placement of the pattern on the quilt. Answers below.

o	b	l	c
i	q	p	h
k	t	r	a
m	d	s	f
g	n	j	e

a. Union Square
b. Pine Tree
c. Water Wheel
d. Crazy Quilt
e. Log Cabin
f. Friendship Ring
g. Tumbling Blocks
h. Mohawk Trail
i. President's Wreath
j. Honeycomb

k. Bear's Paw
l. LeMoyne Star
m. Turkey Tracks
n. Sunburst
o. Weather Vane
p. Joseph's Coat
q. Flower Basket
r. Mariner's Compass
s. Clamshell
t. Pinwheel

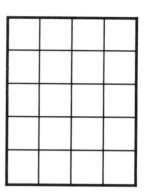

Here's a piece of Americana you can ask your parents about. If they didn't travel Route 66, at least they may have watched the TV show about it.

Travelers May Again Get Kicks on Route 66

from National Geographic

It wound, as Bobby Troup's song put it, "from Chicago to L.A. [actually Santa Monica], more than 2,000 miles all the way." But when the Interstate Highway System came along, U.S. Route 66 faded.

Now the federal government, working with preservation groups, is evaluating ways to commemorate the road that helped shape how Americans travel. Route 66 was the "mother road" for Okies who fled the Dust Bowl of the 1930s for a better life in California. In the 1960s it was celebrated in a television series.

A 1990 law directs the National Park Service to make a two-year study of how to save what is left of Route 66 and interpret its significant features. Aides to the law's sponsor, New Mexico Senator Pete Domenici, say the study may propose saving buildings and signs that remain where the road still exists, encouraging economic renewal in the many small towns where Route 66 was Main Street.

Tom Snyder, a Californian who heads the Route 66 Association, says he would like uniform signs to "create a visual image of continuity" in the eight states the road passes through. "Route 66 was an experience in itself: The going was as important as the destination," he says.

Those of us who once believed that Ms. Oakley was a character straight out of Paul Bunyan Land have much to atone for. Not only was she an authentic sharp-shooter, but she was inclined to give money away to children's charities. A soft touch and a trigger finger—nice mix, don't you think?

Annie Oakley and the Wild West

from Cobblestone

Elsewhere: Stars of the West . . .

by D. P. Brown
from Cobblestone

Johnny Baker was the "Cowboy Kid." Only a boy when he met Buffalo Bill Cody, he soon learned how to rope and shoot. By the time he was 14, he was performing with Buffalo Bill's show. Baker stayed with the show for more than 20 years. After Buffalo Bill died, Baker built a memorial to the showman in Golden, Colorado, that is now a city museum.

Will Rogers was a sometimes cowboy from the Oklahoma Territory. As a trick roper called the "Cherokee Kid" (Rogers was part Indian), he joined a Wild West show in the early 1900s. Although he was an expert roper, it was his humor that made him famous. His observations of life

and politics, related while performing his lasso tricks, propelled him to Broadway and Hollywood. Later he wrote a newspaper column that entertained millions of readers.

In the 1920s, Tom Mix was one of the movies' first cowboy heroes. But Mix started his entertainment career as a riding and roping expert with a Wild West show. After directing and starring in several short films, he began appearing in feature-length movies. He made about 100 Westerns and was wildly popular. He retired from the movies and eventually toured with his own Wild West show.

MIX HELPED MAKE THE 10-GALLON COWBOY HAT FAMOUS.

BRUCE RECENTLY SET THE RECORD FOR "TEXAS SKIPS," JUMPING THROUGH THE LOOP 1,851 TIMES.

Vince Bruce is not a cowboy. He is not a westerner. In fact, he is not even an American. Bruce is an Englishman who has had extraordinary skill with a lasso since he was 12. He travels the world today performing his rope tricks in circuses and nightclubs.

If you wandered through your own attic, or the attic in a relative's house, you'd probably find out plenty about the family—and plenty about yourself. Now you're ready to read:

America's Attic: Hidden Treasures of the Smithsonian

by Curtis Slepian
from 3-2-1-Contact

Remember the last scene in the movie *Raiders of the Lost Ark?* Indiana Jones has brought the ark back in a crate to be stored in a giant government warehouse in Washington, DC. Stretching into the distance are thousands of other crates holding who knows what treasures.

That was just a movie, and the ark probably doesn't exist. But a similar kind of warehouse does. It's called the Paul E. Garber Preservation, Restoration and Storage Facility in Suitland, MD. The Garber Facility, which is used by the Smithsonian museums, may be the world's greatest attic. Its 28 buildings hold more than 16 million amazing items that have to do with U.S. and natural history.

At any one time, only about two percent of what the Smithsonian owns is on display in its museums. The rest is either

on loan to other museums around the world—or in the "attic" in Suitland. Walking down the aisles of the warehouses you'll pass any number of incredible objects, either in crates or cabinets, or out in the open.

A visitor might see a 19th-century sleigh used to deliver bread, an Eskimo seal kayak, a periscope from a German World War II sub, a machine to make screws, a stagecoach, and even a model of a Klingon space ship used in the movie *Star-Trek IV!*

For the people who work at Garber, this isn't just any warehouse. It helps to know how to work a forklift. But it's even more important, William Wyss, a museum specialist, told *Contact,* "to have a feeling for things historical, an interest in collecting. No matter how unimportant an object seems, it has a direct connection with history."

Says museum technician Richard Siday, "Working with the stuff, you're actu-

Here are just some of the 3,000 to 4,000 medallions, buttons, spoons, ashtrays, paperweights, dishes and other World's Fair souvenirs to be found in Garber. The earliest items come from London's 1851 Crystal Palace Exposition. The latest are from the Vancouver World's Fair in 1984.

ally holding a part of history in your hands."

The hands holding these precious items are always covered in white cotton gloves. This is so acids on people's fingers don't harm the surface of the objects. It's by taking this kind of care, says Siday, that "this stuff will be around when the kids reading this article have their own children."

Right now, kids and their parents can tour the part of the Garber Facility devoted to air and space. The rest of the huge storage area is off limits. But *Contact* was allowed to tour the entire place, so we could give you a special peek inside the world's most incredible attic!

Museum specialist William Wyss polishes a rare "fireless" locomotive. Unlike most old steam locomotives, this one didn't produce its own steam. Instead, steam from an outside source was sent through a pipe into the engine's huge boiler. When the boiler filled, the pipe was removed, and the engine ran for a half day.

"Armed Freedom" gets star billing at the U.S. Capitol. That's the sculpture that sits on top of the building's dome. And this is the original plaster model from which that bronze sculpture was made in the 1870's. The 50-foot-high plaster cast had to be cut in half to fit through the Garber Facility's warehouse doors.

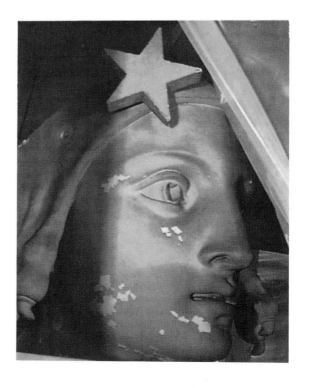

The early cycle here is a 1918 Indian. The car in back is a Pierce Arrow Runabout. Built in 1912, it cost a lot of money in its day: $4,000. It has a "rumble" seat in the back for an extra passenger.

Among the Mercury test capsules, ejector seats, helicopters, fighter planes and other air- and spacecraft in the Garber Facility is this "android." NASA built it to test space suits. The suit was placed over the dummy. Then the robot's arms, legs and joints would move back and forth. This told NASA how well the suit held up.

At the end of an aisle filled with old adding machines and parts from missile guidance systems is a large, cabinet-sized computer. It is a section from ENIAC, the world's first electronic calculator (or "electronic brain," as it used to be called). Built in the early 1940's, before the days of transistors and microprocessors, ENIAC was powered by thousands of vacuum tubes. This and other computers are displayed in "Information Age," an exhibit at the Smithsonian's Museum of American History.

Parked in a cabinet are parking meters from the 1950's and '60's. They are part of a collection given to the Smithsonian by a man who once worked for a parking meter manufacturer.

Here's a shelf from one of 22 cabinets filled with toys, most of them made of cast iron. The Smithsonian collects toys because they can teach us about life in America. For example, when cars came on the scene, kids lost interest in toy wagons—they seemed old fashioned. Later, toy planes and rockets replaced toy cars as kids' fave raves.

The Smithsonian has preserved all kinds of historic vehicles: In the center is a "sprint" car. It was made for racing on sand, and goes up to 90 mph. On its left is a hand-drawn fire engine from 1854. At right is a "turbine" car, which is powered by a jetlike turbine engine. Made by Chrysler in 1963, it is one of only 10 such cars in existence.

What a card! Norcross, a greeting card company, gave the Smithsonian 450,000 of its cards, dating from 1924 to 1974. A volunteer is arranging them by date, theme and price. These cards will offer historians glimpses into the past.

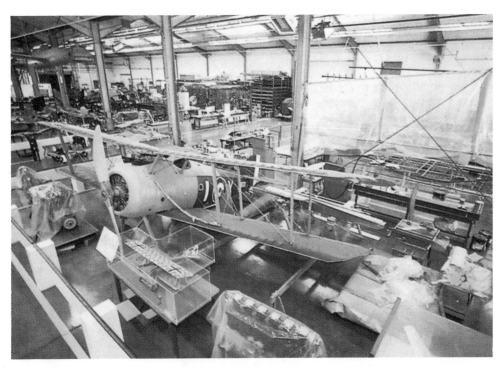

In this large warehouse, craftspeople repair and restore old airplanes for eventual display. Among them is this fighter plane from World War I.

These—and a couple of dozen other—incredibly realistic scale-model wagons were made by an expert model-maker just for the Smithsonian. Why not try to get the real things? Well, you can't fit everything in the storehouses. Both of these models are horse-drawn wagons from the 19th century. On the left is an ice wagon, and the other hauled stones.

13. The Sporting Life: Recreation, Co-operation, Competition

Hall of Fame fans know all about Cooperstown, New York, but here Jon Halter provides a glimpse of its holdings. Drop by if you're in the area!

Baseball's Fabulous Time Capsule

by Jon C. Halter

from Boys' Life

Almost every sport—football, tennis, even harness-racing—has a hall of fame. But *the* Hall of Fame to most fans is the National Baseball Hall of Fame and Museum of Cooperstown, N.Y.

No honor in sports carries more prestige than election to baseball's shrine. Ted Williams called it "the greatest thrill of my life." Williams, who many consider the best hitter of all time, was elected in 1966.

How special is membership? Only 170 of more than 13,000 players in 113 years of major-league competition have been elected to the Hall of Fame. That's exclusive!

The Hall opened in 1939. It attracts more than 300,000 visitors every year. Its museum is a magical time capsule. Some 6,000 baseball treasures are displayed throughout four floors (and many thousands more are kept in storage).

Many exhibits show how the game has changed *and* how it has stayed the same. For example, pitcher Jack Chesbro's tiny 1901 glove looks no bigger than a leather garden glove of today.

But a baseball from 1888 looks just like a baseball of today. Heinie Groh's 1920 "bottle bat" resembles a stretched-out bowling pin. But Hall of Famer Tris Speaker's 1912 bat is as sleek and slender as any used by today's sluggers.

Famous Teams and Events

Great players, famous teams, magic moments, fantastic feats, incredible records are all here.

See the ball Roger Maris hit for his single-season record-breaking 61st home run in 1961. Or the glove Yogi Berra used to catch Yankee pitcher Don Larsen's perfect no-hit game in the 1956 World Series.

There's the shirt Dodger pitcher Orel Hershiser wore while winning the final game of the 1988 World Series. And the ball Henry Aaron hit in 1974 for home run 715, breaking Babe Ruth's career record.

Compare uniforms from different eras.

Players in the early 1900's, like all-time great short-stop Honus Wagner of the Pittsburgh Pirates, wore bulky warm-up sweaters that would be out of place today. Ted Williams's trim 1946 Boston Red Sox uniform, however, looks much like today's Red Sox uniform.

You'll see some unusual outfits too. Like the green-and-white Cincinnati Reds uniforms used for the 1978 St. Patrick's Day game. Or the 1948 Boston Braves' special night uniforms, made of shiny satin to look flashy under the lights.

Each part of baseball's past has its own memorabilia-filled exhibit. There are special displays for the World Series, All-Star games, no-hit games, all-time record holders, and more.

One exhibit honors great black Hall of Famers—like speedy center fielder James "Cool Papa" Bell and slugging catcher Josh Gibson—who starred in the old Negro leagues. The display reminds visitors of an injustice from baseball's past: African-American players weren't allowed to compete in the major leagues until 1947.

Legendary ball parks of the past live on. You can see dugout benches, grandstand seats, and ticket booths and turnstiles from long-gone stadiums like Ebbets Field in Brooklyn and the Polo Grounds in New York.

Sports card and stamp collectors head for a third-floor exhibit. The showcase item is the ultra-rare 1909 Honus Wagner "T-206" tobacco card. (The great shortstop, a nonsmoker, asked that the card be withdrawn from circulation.)

Got a baseball question? The Hall's National Baseball Library is open to visitors. The reference department will also answer questions by mail or telephone.

Enter the solemn Hall of Fame Gallery and you're among baseball's all-time stars. Bronze plaques honor the 170 players, 20 executives, 10 managers and 6 umpires elected to membership since 1936.

Most fans know of legends like Babe Ruth, Willie Mays and Hank Aaron. But how many recognize the likes of Elmer Flick (.315 lifetime batting average) or Ted Lyons (260 victories)? Or have heard of 19th-century stars like Kid ("No Windup") Nichols, hit-and-run pioneer King Kelly, or curveball innovator Candy Cummings? Each star's Hall of Fame plaque describes his contribution to the game.

Every generation has heroes who become Hall of Famers. Your great-grandfather's favorite player may have been the legendary pitcher Christy ("Big Six") Mathewson, or Honus ("The Flying Dutchman") Wagner. Your grandfather's heroes probably included Babe ("The Sultan of Swat") Ruth, or his Yankee teammate Lou ("The Iron Horse") Gehrig. And your father probably admired home run champions like Mickey ("The Mick") Mantle and Willie ("Say Hey") Mays.

Some players you root for today will also earn a place in the Hall of Fame. Their accomplishments, along with those of yesterday's stars, will live on in Cooperstown for future fans to enjoy.

It wouldn't be "cricket" to give away here the information in this article, but you may be surprised at how universal—and ancient—the great American pastime is.

It Wasn't Always Called Baseball

by Vicki McClure, illustration by Les Grey
from Children's Digest

Did you know that baseball, one of the most popular games in the United States and Japan, was originally called "rounders"? That may sound strange, but it was so named because posts were used instead of bases, and the runners ran *around* them. Batters weren't called batters, either. They were called "strikers." Runs were called "aces," and whichever team made twenty-one aces won the game. Innings didn't exist then—quite a difference from how things are today!

Sports have been a big part of people's entertainment for thousands of years. Many popular games have changed dramatically from the way they were played when they first started.

Baseball was played by the Egyptians, the Greeks, and the Romans many centuries ago, but the game didn't start looking like the baseball we know until about a hundred years ago in England. Even as it was then, you probably wouldn't recognize the game. Twelve people were on the field instead of the nine to which we're ac-

customed. The pitcher was called the "thrower," and the opposing team would actually throw the ball at the runner and try to hit him! Instead of one catcher, there were two, one behind the other.

The playing field was strange, too. There were no regulations for the distance between bases, and all sorts of shapes were used. In fact, five bases were used instead of four.

A man named Alexander Cartwright finally came up with the field design we know. He also devised the diamond-shaped running area. Posts were replaced by flat bases because posts had proved to be too dangerous. Because of the bases, the game's name was changed to baseball.

Bowling is another sport that has gone through many changes. Did you know that bowling was once a religious ceremony in ancient Germany? Church people rolled a large, round stone at a pin called a *Heide,* or heathen. If the thrower knocked down the pin, it was believed that he had overpowered the heathen and was leading a

good, clean life. Afterward, a huge party would take place to honor the successful *kegelspielers*, or bowlers.

The popularity of the game spread to England, and people started to play it all the time. To play, you had to bring your own pin! The number of pins changed with the number of people playing. Eventually, the rule was made that only nine pins would be used in a game. Bowling was then called "ninepins."

The king of England was concerned that the new game was taking up the people's time and that they wouldn't practice archery. Bows and arrows were the country's main defense. Also, since gambling was popular at the games, all sorts of dreadful people began to mingle there. So, the king outlawed ninepins.

To bypass the new law, a game called "tenpins" was invented. The people added a pin and rearranged the pins' positions. After all, the law was only for *nine*pins — not *ten*pins!

Bowling wasn't the only sport to be outlawed. Boxing had been, too, but for different reasons.

Boxing used to be a "fight-to-the-death" game, although the only people who were allowed to watch it at first were the rulers of ancient Greece and Rome. To entertain these people of royalty, gladiators were matched against each other, fighting and punching with their hands encased in leather. The game was over when one of them was killed. As time passed, the leather hand coverings had fancy metal spikes attached to them. Without doubt, the "game" was bloody and horrid.

Over and over again, boxing was banned, but popular demand kept bringing it back. Finally, a man named James Figg decided to clean up the image of boxing.

He was the bareknuckle champion in England. He introduced footwork, thrusts, and defense into the game, and eliminated all the kicking and gouging that had been a part of the sport. He proved that boxing could be entertaining without being so violent. Other boxers began to imitate him. The sport became less dangerous. James Figg started the first school for boxers.

Unlike many other games, basketball is a very young sport. It was created in 1891 in the United States by a physical education teacher at the YMCA. Dr. James Naismith needed a sport that could be played indoors during the cold, snowy months in Massachusetts. All the indoor games around at the time were dull. He wanted one that would be competitive and fun.

Dr. Naismith hung two peach baskets, one at each end of the gym's balcony. He divided the athletes into two teams and instructed them to try to throw a ball into one of the baskets. As they played, different rules were formed. Many of the rules today are still the same.

Basketball was an immediate success. People liked to go and watch the competitions because the gyms were warm and comfortable. The bottoms of the peach baskets were cut away to speed up the game.

The game spread across the United States in just a few years. The peach baskets were replaced with metal hoops. Backboards had to be installed because the spectators often interfered with shots the players were making.

Volleyball was born four years after basketball. William Morgan decided that a second indoor game would be good for the YMCA. He strung a tennis net across the gym and lined up six players on each side. He tossed a "bladder" from a soccer ball to the players and told them to bat it back and forth. Later, standard rules were made. Mr. Morgan called his new game "mintonette," but the officials of the YMCA exhibitions didn't like the name. Mr. Morgan renamed it "volleyball."

Sports are fun to play and to watch. People have enjoyed them for centuries. But nobody knows *everything* about how they started. For instance, did you know that golf balls were once called "featheries"? That's because the first golf balls were made of leather and they were stuffed with goose feathers!

Illustration by Don Page, from Children's Playmate.

Curveballs: Wacky Facts to Bat Around

illustrated by Andy Levine

from Sports Illustrated for Kids

DO YOU KNOW WHAT A **wormburner** or a **bench jockey** is? These crazy baseball terms have been around for a long time. Baseball has many colorful expressions, and their meanings and origins may surprise you. Here are our favorites.

Lefthanded pitchers have been called **southpaws** since the late 1800s. Home plate was usually placed at the western end of a ballpark in those days, so when a lefty was on the mound, his pitching arm was the one on the *south* side of his body.

When a third baseman throws to the second baseman, who then throws to first, people say the double play was made **around the horn**. Sailors once used this phrase to describe the long sail around South America's Cape Horn, the route used to get from the Atlantic Ocean to the Pacific Ocean.

A sharply hit groundball that doesn't bounce very high is called a **wormburner** because of what it could do to any ooey-gooeys that happen to be in the ball's path.

When a team has men on base, it has **ducks on the pond**. Broadcaster Arch McDonald used this phrase first, in 1939. He thought that driving in runners should be as easy as shooting ducks on a pond.

A jockey is someone who rides a horse in a horse race. Baseball has its own kind of jockeys. Players who "ride," or tease, the other team's players from the dugout are called **bench jockeys**.

© 1990 BY ANDY LEVINE

Room with a Zoo

illustrated by David K. Sheldon
from Sports Illustrated for Kids

From the January 1991 issue of *Sports Illustrated for Kids*. Reprinted by permission. Copyright © 1990 by *Sports Illustrated for Kids*, a division of The Time Inc. Magazine Company.

THIRTEEN ANIMALS in (or peeking into) this room share their names with teams in the National Football League, the National Basketball Association, Major League Baseball, or the National Hockey League. Find them?

TEAMS

NFL
Chicago
Detroit
Indianapolis
Los Angeles
Miami
Philadelphia

NBA
Chicago
Minnesota

Baseball
Chicago
Detroit
St. Louis
Toronto

NHL
Pittsburgh

ILLUSTRATION BY DAVID K. SHELDON

NFL: Chicago *Bear*, Detroit *Lion*, Indianapolis *Colt*, Los Angeles *Ram*, Miami *Dolphin*, Philadelphia *Eagle* **NBA:** Chicago *Bull*, Minnesota *Timberwolf* **Baseball:** Chicago *Cub*, Detroit *Tiger*, St. Louis *Cardinal*, Toronto *Blue Jay* **NHL:** Pittsburgh *Penguin*

Here's a way to pass those frigid winter months—ice hockey! Now some girls' teams have the opportunity to crash around in the rink, bash other players, elbow the ump—just like the boys.

Great Skates!

by Mikki Morrissette

photograph by Manny Millan

from Sports Illustrated for Kids

Whoosh! Clack! *Thud!* Two all-girl pee-wee hockey teams are battling it out at a cold, drafty rink in Stillwater, Minnesota. Shots zip across the ice. Elbows fly and skates scrape as the players chase the puck.

The action is wild. One player snares the puck with her stick and tries to skate around a defender. But the player gets cut off, crashes into the boards, and falls butt-first to the ice.

"Shake it off, Candy!" a fan yells, as the player scrambles to her feet and rejoins the action.

These days, girls are playing hockey — good, fast, fun hockey — in states across the country. This game is between the St. Croix Fillies and the Anoka Wildcats, two of eight teams in a Minnesota peewee league for girls age 15 and younger. There also are girls' peewee teams in nine other states.

The sport is growing steadily. USA Hockey, the national governing body for the sport, sanctions about 150 girls' and women's teams, and it hopes someday to have female leagues in every state in which men's hockey is played.

© 1991 BY MANNY MILLAN

Girls and women now play hockey in at least 11 countries. The first women's world ice hockey championships were held last year. (The U.S. team finished second, behind Canada.) Women's hockey might even become an Olympic sport in 1994!

The Fillies are one of the most enthusiastic teams anywhere. Their state, Minnesota, is *crazy* about hockey. The boys' state high school tournament is one of Minnesota's biggest sports events. The Fillies were formed in 1986 because girls wanted to play hockey, too.

The Fillies have won three Minnesota girls' peewee championships in the past four seasons. In 1989–90, they had a record of 36-8-2 and won the state title.

Many of the Fillies used to compete on boys' teams. Kenzie Stensland, now 10, played on a boys' team last year with her 8-year-old brother, Isaac. In 40 games, Kenzie scored 40 goals—more than any boy on the team! Almost every night, Kenzie practices with Isaac and her other brother, Zachary, 14, on their backyard rink.

Boys in Stillwater like to talk about hockey with the girls who play. "The guys basically think it's cool that we're playing," says the Fillies' Dani Alm, 14.

Sometimes boys don't treat girl players very well on the ice, however. "Boys don't always pass the puck to girls, because they think you stink," says the Fillies' Jessie Kunkel, 12. That's one reason girls like to have their own teams.

People who have coached boys and girls say that boys have more upper-body strength, so they are generally better at stickwork and at shooting the puck hard. Girls, they say, usually are better skaters and listen to the coach more.

When they reach the peewee level, players on boys' teams learn to bodycheck opponents. To bodycheck an opponent, a player uses the upper part of his body to bump the opponent from the front or side. Body-checking is not allowed in girls' or women's hockey.

The girls aren't afraid to get tough, though. Fillies defenseman Jenny Duis has used bodychecks on boys in pickup games, and she loves it. "I'm about as tall as they are," says Jenny, who is 5'7". "When they try to squish me, I can squish them back!"

None of the Fillies has ever had a serious injury. They are required to wear helmets, face masks, mouthpieces, gloves, shoulder pads, elbow pads, shin pads, and padded shorts. At worst, players sometimes get the wind knocked out of them.

Still, some parents worry that their daughters will get injured. "I don't think most of the parents realize how resilient girls are," says Fillies coach Larry Alm, Dani's dad. "Girls are as tough as they have to be."

The Fillies often play boys' teams for fun—and often beat them. "When the boys lose to the girls, you have never heard such complaining in your life," says Coach Alm. "The boys come up with every excuse in the book to explain why they lost the game."

Hockey can lead to great opportunities for girls. Fifteen U.S. colleges have varsity programs for women, and at least three of those schools offer scholarships to players. But most of the Fillies play hockey just because they enjoy it.

"It's more fun playing on an all-girls team than with the guys," says 13-year-old Erin Yoho. "You feel very proud about it and want everyone to know there is such a thing as ice hockey just for girls."

Last year, the Fillies played in the USA Hockey's Girls' and Women's National Championships in Detroit, Michigan. The

Fillies didn't do very well *on* the ice—they lost all three games they played—but they had a blast off it. They stayed at a hotel, ate a lot of pizza, soaked in a hot tub, and made up a song called "The Funky Chicken."

A visit to the Fillies locker room shows what a blast the team has. The Fillies have just won another game, and they're passing around a pan of brownies that someone's mother made. The players are joking about whose parents yelled the loudest during the game. Huge bags waiting to be filled with equipment cover the floor.

After the coaches leave the room, goalie Lynn Broberg pops a tape into her cassette player. The rap song "U Can't Touch This" by M.C. Hammer comes on, and each player starts unlacing her skates to the beat. Soon, the whole team is singing and dancing. To the Fillies, being on a girls' hockey team means having a great time with some of your best friends.

Winter Wackyland

illustration by Jared D. Lee

from Kid City

It's fun to be outdoors on a beautiful winter day. But there are ten things wrong with this picture. Can you spot them all? We circled one for you.

CAMP WO-BE-GON

17

Illustration by Jared D. Lee

282

Like, do you think this goes back to all that identity stuff? Do you think it's a problem that there were no "Mom's" uniforms for kids to put on? Do you think that's just too much thinking? Yeah.

Suit 'Em Up!: Kids Raid Their Dads' Lockers

by J. B. Morris

from Sports Illustrated for Kids

What kid wouldn't want to try on a real National Football League jersey or a major league baseball uniform or a jersey and shorts from the National Basketball Association? For the kids on these pages, borrowing professional sports uniforms is as easy as reaching into their dads' lockers. That's because their fathers are athletes. As a special Father's Day surprise, these kids put on their dads' work clothes and posed for *Sports Illustrated for Kids*. They also told us a few things about their dads that most of the world may not know. Can you use the clues to figure out the names of their famous fathers? The answers are on page 286. And don't forget: Father's Day is June 16!

What do you do when your dad stands 6'6" and weighs 300 pounds? You do anything he says! Actually Austin (left) and Brandon like having an NFL-sized dad.

© GEORGE B. FRY III

Austin and Brandon

"He's fun to wrestle with," Austin says. "Dad wrestles with me and my brothers [Austin and Brandon have two brothers and two sisters], and *he* always gets hurt. We all jump on his head."

Dad's job is to block for Joe Montana. In backyard football games, he blocks for Brandon. "Then I get to run for the touchdown," Brandon says.

Who is their dad? Here's one more clue: Austin and Brandon's last name sounds like a city in France.

H e shoots! He scores! Brian gets to go one-on-one with a National Hockey League goaltender whenever he wants. He plays floor hockey with his dad, a Boston Bruins goalie, in the family's basement.

Brian plays right wing on a youth hockey team. He says he wouldn't want to play his dad's position. "One time after a Bruins game, I put on my dad's helmet and it was really weird," Brian says. "It felt all big and gooey. Totally gross!"

Mickey and Kristen

Brian

T he father of Mickey (left) and Kristen has been on the pro golf tour for 15 years. But he's not just a good golfer—he's also a good sport. Their dad loves telling jokes, and he can do impersonations of other golfers.

Kristen thinks her father is even funnier *off* the course. "My dad sometimes sings with two other golfers in a band called Jake Trout and the Flounders," she says. "They sing rock songs with the words changed so they're about golf." Adds Kristen, "He's a better golfer than a singer."

Austin

I like it when my dad takes us to the batting cages," says Austin. "He teaches us to hit the right way and to field with two hands."

That's a hint about Austin's father. These days, he plays guard for the Portland Trail Blazers, but he used to be an infielder for the Toronto Blue Jays! Ashlee says her dad is great. "He's not extra strict and he's fun to be with," she says. So who is he? Two hints: He used to wear a Celtics uniform, and he is one of the most accurate three-point shooters in the NBA.

Ashlee

Tanner

© GARY NOLTON

Answers to "Suit 'Em Up" pp. 283–285

Bubba Paris is an offensive tackle for the San Francisco 49ers. His sons Austin and Brandon share their dad's "work shirt" on p. 283.

Reggie Lemelin, a goalie for the Boston Bruins, is the father of Brian, who is dressed for the ice on p. 284.

Danny Ainge of the Portland Trail Blazers is the father of Austin, Ashlee, and Tanner, who are suited up in their dad's court clothes on p. 285.

Peter Jacobsen has earned more than $2.5 million on the pro golf tour. His kids Mickey and Kristen appear on p. 284.

The boomerang may be 30,000 years old, but Alan Adler thought it could be improved upon. Perhaps his invention will replace the Frisbee.

Scientist Develops Unusual Boomerang

from Current Science

A boomerang flutters overhead, tracing a low, graceful path through the air. Humans first threw boomerangs, or 'rangs, as they are sometimes called, about 30,000 years ago. They've been coming back ever since. The boomerangs, that is, not the humans.

Most boomerangs are shaped like a bent elbow, are made of wood or plastic, and weigh as much as 6 ounces (168 grams). The design and weight of these boomerangs make it both difficult and a bit dangerous to catch the 'rangs in midair.

An engineer at Stanford (Calif.) University, however, recently developed a triangular boomerang—the Aerobie Orbiter—that weighs just 2 ounces (56 grams). Inventer Alan Adler says the Orbiter can be thrown more easily and caught more safely than can conventional 'rangs.

"I was afraid to catch wooden boomerangs," says Mr. Adler. "I wanted something easier to throw and safer to catch." So he built the Orbiter from lightweight plastic, then coated the plastic with soft rubber to protect the person catching it.

The Orbiter flies easily because it has wing flaps at each corner. These wings, explains Mr. Adler, provide the new boomerang with better aerodynamic lift. *Aerodynamic lift* is a force that pushes an object upward through the air.

An airplane, for instance, flies because air moving past the wings flows faster over the wings than it does under them. The difference in air flow produces a greater pressure against the underside of the wings. This higher pressure lifts the plane into the air.

In an Aerobie Orbiter, lift is produced when air flows past the wing flaps as the Orbiter tumbles end over end. Airflow is fastest when a wing-tip cuts directly into the wind at the top of the spin. The lift produced by the faster airflow at the topmost wing flap causes the boomerang to lean leftward. According to Mr. Adler, the extra lift from the wing flaps makes it twice as easy to fly the Orbiter as it is to fly a wooden 'rang.

If aerodynamic lift were the only force at work on the tumbling boomerang, the

Orbiter would only lean to the left and not come back to the thrower. However, another force, called gyroscopic precession, causes the Orbiter to follow a curved path back to the thrower. *Gyroscopic precession* (jigh-rə-SKOP-ik pree-SESH-uhn) causes the Orbiter to keep turning left until it completes a circle and returns to the thrower.

It took practice, but we here at *Current Science* got pretty good at making the Orbiter come back. Which is just what we plan to do—keep coming back to play with this nifty little toy.

When all is said and done, it's more fun to be with others, and the best way to do that is pretty simple. Whether you participate in games, read out loud to each other, or build something—like a snowman—it's nice to play together.

Playing Together

illustration by Laura Cornell

from U*S* Kids

289

DIRECTORY OF MAGAZINES

Boys' Life
P.O. Box 152079
1325 West Walnut Hill Lane
Irving, TX 75015-2079

Calliope
Cobblestone Publishing, Inc.
30 Grove Street
Peterborough, NH 03458

Career World
Weekly Reader Corporation
4343 Equity Drive
Columbus, OH 43228

Child Life
Children's Better Health Institute
P.O. Box 7133
Red Oak, IA 51591-0133

Children's Digest
Children's Better Health Institute
P.O. Box 7133
Red Oak, IA 51591-0133

Children's Playmate
Children's Better Health Institute
P.O. Box 7133
Red Oak, IA 51591-0133

Cobblestone: The History Magazine for Young People
Cobblestone Publishing, Inc.
30 Grove Street
Peterborough, NH 03458

Cricket
P.O. Box 51144
Boulder, CO 80321-1144

Current Events
Weekly Reader Corporation
4343 Equity Drive
Columbus, OH 43228

Current Health
Weekly Reader Corporation
4343 Equity Drive
Columbus, OH 43228

Current Science
Weekly Reader Corporation
4343 Equity Drive
Columbus, OH 43228

Dolphin Log
The Cousteau Society Membership
Center
930 West 21st Street
Norfolk, VA 23517

Faces: The Magazine About People
Cobblestone Publishing, Inc.
30 Grove Street
Peterborough, NH 03458

Highlights for Children
2300 West Fifth Avenue
P.O. Box 182347
Columbus, OH 43218-2347

Humpty Dumpty's Magazine
Children's Better Health Institute
P.O. Box 7133
Red Oak, IA 51591-0133

International Wildlife
National Wildlife Federation
1400 Sixteenth Street, N.W.
Washington, DC 20077-9964

Jack and Jill
Children's Better Health Institute
P.O. Box 7134
Red Oak, IA 51591-0134

Kid City
P.O. Box 53349
Boulder, CO 80322

National Geographic
National Geographic Society
P.O. Box 2895
Washington, DC 20077-9960

National Geographic World
National Geographic Society
P.O. Box 2330
Washington, DC 20077-9955

National Wildlife
National Wildlife Federation
1400 Sixteenth Street, N.W.
Washington, DC 20077-9964

Plays: The Drama Magazine for Young People
Plays, Inc.
120 Boylston Street
Boston, MA 02116-4615

Ranger Rick
National Wildlife Federation
1400 Sixteenth Street, N.W.
Washington, DC 20077-9964

Scienceland
Suite 2108
501 Fifth Avenue
New York, NY 10017-6102

Sesame Street Magazine
P.O. Box 52000
Boulder, CO 80322-2000

Sports Illustrated for Kids
P.O. Box 830609
Birmingham, AL 35283-0609

3-2-1 Contact
P.O. Box 53051
Boulder, CO 80322-3051

*U*S* Kids*
P.O. Box 8957
Boulder, CO 80322

*Wee Wisdom**
Unity School of Christianity
Unity Village, MO 64065

Zillions
P.O. Box 54861
Boulder, CO 80322-4861

*Ceased publication with December 1991 issue.

COPYRIGHT NOTICES

From *National Geographic:*

November 1990, "Six Across Antarctica" by Will Steger, pp. 66–93, and "Six Men, Six Nations, One Quest" p. 75; excerpted and reprinted by permission of the author. Copyright © 1990 Will Steger.

December 1990, "Some Tasty Recipes for a Babylonian Feast" from the Geographica page; reprinted by permission. Copyright © 1990 by the National Geographic Society.

June 1991, "The Wonderland of Lewis Carroll" by Cathy Newman, pp. 100–129; excerpted by permission. Copyright © 1991 by the National Geographic Society.

July 1991, "Travelers May Again Get Kicks on Route 66" from the Geographica column and "Symbols of the South Grow Thin in Louisiana" from the Earth Almanac column; both reprinted by permission. Copyright © 1991 by the National Geographic Society. "The Wyeth Family: American Visions" by Richard Meryman, pp. 78–109; excerpted by permission. Copyright © 1991 by the National Geographic Society.

August 1991, "Persian Gulf: Tide of Destruction" pp. 14–15; reprinted by permission. Copyright © 1991 by the National Geographic Society. "L'Enfant's Washington" by Alice J. Hall, pp. 122–134; excerpted by permission. Copyright © 1991 by the National Geographic Society.

From *National Geographic World:*

September 1990, "Don't Houseclean . . . Airclean!" p. 13; reprinted by permission, National Geographic WORLD. Copyright © 1990 by the National Geographic Society. Photographs from "Postal Pickups," pp. 32–35; captions reprinted by permission, National Geographic WORLD. Copyright © 1990 by the National Geographic Society. All accompanying photographs reprinted by permission.

November 1990, "Shooting for a Dream," pp. 20–25; text reprinted by permission, National Geographic WORLD. Copyright © 1990 by the National Geographic Society. Photograph by Columbia Thomas reprinted by permission of Shooting Back, Washington DC 20009.

December 1990, "Dictionary for Dudes" p. 7; reprinted by permission, National Geographic WORLD. Copyright © 1990 by the National Geographic Society. "Now Say Cheese! Eye to Eye with Wildlife," pp. 28–29; text reprinted by permission, National Geographic WORLD. Copyright © 1990 by the National Geographic Society. Photographs reprinted by permission of the photographers.

January 1991, "The Secret World of Termites," pp. 23–24; text reprinted by permission, National Geographic WORLD. Copyright © 1991 by the National Geographic Society. Photograph of aardwolf reprinted by permission of the photographer. Copyright © 1991 by Alan Root. "How Sweet It Is" p. 29; reprinted by permission, National Geographic WORLD. Copyright © 1991 by the National Geographic Society.

February 1991, "Why Do X's Stand For Kisses," p. 3; reprinted by permission, National Geographic WORLD. Copyright © 1991 by the National Geographic Society. "Sweet Jobs: Kids in Business," pp. 11–15; text reprinted by permission, National Geographic WORLD. Copyright © 1991 by the National Geographic Society. Photograph of three sisters reprinted by permission.

March 1991, "They're in Clover" p. 18; text reprinted by permission, National Geographic WORLD. Copyright © 1991 by the National Geographic Society. Photograph reprinted courtesy of Rose Purrington.

April 1991, "Why Do People Count Sheep to Fall Asleep?" p. 3, "Touch-Tone Translation," p. 10, and "Fiddle Faddle," p. 30; all reprinted by permission, National Geographic WORLD. Copyright © 1991 by the National Geographic Society. Bass fiddle telephone booth reprinted by permission of Gamma-Liaison, New York.

June 1991, "Soap Box Speedsters," pp. 12–13; reprinted by permission, National Geographic WORLD. Copyright © 1991 by the National Geographic Society.

From *National Wildlife:*

August-September 1990, "Farewell to a True Friend" by Jay D. Hair, p. 26, "Sea Creatures Thrive on Oceans' Oil Seeps," p. 28, and "Test Tube Tigers Born in Omaha Zoo," p. 28; all copyright © 1990 by the National Wildlife Federation. Reprinted from the August-September 1990 issue of *National Wildlife*. Illustration for "Sea Creatures" reprinted by permission of the artist. Copyright © 1990 Charles Peale.

December-January 1991, artwork from "Out for the Count" pp. 38–39, reprinted by permission of the artist. Copyright © 1991 by Charles Peale. "In Search of the Barnyard Ark" by Lisa Drew, pp. 42–43; text copyright © 1991 by the National Wildlife Federation. Reprinted from the December-January 1991 issue of *National Wildlife*. Photograph of Tamworth pig reprinted by permission of the photographer.

From *Plays:*

May 1991, "The Western Civ Rap" by Nancy Porta Libert, p. 44; reprinted by permission of the publisher. Copyright © 1991 by Plays, Inc.

From *Ranger Rick:*

September 1990, "Whatta Buncha Junk!" pp. 26–29; reprinted from the September 1990 issue of *Ranger Rick* magazine, with the permission of the publisher, the National Wildlife Federation. Copyright © 1990 by National Wildlife Federation. Illustrations reprinted by permission of the artist. Copyright © 1990 by Terry Sirrell.

October 1990, "Dinosaurs Were Babies Too!" by Petra de Groot, pp. 30–34; reprinted from the October 1990 issue of *Ranger Rick* magazine, with the permission of the publisher, the National Wildlife Federation. Copyright © 1990 by National Wildlife Federation.

February 1991, "Will You Be Mine?" by Kay Ingalls, pp. 46–47; reprinted from the February 1991 issue of *Ranger Rick* magazine, with the permission of the publisher, the National Wildlife Federation. Copyright © 1991 by National Wildlife Federation. Illustrations reprinted by permission of the artist. Copyright © 1991 by Jean Pidgeon/Light Flight, Inc.

April 1991, "Critter Crackups" by Anthony Taber, p. 28; reprinted by permission of the artist. Copyright © 1991 by Anthony Taber.

SUBJECT INDEX

Worms
SEE Earthworms
Writing
Why Do X's Stand for Kisses? (*National Geographic World* Feb 1991) p199

Wyeth, Andrew
The Wyeth Family: American Visions. R. Meryman. (*National Geographic* Jul 1991) p251–252

Wyeth, N.C.
The Wyeth Family: American Visions. R. Meryman. (*National Geographic* Jul 1991) p251–252